PERPETUITIES LAW IN ACTION

A UNIVERSITY OF
KENTUCKY STUDY

Perpetuities Law in Action

KENTUCKY CASE LAW AND THE
1960 REFORM ACT

by

Jesse Dukeminier, Jr.

UNIVERSITY OF KENTUCKY PRESS

Copyright © 1962 by the University of Kentucky Press
Printed in the United States of America by the
University of Kentucky Printing Division
Library of Congress Catalog Card
No. 62-13459

The publication of this book has been made possible partly through a grant from the Margaret Voorhies Haggin Trust, established in memory of her husband, James Ben Ali Haggin.

FOREWORD

THIS BOOK is a rare jewel of scholarship with nationwide practical importance to lawyers, professors, and legislators faced with problems in the Rule against Perpetuities.

Professor Dukeminier has analyzed in detail every perpetuities case in Kentucky, including excursions into unpublished court papers, both as an exposition of the law of one representative jurisdiction and as a brief for the legislature in support of the bill which became law as the 1960 Perpetuities Act. Some seventy-seven cases, comprising practically complete coverage of perpetuities doctrine, are analyzed with reference to (a) conformity to standard applications of the Rule and (b) effect of the recommended Perpetuities Act. No equivalent treatment in depth of the law of one or many jurisdictions has heretofore been published, and I say this after having participated in a similar enterprise for English and Commonwealth law.[1]

As an exposition of the quirks and quiddities of perpetuities doctrine, it should be a caution to estate planners and draftsmen in any jurisdiction and a rich source for those who find themselves litigating perpetuities cases. As an argument for perpetuities reform, it is overwhelming, though I confess to some predisposition to being overwhelmed on this subject; yet it must be added that it *was* successful in producing enactment of the reform statute which, in my judgment, is the most workable of those which have been passed by some dozen state legislatures, beginning with the Pennsylvania Estates Act of 1947.

The book is short enough to be read in two or three hours and is couched in a literary style that defies the tradition that writings on perpetuities must read like sections from the Internal Revenue Code.

A recently decided case should shock the bar into a realization that legislative reform of the Rule is a necessity as a matter of vital self-interest as well as professional responsibility and that the utmost care must be taken to master and conform to the Rule until reform is achieved. In a California Appeals case[2] a unanimous court held that where an attorney so drafts an instrument as to violate the Rule, the bereft intended beneficiaries have a right of action against him by application of the doctrine of *MacPherson v. Buick Motor Co.*[3] On appeal,[4] the Supreme Court of California agreed that an attorney for a testator is liable to a beneficiary who loses an intended bequest because of the attorney's negligence, but at the same time it also held that the Rule against Perpetuities is so esoteric that as a matter of law it is not actionable negligence to violate it. If the view of the lower court is followed in other jurisdictions—as well it might be—the bar simply has got to take protective measures. One of these, a boilerplate saving clause, I have recently suggested in collaboration with Professor James K. Logan.[5] But the more comprehensive protection, to client and

---

[1] Morris & Leach, The Rule against Perpetuities (1956) had a similar dual motivation—to provide a current text on English and Commonwealth law, and to serve as documentary background for the deliberations of the British Law Reform Committee. See British Law Reform Committee, Fourth Report (The Rule against Perpetuities), Cmd. No. 18 (1956); Leach, "Perpetuities Reform by Legislation: England," 70 Harv. L. Rev. 1411 (1957), in Leach & Tudor, The Rule against Perpetuities 217 (1957).

[2] Lucas v. Hamm, 11 Cal. Rep. 727 (1961).

[3] 217 N.Y. 382, 111 N.E. 1050 (1916). It will be recalled that prior to this decision the doctrine of Winterbottom v. Wright, 152 Eng. Rep. 402 (1842) ruled there could be no action against a manufacturer of a defective product by an ultimate purchaser from a retailer because of absence of "privity" between the parties. This has heretofore been the shield behind which the bar has protected itself in various cases where wills and trusts have failed through legal incompetence.

[4] Lucas v. Hamm, 15 Cal. Rep. 821 (1961).

[5] Leach & Logan, "Perpetuities: A Standard Saving Clause to Avoid Violations of the Rule," 74 Harv. L. Rev. 1141 (1961). The clause also appears in the model will in Leach & Logan, Cases and Text on Future Interests and Estate Planning, c. 28, at 982 (1961).

lawyer alike, is a type of reform statute which Professor Dukeminier successfully urged upon the Kentucky legislature. This volume should be as persuasive in other states as it has proved to be in Kentucky.

Pending reform, the practitioner would be well advised to spend the time necessary to refresh his understanding of the Rule by perusing this book.

Harvard Law School W. BARTON LEACH
September, 1961

CONTENTS

FOREWORD *by* W. *Barton Leach*	*page* v
INTRODUCTION	1
1. WHAT THE RULE AGAINST PERPETUITIES IS IN KENTUCKY	6
1. What the Common Law Rule against Perpetuities Is	6
A. *Lives in being*	7
B. *The remote possibilities test*	9
2. The Meaning of "Vest": Myth and Reality	14
A. *Vest in possession*	19
B. *Indefeasibly vest in interest*	21
C. *Vest in interest with possession postponed*	24
D. *Vest in interest subject to open (or subject to partial divestment)*	26
E. *Vest in interest subject to total divestment*	27
2. APPLICATION OF THE RULE AGAINST PERPETUITIES TO VARIOUS INTERESTS	31
1. Gifts to Classes	31
2. Powers of Appointment	36
3. Options	39
4. Gifts to Charity	41
5. Trusts for Employees	42
6. Trusts for Accumulation	43

7. Consequences of Violating the Rule	44
A. *Preceding estates stand; invalid interest passes by intestacy*	44
B. *Preceding estates stand; invalid interest passes to the last person(s) entitled to the income*	45
C. *Infectious invalidity; preceding valid estates fall with invalid remainder*	46
D. *Reform of invalid interest by cy pres*	50

3. THE TROUBLES CAUSED BY THE STATUTE PROHIBITING SUSPENSION OF THE POWER OF ALIENATION . . . 52

   1. The Meaning of KRS 381.220, Prohibiting Suspension of the Power of Alienation (Applicable to Transfers That Took Effect prior to July 1, 1960) . . . 52
   2. Is There a Rule Limiting the Duration of Trusts? . . . 57

4. REFORMS OF THE 1960 PERPETUITIES ACT . . . 66

   1. Why Reform? . . . 66
      A. *The Rule against Perpetuities is essentially incomprehensible* . . . 68
      B. *The statutory language in KRS 381.220 prohibiting suspension of the power of alienation confused both bench and bar* . . . 70
      C. *The remote possibilities test, in about three-quarters of the cases, deprived beneficiaries of gifts which in fact would have vested in due time; we concluded this was unfair and unjustifiable in policy* . . . 70
      D. *The consequences of violating the Rule were harsh and unsettled* . . . 75
      E. *Confusion surrounds the meaning of "vest"* . . . 76
   2. Adoption of the Common Law Rule against Perpetuities . . . 78
   3. The Wait-and-See Doctrine and Cy Pres . . . 79
      A. *The wait-and-see doctrine* . . . 79
      B. *Reformation by cy pres* . . . 83
   4. Illustrations of How KRS 381.216 Applies . . . 84
   5. Drafting to Avoid Perpetuities Problems . . . 91

5. ABOLITION OF POSSIBILITIES OF REVERTER AND TERMINATION OF RIGHTS OF ENTRY . . . 96

   1. The Purpose of the Statute . . . 96
   2. Good Riddance: The Determinable Fee and Possibility of Reverter Abolished . . . 99
   3. Termination of Rights of Entry after Thirty Years . . . 106
   4. Termination and Preservation of Possibilities of Reverter and Rights of Entry Created prior to July 1, 1960 . . . 109
   5. Exceptions to the Thirty-Year Termination Rule . . . 111

6. THE RULE AGAINST DIRECT RESTRAINTS ON ALIENATION — 114
   1. The Rule against Restraints Distinguished from the Rule against Perpetuities and the Rule against Suspension of the Power of Alienation — 114
   2. Restraints on Legal Life Estates and Remainders — 119
   3. Restraints on a Legal Fee in Possession: The Doctrine of Reasonable Restraints — 120
   4. Restraints upon Equitable Interests — 127
   5. Options Treated as Direct Restraints — 127
   6. Consequences of Violating a Valid Restraint: Forfeiture and Disabling Restraints Distinguished — 131
   7. Creditors' Rights — 134
   8. Sale for Reinvestment under Court Order — 140
   9. Critique of Kentucky Doctrine of Reasonable Restraints — 142

APPENDIXES
   1. Kentucky Perpetuities Act of 1960 — 147
   2. Analysis of Kentucky Perpetuities Cases — 150
      Table 1. Cases consistent with orthodox perpetuities doctrine in result — 150
      Table 2. Cases holding contrary to orthodox perpetuities doctrine — 151
      Table 3. Doubtful cases under orthodox perpetuities doctrine — 156
      Table 4. Cases holding interests valid under the remote possibilities test: the results are not affected by the 1960 perpetuities act, since it is not necessary to wait and see to save the gifts — 157
      Table 5. Cases holding interests void which actually did, or very probably would, vest in time: how KRS 381.216 would have saved them — 158
      Table 6. Cases holding interests void which did not or might not vest in due time: how KRS 381.216 would have applied — 160
      Table 7. Cases on options: application of KRS 381.216 — 161
      Table 8. Cases on rights of entry, possibilities of reverter, and executory interests after determinable fees: application of KRS 381.218 and KRS 381.219 — 161

TABLE OF CASES — 163

INDEX — 167

INTRODUCTION

ANYONE who has tried to explain the Rule against Perpetuities to laymen finds it very like trying to picture Marianne Moore's imaginary garden with real toads in it. Full of illusion and deception, it is the abode of such fantastical characters as the fertile octogenarian, the unborn widow, the precocious toddler, the slothful executor—all imaginary beings with power to bring the Rule down hard on the head of any trespasser. This extraordinary power in imaginary hands is the result of one of the most arbitrary rules known to the common law: the rule that any possibility, however preposterous, that a gift might vest beyond lives in being plus twenty-one years defeats the gift. The purpose of the Rule— to prevent property from being tied up in trust or otherwise for too long a period of time—laymen can understand. But all those delightful characters that populate the Rule are looked upon as the strangest aberrations of the legal mind.

Despite the difficulties in explaining the Rule to laymen, few rules of property have been so widely celebrated by lawyers as the Rule against Perpetuities. The proper application of the Rule requires an unerring technical virtuosity, together with a sure sense of the underlying policy, and mastery of its subtleties breeds devotion. One lawyer, in a brief of fifty years ago, expressed the attitude of the times. The Rule, he said, "almost has the force and dignity of a constitutional provision."[1] Yet in the last fifteen years there has arisen widespread dissatisfaction with the mischievous applications of the Rule and with its intricate refinements. Reverence has turned into skepticism and, in many states, into reform.

Several states have moved to reform the Rule by eliminating through legislation the arbitrary rule referred to above: the rule which invalidates an interest that possibly may vest too remotely regardless of whether it does so in fact. The Pennsylvania legislature in 1947 led the way with an act that determines the validity of interests by what actually happens, not by what might happen. If the interest in fact vests within the perpetuity period, it is valid. Professor Barton Leach of Harvard, with his usual felicity, christened this the "wait-and-see" test, and the name stuck. Following Pennsylvania came Massachusetts, Maine, Connecticut, Maryland, Vermont, and Washington with statutes adopting in whole or in substantial part the wait-and-see principle. The last two states coupled it with a cy pres provision. Idaho and New York followed with acts reforming the Rule in different ways. As befits a state which has been a leader in sloughing off common law archaisms, Kentucky recently joined the reform movement by enacting the Perpetuities Act of 1960.[2]

The genesis of this act was a study by the author of all the perpetuities cases decided by the Kentucky Court of Appeals, including examination of the briefs and records on appeal. The purpose of this study was to get beneath the surface of the Rule and find out how the Rule was working in practice. Among other things, it revealed some striking departures from orthodox doctrine: in the meaning of "vest," in the consequences of violating the Rule, in refusing to apply the rule of convenience and the doctrine of severed shares to save class gifts. These departures resulted in 27 percent of the cases being wrongly decided and another 22 percent being of doubtful correctness under the orthodox interpretation of the Rule.[3] In these cases, tradition and innovation are so fused that, to the court at least, they exist in identity with one another.

[1] Brief for Appellant, p. 8, Curd's Trustee v. Curd, 163 Ky. 472, 173 S.W. 1148 (1915).
[2] Ky. Acts 1960, c. 167, compiled as Kentucky Revised Statutes §§ 381.215-.223, reproduced in Appendix 1 *infra*. The Kentucky Revised Statutes are hereinafter cited as "KRS."
[3] See Appendix 2, Tables 2 and 3 *infra*.

While some may dismiss these cases as judicial blunders or temporary lapses of faith which do not change "the law," at the very least they show the chaotic state of the law in practice. They also exist as perilous precedents for the practicing lawyer. Perhaps as a result of these cases, we found in our discussions with lawyers about reform that there were almost as many opinions as to what the Rule against Perpetuities was in Kentucky as there were practicing lawyers.

In addition to doctrinal confusion, the study disclosed some exceedingly harsh results for the parties concerned. In more than half of the three dozen cases holding interests void, the court knew at the time of decision that the interest would in fact vest within the period. Nonetheless, the Rule required the interest be struck down because some remote event might have happened, although in fact it did not. Usually the draftsman had overlooked the presumption of fertility or had put in an age or time condition of more than twenty-one years. To make matters worse, the court added to the carnage by vigorously applying infectious invalidity.

The results of this study, which are set forth in Chapters 1, 2, and 3 and in Appendix 2 of this book, showed the operation of the Rule to be unpredictable and to be unfair to the intended beneficiaries. The author then undertook to draft appropriate remedial legislation. Alternative drafts were prepared and circulated among various members of the bar, one containing changes in presumptions of law or fact to cure specific anomalies, the other adopting wait-and-see and cy pres with the Vermont statute serving as a model. Both contained identical provisions terminating rights of entry and possibilities of reverter. The first alternative draft ran into many objections—mainly to its complexity—and proved unsalable. The second was agreed upon as the fairest and simplest solution, but the demand for simplicity required further compromise and concision, especially in the sections dealing with forfeiture restrictions on land use.

The second alternative draft ultimately became the Kentucky Perpetuities Act of 1960. This act repealed the old statute prohibiting suspension of the power of alienation, adopted the common law Rule against Perpetuities as modified by the wait-and-see test, and further provided for reformation of invalid interests by cy pres. The act also abolished two common law anachronisms, the determinable fee and the possibility of reverter, converting them respectively into a fee simple subject to a right of entry and into a right of entry; it then terminates after thirty years rights of entry, which traditionally have been exempt from the perpetuity rule. Except with respect to rights of entry, the effect of the act is to limit the destructive force of the Rule and save many reasonable family dispositions previously held void under the remote possibilities test.

The changes made by the 1960 Perpetuities Act were purposely conservative. Perpetuities law, like most of property law, is judge-made, and detailed and complex legislative changes in property law have not often been notable successes. It was our purpose, in limiting the act to essential reforms, to leave the courts in their traditional position as the main source of perpetuities law.

Chapters 1, 2, and 3 of this book contain an analysis of Kentucky perpetuities law prior to July 1, 1960, the effective date of the new act. Except as modified by this act, the old law remains in force. These chapters have a dual purpose. First, they are designed to show that perpetuities law in practice is not the same as it is in the books. It is, in Kentucky, much more chaotic and inconsistent than any writer has ever suggested. In this field it is commonly assumed that the law is unchanging and that doctrine is fixed. Yet, as we shall see, while the words remain the same, the meaning shifts. The courts seemingly are working the law slowly and tortuously to a new and sounder policy base.

These first three chapters are also designed to provide the practicing lawyer with a simplified statement of the Rule, with citations to and analyses of Kentucky cases. They purport to be comprehensive in that every perpetuities case decided by the Court of Appeals is cited, and many of them are discussed. They do not pretend to cover all the complexities of the subject, however. For that the reader is referred to the many excellent treatises[4] (with the warning that Kentucky law differs in several important particulars from that stated in the texts). In view of the abstract

---

[4] 6 American Law of Property, pt. 24, by Leach & Tudor (Casner ed. 1952); Gray, The Rule against Perpetuities (4th ed. by Roland Gray, 1942); 5 Powell on Real Property ¶¶ 759-90 (1956); 4 Restatement of the Law of Property, cc. 26-28 (1944); Simes & Smith, The Law of Future Interests §§ 1201-480 (2d ed. 1956). These works are hereinafter cited respectively as "Am. L. Prop.," "Gray," "Powell," "Restatement of Property," and "Simes & Smith." Citations to pt. 24 of Am. L. Prop. also refer to identical sections in Leach & Tudor, The Rule against Perpetuities (1957). For a concise treatment of the Rule, see Leach, "Perpetuities in a Nutshell," 51 Harv. L. Rev. 638 (1938).

terminology in this area, the discussion is illustrated by brief hypothetical cases.[5]

Chapters 4 and 5 deal with the 1960 Perpetuities Act. The reasons for, and the purposes of, the act are set forth, as well as how the act will apply in all the commonly recurring situations. By way of further illustration, the act is applied to every perpetuities case decided in Kentucky in Appendix 2, Tables 4-8. As will be seen, the act is of easy application in every one of these cases and, had it been in force, would have wholly saved at least three-quarters of the invalid dispositions. Chapters 4 and 5 were submitted in an abbreviated form to the Senate Judiciary Committee and the House Rules Committee in support of the act. A draft of the act and an explanation were also submitted informally to the Court of Appeals.

Chapter 6 contains a presentation of the unique Kentucky law of direct restraints on alienation. This law has often been confused with perpetuities, and the purpose of stating it here is to show it as a distinct body of doctrine. It is hoped this discussion will serve the needs of lawyers, judges, and students having problems involving this peculiar Kentucky law, which has neven been treated adequately by legal writers.[6]

[5] A method borrowed from Professor Leach.
[6] The subject matter of this book was treated earlier in abbreviated form in an article by the author entitled "Kentucky Perpetuities Law Restated and Reformed," 49 Ky. L.J. 1 (1960). The Kentucky Law Journal has kindly consented to the use of the original material, a substantial portion of which has been completely reorganized, rewritten, and expanded.

1

WHAT THE RULE AGAINST PERPETUITIES IS IN KENTUCKY

1

WHAT THE COMMON LAW RULE AGAINST PERPETUITIES IS

THE CLASSIC statement of the Rule against Perpetuities, formulated by John Chipman Gray, reads:

No interest in real or personal property is good unless it must vest, if at all, not later than twenty-one years after some life in being at the creation of the interest.[1]

Although Gray put the Rule in this one sentence, he required more than four hundred scrupulously detailed pages to explain what it meant. His exegesis, of almost Byzantine complexity, was so impressive, his mastery of ancient cases so apparently complete, that the Rule has sometimes been treated as if it were laid down at one time by one man. But of course nothing is further from the truth. As was common with scholars in the late nineteenth century, Gray's energies were fired by an elan to understand multiplicity in terms of a few basic ideas, and to order experience by inventing compendious theorems. Gray's statement of the Rule was merely a succinct synthesis of generations of cases, mainly English. While his mind subsequently became infected with an eager dogmatism about his own theorem, the great merit of his original scholarship was that he went to the cases (not the treatises) for the law.

The Rule against Perpetuities did not stop developing with the first edition of Gray's book in 1886. No photograph of the law can stop it from changing. It has changed in Kentucky as it has changed elsewhere. And to discover these changes—to find out what really comprises the Rule against Perpetuities in this state—we must, like Gray, turn to the cases and examine them afresh. To accept the general treatises as stating Kentucky law is a dangerous credulity.

The Kentucky Court of Appeals subscribes to Gray's words as a proper statement of the Rule, but when the cases are examined, it will be found that the court uses the word "vest" in a different way. "Vest" is the key word, and how it is used by the court is so important to understanding the Rule in Kentucky that its meaning will have to be treated in detail. Before turning to the meaning of "vest," however, two other important aspects of the Rule require brief discussion: lives in being and remote possibilities.

A. *Lives in being*

Who is a life in being? This is usually the first question students ask when they meet the Rule. The answer is that it can be any person alive (or in the womb) at the creation of the interest, so long as his death or some event which will necessarily happen or fail to happen within his life will *insure*[2] vesting or failure of the interest within twenty-one years of his death. The lives in being "may be any lives which play a part in the ultimate disposition of

---

[1] Gray § 201. The phrase, "in real or personal property," is added to Gray's statement. This definition is enacted by Ky. Acts 1960, c. 167, § 1; KRS 381.215.

[2] It is the remote possibilities test which requires that the measuring lives be lives which will *insure* vesting. Under wait-and-see (KRS 381.216) the measuring lives must be connected with the gift, but they do not have to insure vesting. See pp. 80-81 *infra*.

the property."[3] They need not be given any beneficial interest in the property nor be referred to in the instrument, but the causal connection which insures vesting must be express or implied. Thus:

Case 1 (Causal connection express). T devises property in trust "to pay income to my issue per stirpes from time to time living until twenty-one years after the death of X, Y, and Z, at which time the corpus is to be distributed among my issue per stirpes then living." X, Y, and Z are the measuring lives. The causal connection is express; their deaths will cause the twenty-one-year period to begin running, at the end of which the gift of corpus vests. Whether they are T's issue and have a beneficial interest in the income or are persons unrelated to T is irrelevant. The gift is good. If X, Y, and Z had not been referred to by name, but were the only members of a class of measuring lives in being at T's death and such class were closed at T's death (*e.g.*, "after the death of the last survivor of my issue living at my death"), X, Y, and Z would likewise serve as measuring lives.[4] The members of a class may serve as measuring lives if the class is closed at the beginning of the perpetuity period.

Case 2 (Causal connection implied). T devises property "to my wife for life, remainder to my grandchildren whenever born." T's children, though not mentioned in the instrument nor given any beneficial interest, are the measuring lives by implication. All T's children are in being at his death, and the remainder to his grandchildren is bound to vest on the death of his last surviving child. If the transfer were by deed, however, the grantor could have a child after the date of the deed, who could produce a grandchild long after all persons in being are dead. This grandchild would share in the gift and the remainder is void.[5] When the class of children is not closed, the children cannot be used as measuring lives because the death of those children in being will not necessarily cause the remainder to vest.

Sometimes the perpetuity period is said to be lives in being plus twenty-one years *plus* actual periods of gestation. This is simply another way of stating that a child *en ventre sa mère* is a life in being. For purposes of the Rule (and for practically all purposes of property law) a person is considered to be in being from time of conception, if he is later born alive.[6]

Where there are no lives causally connected with the vesting

[3] Bach v. Pace, 305 S.W.2d 528, 529 (Ky. 1957). See 5 Powell ¶ 766.
[4] Gray v. Gray, 300 Ky. 265, 188 S.W.2d 440 (1945); Clay v. Anderson, 203 Ky. 384, 262 S.W. 604 (1924); Russell v. Meyers, 202 Ky. 593, 260 S.W. 377 (1924); Gillespie v. Winston's Trustees, 170 Ky. 667, 186 S.W. 517 (1916).
[5] Bach v. Pace, *supra* note 3.
[6] Gray § 220; Note, 33 Mich. L. Rev. 414 (1935).

or failure of the interest, then no lives in being can be used. The interest is void if it will not necessarily vest or fail within twenty-one years.

In *Farmers National Bank v. McKenney*,[7] the draftsman called upon the court to supply the measuring lives. He attempted to set up a testamentary trust to pay income to the testator's three half-sisters for life, and on the death of each to pay her share of the income to "her heirs, if any, as long as the law allows." What measuring lives is the law to allow, is the court to supply? After remarking that for "such a formidable task we are given little help by counsel for the trustee (who, incidentally, appears to have drawn this will),"[8] the Court of Appeals held the entire trust void for uncertainty. Although in this case the court declined to fill in what period "the law allows," it implied that if there had been a gift of the corpus or some clear evidence of testator's intention, it would have done so. In other jurisdictions, courts have held that this wording means for the lives of the primary beneficiaries (the three half-sisters above) and twenty-one years thereafter,[9] or, where there are no primary beneficiaries, for twenty-one years.[10]

B. *The remote possibilities test*

Under the common law Rule against Perpetuities, *any* possibility at the date of creation of the interest that the interest might vest beyond the period invalidates the interest. This is known as the remote or fantastic possibilities test. It is this test, which has brought so many draftsmen grief, that is done away with by the 1960 act. The following cases illustrate the operation of the remote possibilities test in its extreme, but orthodox, form. In all these

Drawing by Steinberg;
© 1961 The New Yorker Magazine, Inc.

[7] 264 S.W.2d 881 (Ky. 1954).
[8] *Ibid.*
[9] Fitchie v. Brown, 211 U.S. 321 (1908); Re Vaux, [1939] Ch. 465; 6 Am. L. Prop. § 24.13; Simes & Smith § 1227.
[10] Re Hooper, [1932] 1 Ch. 38.

cases the gifts are essentially innocent and the violation one of a technical premise rather than of policy.

Cases 3 and 4 are quite common and have been the subject of many gibes as well as more affectionate raillery.

Case 3 (The unborn widow).[11] T devises property "to my son for life, then to my son's widow, if any, for life, then in fee to my son's issue per stirpes then living." The gift to the son's issue is void. It will

Drawing by Steinberg; © 1961 The New Yorker Magazine, Inc.

not vest until the death of the son's widow, and she may not be a person now in being. If the son is presently married, his wife may die or be divorced, and he may then take as a second wife a woman not now alive who might survive him and be his widow. The chance of this happening may be very slight indeed, but the chance invalidates the gift.[12]

Case 4 (The fertile octogenarian). T devises property "to my sister A for life, remainder to A's children for their lives, remainder in fee to

[11] The descriptive names—"unborn widow," "fertile octogenarian," and "precocious toddler"—were concocted by Professor Leach.
[12] Chenowith v. Bullitt, 224 Ky. 698, 6 S.W.2d 1061 (1928). *Cf.* Goodloe's Trustee v. Goodloe, 292 Ky. 494, 166 S.W.2d 836 (1942). For a case where an unborn widow was taken care of by a saving clause, see Gilbert v. Union College, 343 S.W.2d 829 (Ky. 1961).

A's grandchildren." A is eighty years old at T's death and is living out her days in Florida. Because the law conclusively presumes A to be capable of bearing further children, the remainder in fee might not vest until the death of her children born after T's death, which is too remote. The remainder in fee is void.[13] Now this is of course absurd, but not so absurd as it seems. At what age is a woman or a man presumed to be sterile? Is medical testimony on A's procreative capacity to be admitted? What would prevent A from adopting a child at any age?

Drawing by Steinberg;
© 1961 The New Yorker Magazine, Inc.

Here is a delightful case which occurred in England. It presents the converse question to that of the fertile octogenarian: What is the minimum age at which a person can have a child?

Case 5 (The precocious toddler). T bequeathed property in trust "to pay the income to A for life, and then to pay the principal to such of A's grandchildren living at my death or born within five years thereafter as shall attain the age of twenty-one." The gift of principal will vest too remotely only if A has a child (X) born after T's death, and that child (X) marries and has a child (Y) within five years after T's death. An English court upheld the gift, though not on the ground that procreation before age five is impossible. Instead, the court held a marriage under age sixteen was void under English law and any children born of it illegitimate.[14] And of course illegitimates do not take as "grandchildren."

Drawing by Steinberg; © 1961 The New Yorker Magazine, Inc.

[13] See sixteen Kentucky cases cited in Appendix 2, Table 5, fact patterns (1) and (2), and Table 6, fact pattern (1) *infra*.
[14] Re Gaites' Will Trusts, [1949] 1 All E.R. 459 (Ch.) The reasoning of the court has been criticized. See Morris & Leach, The Rule against Perpetuities 81-83 (1956); 6 Am. L. Prop. § 24.22.

The following cases fortunately have never arisen in Kentucky, but they have bothered courts elsewhere.

Case 6 (The slothful executor). T devises property to A "upon probate of my will," "when my estate is settled," "after payment of debts," or upon some similar event related to administration. Courts have sometimes struck down these gifts on the theory the event was a condition precedent which might not happen within lives in being and twenty-one years.[15] No case has been found in Kentucky where such an unflinching application of the Rule has been made.[16]

Case 7 (Wars that never end, and such). T devises property to his issue per stirpes living "when World War II ends," "when the gravel pits are exhausted," or upon some similar event very likely, but not certain, to happen within twenty-one years. Such devises have been held void.[17] A similar type of transfer is a lease of property to commence "when the building is finished." Such a lease was held void in a recent case.[18]

The newest addition to Mr. Leach's collection of queer characters is this one.

Case 8 (The superannuated minor). T devises property "to A for life, remainder to such of A's children as shall reach their respective twenty-first birthdays." (Twenty-one was fixed by common law as "full age" because it was believed that males of that age could bear the heavy armor of a knight and thus could be tenants by knight's service.) Since a person reaches twenty-one at the first moment of the day before his birthday,[19] in effect this remainder is to "such of A's children as shall be living one day after they reach the age of twenty-one." It is arguable that this gift exceeds by one day the Rule against Perpetuities.[20]

These cases do not exhaust the extravagant possibilities which can be dreamed up to invalidate gifts. But they suffice to show how the remote possibilities test works. Some writers have expressed

---

[15] See 6 Am. L. Prop. § 24.23.

[16] Compare Ford v. Yost, 299 Ky. 682, 186 S.W.2d 896 (1944), where the court invalidated a devise in trust for thirty years "from date of probate" upon another theory. KRS 381.220 was amended in 1956 to cure some administrative contingencies. Ky. Acts 1956, c. 175. The amendment, along with the rest of the section, was repealed by the 1960 act.

[17] Brownell v. Edmunds, 209 F.2d 349 (4th Cir. 1953); In Re Wood, [1894] 3 Ch. 381. See 6 Am. L. Prop. § 24.21; Simes & Smith § 1228.

[18] Haggerty v. City of Oakland, 161 Cal. App. 2d 407, 326 P.2d 957, 66 A.L.R.2d 718 (1958), criticized by Professor Leach at 73 Harv. L. Rev. 1318 (1960). Can the principle of this case be extended to invalidate forward commitment agreements and other procedures currently used in mortgage financing?

[19] Erwin v. Benton, 120 Ky. 536, 87 S.W. 291 (1905); Annot., 5 A.L.R.2d 1143 (1949).

[20] Leach, "The Careful Draftsman: Watch Out!" 47 A.B.A.J. 259 (1961).

Drawing by Steinberg; © 1961 The New Yorker Magazine, Inc.

concern that emphasis on these odd cases presents a distorted and unwholesome picture of the Rule, and so tends to delude people into thinking the possibilities test is ridiculous. They assume these cases are exceptional, and not usual. However that may be in other states, Appendix 2 shows that practically all the gifts held void in Kentucky were held void because of one of the possibilities exemplified above.

2

THE MEANING OF "VEST": MYTH AND REALITY

The tendency to assume that a word which appears in two or more rules, and so in connection with more than one purpose, has and should have precisely the same scope in all of them runs all through legal discussions. It has all the tenacity of original sin and must constantly be guarded against.—Walter Wheeler Cook.

The word "vest" is the key word in applying the Rule against Perpetuities. If an interest will "vest" in due time, it is valid. If it may "vest" too remotely, it is void. Where such important legal consequences turn on the use of this particular collocation of four letters, it behooves us to ascertain, as far as may be possible, what this four-letter word means.

An obstinate mythology has made "vest" into a ventriloquism. Though seemingly pronounced by the court, the true source, it is said, is the apt language of the instrument creating the interest. Since words of the instrument control—regardless of the problem before the court—"vest" may be defined solely by reference to such words. History has seen some remarkable efforts to frame definitions which would classify whatever words man could produce; yet none of them gives us any reliable prediction of how the courts will use the word "vest." It has been obvious for many years—at least since Myres McDougal's classic debunking of this myth[21]—that "vest" cannot be given any realistic meaning by referring solely to the words of the instrument. Still there persists this belief in the power of a dead man's words to conquer whatever problem may arise.

This notion that "vest" is a talismanic word seems to rest on

[21] McDougal, "Future Interests Restated: Tradition versus Clarification and Reform," 55 Harv. L. Rev. 1077 (1942).

ignorance of elementary semantics as well as on fallacious logic. At any rate, these matters need some looking into before we turn to the cases and attempt to discover the meaning of "vest." For anyone with a fixed belief in an all-embracing definition of "vest" cannot begin to hope to understand Kentucky perpetuities cases. He will find they stubbornly resist analysis.

It is a truism that the meaning of a word depends upon its context. A pass at the bridge table, for example, is quite different from a pass at a good-looking blonde. And even within the limits of a game of bridge, "pass" can have several different meanings to a partner depending upon the context of prior bids, even though the consequence of passing under the rules of the game is always the same. So it is with "vest." It can have many meanings depending upon the sense and context in which it is used.

In addition to being like all words in that it depends upon a factual context for meaning, "vest" is a word which invokes the sanction of the law. It is a focus of a scheme of relationships between a miscellany of facts on the one hand and an assortment of legal consequences on the other. To say that an interest is "vested" means both that certain factors are in view and that certain legal consequences follow. Because of this—if we are seeking a meaning which will allow us to predict judicial response—we must distinguish between different legal problems in which "vest" is used. It is impossible to say why the court found (or will find) the interest to be "vested" without knowing what the problem is and what policies are germane thereto.[22]

The court may set up a "vested"-"contingent" dichotomy to deal with all sorts of different problems: whether the taker of the interest must survive to the time of possession, whether the interest will "accelerate" upon renunciation, whether the holder of the interest may partition, whether the interest violates the policy against perpetuities. In determining whether the court is going to protect the taker of the interest, and call the interest "vested," each of these problems must be examined separately to determine what facts and policies are relevant to this decision. Relevant policies may include: carrying out the donor's intent, keeping property in the bloodlines, equality of distribution among children, fostering alienability of property, restricting dead-hand control,

---

[22] See *ibid.*; McDougal & Haber, Property, Wealth, Land 309 (1948). *But see* Simes & Smith § 134.

protecting creditors, preventing tax evasion. Where the only policy involved is carrying out the donor's intent, the language of the donor may be the part of the factual context that is most important. The interest may be called "vested," and certain consequences follow, because the grantor clearly intended those consequences to follow. But where the donor's language gives no clear direction or where there are other policies involved (as is obviously the case where a gift is alleged to create a perpetuity), then the donor's language cannot be controlling. It can have at most an indirect effect upon the issue.[23] The myth of ventriloquism assumes the single policy norm is donor's intent and further assumes his intent is clear. Where that is so, litigation is most unlikely. In practically all cases which come to court, the court must resolve an issue where there are competing claimants invoking competing policies. To give "vest" realistic meaning, we must put it in the context of the particular issue involved.

The failure to distinguish between the meaning of "vest" for perpetuities purposes and its meanings in other contexts can lead only to confusion. This is a human failure and one with long precedent in the field of future interests. The treatises are full of definitions of "vest" indiscriminately applied to all problems.[24] These definitions, however, have little place in the context of reality. They are false coin. Their purveyors have assumed that if an interest is "vested" for one purpose, it is "vested" for all purposes. But this is neither logically necessary nor empirically verifiable by the cases.[25] It involves a type of fallacious reasoning John Dewey called "the fallacy of unlimited universalization," and that Moffatt Hancock has more recently called "the fallacy of the transplanted category."[26] It does not take into account

---

[23] For a discussion of factors other than the donor's language which influence construction of the word "heirs," see Simes, "The Meaning of 'Heirs' in Wills—A Suggestion in Legal Method," 31 Mich. L. Rev. 356 (1933).

[24] The most famous is that of Gray § 108: "Whether a remainder is vested or contingent depends upon the language employed. If the conditional element is incorporated into the description of, or into the gift to, the remainderman, then the remainder is contingent; but if, after words giving a vested interest, a clause is added divesting it, the remainder is vested."

[25] See Lynn & Van Doren, "Applying the Rule against Perpetuities to Remainders and Executory Interests: Orthodox Doctrine and Modern Cases," 27 U. Chi. L. Rev. 436 (1960); Schuyler, "Should the Rule against Perpetuities Discard Its Vest?" 56 Mich. L. Rev. 887, 888-926 (1958); Jones, "Vested and Contingent Remainders, a Suggestion Concerning Legal Method," 8 Md. L. Rev. 1 (1943).

[26] Hancock, "Fallacy of the Transplanted Category," 37 Can. B. Rev. 535 (1959).

that the context limits the meaning of a word. It ignores the fact that the purposes and policies of a rule affect the meaning of the words used in stating the rule.

The problem we are concerned with here is violation of the Rule against Perpetuities, and meanings of "vest" derived from its use in other contexts (problems of survivorship, acceleration, destructibility, etc.) involving different policies have no necessary application. This is to a fair degree demonstrable by a brief comparison of perpetuities cases with cases raising the questions of survivorship and acceleration. It should be kept in mind that these latter questions are supposedly controlled by testator's intent, whereas the Rule against Perpetuities is expressly designed to curtail that intent.[27]

In *Clay v. Security Trust Co.*[28] testator devised property in trust to pay the income to Laura for life, and at her death, "I direct my trustee to hold the said estate until my nephew John Ireland Macey ... arrives at the age of thirty-five years, and direct that the income shall be paid to him in monthly installments until the said fund is turned over to him." John predeceased Laura before he reached the age of thirty-five. At Laura's death, John's executor claimed the fund. "The sole question," said the court, "is whether the remainder interest given to John I. Macey in the third clause of the will was a vested or contingent remainder." This is precisely the same vague way perpetuities issues are phrased; more accurately, the question was whether there was a requirement that John survive to age thirty-five. The court held the remainder was "vested with possession postponed"; that is, there was no requirement of survival and the fund passed to John's executor on Laura's death. Two rules of construction designed to find testator's intent were invoked: (a) the absence of a gift over in the event the designated person fails to survive to the time of distribution "vests" the gift; and (b) a gift of income to a person "vests" a gift

---

[27] Failure to distinguish between the use of "vest" for acceleration purposes and for destructibility purposes, which involved an intent-defeating rule like the Rule against Perpetuities, led courts and text writers into one of the most famous hair-splitting distinctions of all times. *Compare* Edwards v. Hammond, 3 Lev. 132, 83 Eng. Rep. 614 (C.P. 1683) (acceleration case) *with* Festing v. Allen, 12 Mees. & W. 279, 152 Eng. Rep. 1204 (Ex. 1843) (destructibility case). The distinction is discussed in 5 Am. L. Prop. § 21.32 without reference to the different problems with which each of these cases dealt. For a careful examination of the context, see Gulliver, Cases on Future Interests 234-39, 244-46 (1959).

[28] 252 S.W.2d 906 (Ky. 1952).

of principal to the same person. In numerous cases involving similar language, where either one or both of these constructional guides could be invoked, but where the issue was not requirement of survival but violation of the Rule against Perpetuities, the court has classified the interest as "contingent," not "vested."[29]

That "vest" takes on a different meaning in accordance with the rule it is used in is strikingly apparent in a comparison of perpetuities cases with cases involving accelerating the remainder upon renunciation of a life estate. In acceleration cases the distinction between "vested" and "contingent" remainders is, according to Professor Richard Powell, of "decisive importance,"[30] just as it is in perpetuities cases. "Contingent" remainders do not accelerate, whereas "vested" remainders do.[31] There are many acceleration cases in Kentucky. Most of them involve interpretation of dispositive language similar to this: "to W for life, and at her death to my children, the issue of any then deceased child to take his parent's share." At testator's death, W renounces her life estate. Invariably the court has held the remainder to children is "vested" and accelerates.[32] The supplanting limitation is not regarded as requiring survival to the death of the widow. On the other hand, supplanting limitations have not been construed so benevolently in perpetuities cases. There they have been held to make the preceding gifts "contingent."[33]

Even Gray recognized that a class gift could be "vested" for many purposes when it is not "vested" under the Rule against Perpetuities. Relying heavily upon eighteenth and nineteenth century English cases, Gray simply restated the decision of English

---

[29] Curtis v. Citizens Bank, 318 S.W.2d 33 (Ky. 1958); Ford v. Yost, 299 Ky. 682, 186 S.W.2d 896 (1945); Hussey v. Sargent, 116 Ky. 53, 75 S.W. 211 (1903); Coleman v. Coleman, 23 Ky. L. Rep. 1476, 65 S.W. 832 (1901); Stevens v. Stevens, 21 Ky. L. Rep. 1315, 54 S.W. 835 (1900).

[30] 2 Powell ¶ 310, at 632.

[31] *Ibid.*; 2 Restatement of Property § 233. *But cf.* Simes & Smith § 796.

[32] Farmers Bank v. Morgan, 308 Ky. 748, 215 S.W.2d 842 (1948); Baldwin's Coex'rs v. Curry, 272 Ky. 827, 115 S.W.2d 333 (1938); Ruh's Ex'rs v. Ruh, 270 Ky. 792, 110 S.W.2d 1097 (1937). See Note, 38 Ky. L.J. 291 (1950), discussing other cases accelerating remainders that orthodoxy would surely classify as contingent.

[33] Curtis v. Citizens Bank, 318 S.W.2d 33 (Ky. 1958); Fidelity & Columbia Trust Co. v. Tiffany, 202 Ky. 618, 260 S.W. 357 (1924); *cf.* Curd's Trustee v. Curd, 163 Ky. 472, 173 S.W. 1148 (1915); Stevens v. Stevens, 21 Ky. L. Rep. 1315, 54 S.W. 835 (1900). *Compare* Breckinridge v. Breckinridge's Ex'rs, 264 Ky. 82, 94 S.W.2d 283 (1936) (acceleration case), *with* Coleman v. Coleman, 23 Ky. L. Rep. 1476, 65 S.W. 832 (1901) (perpetuities case)—gift to remaindermen "if then living," with supplanting limitation, accelerated as vested remainder in former case, held void as contingent remainder in latter.

judges to treat class gifts which can increase in membership as not "vested" under the Rule, even though for most other purposes a class gift subject to open (and not subject to any other contingency) was treated as "vested" as soon as one member qualified. The decisions of Kentucky judges treating remainders subject to total as well as partial divestment as not "vested" under the Rule are but a natural development of this limited English attempt to find definitions appropriate to the perpetuities context. It reflects, as it should, a strong sense of the policy against extended deadhand control and of what practically lessens alienability. The Court of Appeals has, with great good sense, steered remarkably clear of the fallacy of unlimited universalization based upon feudally oriented definitions.[84]

From the preceding discussion it should be clear that the word "vest" is not merely a word to be defined by a text. It is the working tool of the court in applying the Rule against Perpetuities. To discover its meaning requires us to see how the court works with it.

Five meanings of "vest" will be examined below: "vest in possession," "indefeasibly vest in interest," "vest in interest with possession postponed," "vest in interest subject to open," and "vest in interest subject to divestment." The question is, which of these meanings are used in applying the Rule against Perpetuities in Kentucky to future interests in transferees?

A. *Vest in possession*

An interest in property vests in possession when the holder of the interest becomes entitled to possession or enjoyment of the property. Applied to future interests, this meaning involves no substantial difficulty. A remainder or executory interest satisfies the Rule if it necessarily will take effect in possession and enjoyment within the period. Both standard perpetuities doctrine and the Kentucky cases so hold.

---

[84] Because "vested" as used in most other contexts is an inaccurate word to describe what interests are valid under the Rule, and because the word "vested" conceals the important social policy underlying the Rule, Professor Powell believes the Rule should not be formulated as a rule against remote vesting at all, but as a rule against specific fetterings of property found socially inconvenient. His position is cogently stated at 5 Powell ¶ 767 and is adopted by 4 Restatement of Property §§ 370-82.

Case 9. T devises property in trust "to pay the income to my issue per stirpes from time to time living until twenty-one years after the death of my last surviving child or grandchild who was alive at my death, then to pay principal to my issue then living per stirpes." The gifts of income and principal are valid.[35] They are bound to become possessory within twenty-one years of the death of a person alive at T's death, though it will not be known who will enjoy the gifts until they become possessory. The gift of principal does not vest prior to possession.

Is this the only meaning of "vest" that satisfies the Rule? That is, must an interest become possessory within the period, or is the Rule satisfied if it merely vests in interest within the period? According to many writers, a *remainder* is valid if it vests in interest, but an *executory interest* must vest in possession. The reason given is that an executory interest did not have the "capacity" to vest in interest under feudal law. The Court of Appeals has ignored this distinction and has not attempted to classify future interests in transferees as remainders or executory interests. Along with many courts, it has called them all remainders. Because the court has ignored the distinction, and because application of this feudal dichotomy to modern dispositions is impossible to justify,[36] it would not be profitable to set forth an analysis of Kentucky cases in these terms.

In the early cases it was apparently assumed that a future interest in a transferee must become possessory within the period of the Rule or fail. In *Moore's Trustees v. Howe's Heirs*,[37] Chief Justice Boyle, in a frequently cited opinion, referred to the Rule and stated, "A man cannot, therefore, devise over an estate to take effect after that period, and if he does so the limitation over will be void." The requirement that an interest become possessory was said to apply to remainders as well as to executory interests.[38]

---

[35] First Nat'l Bank v. Purcell, 244 S.W.2d 458 (Ky. 1951); Gray v. Gray, 300 Ky. 265, 188 S.W.2d 440 (1945); Emler v. Emler's Trustee, 269 Ky. 27, 106 S.W.2d 79 (1937); Clay v. Anderson, 203 Ky. 384, 262 S.W. 604 (1924); Russell v. Meyers, 202 Ky. 593, 260 S.W. 377 (1924); Gillespie v. Winston's Trustee, 170 Ky. 667, 186 S.W. 517 (1916).

[36] See Dukeminier, "Contingent Remainders and Executory Interests: A Requiem for the Distinction," 43 Minn. L. Rev. 13 (1958).

[37] 20 Ky. (4 T.B. Mon.) 199, 201 (1827); *accord*, Coleman v. Coleman, 23 Ky. L. Rep. 1476, 1477, 65 S.W. 832, 833 (1901); Armstrong v. Armstrong, 53 Ky. (14 B. Mon.) 269, 277-80 (1853).

[38] U.S. Fidelity & Guaranty Co. v. Douglas' Trustee, 134 Ky. 374, 385, 120 S.W. 328, 331 (1909): "The rule in question is that an estate in remainder cannot be created to take effect beyond the end of a life or lives in being and 21 years and 10 months thereafter."

This theory was applied in an extraordinary way two years before the Civil War. The court had before it a deed granting freedom to the children of Martha (a slave) when each reached the age of twenty-five. Some years after the deed was executed, Martha gave birth to a son who, upon reaching twenty-five, brought suit for his freedom. James Harlan, the father of Mr. Justice Harlan I (he of "The Constitution is color-blind"), argued for the slaveowner that the grant of freedom violated the Rule against Perpetuities. The court agreed, holding the limitation might not have "taken effect" during the period.[39] The son remained a slave. If a grant of freedom can be analogized to a per capita gift of money, the decision may be technically correct; but the complete answer to Harlan's argument is the Rule should not apply to a grant of freedom at all. It is monstrous irony that a rule invented to keep property free kept it slave.

More recent cases do not make it wholly clear that a remainder is void if it might vest in possession beyond the period. But, as subsequent discussion reveals, it is perilous for any draftsman to rely on any other assumption.

B. Indefeasibly vest in interest

A *remainder* is, in orthodox vernacular, indefeasibly vested in interest if all the takers are *presently ascertained* and are *certain* to acquire *permanent* possession of the property at some future time. All three of the italicized requirements must be met. Thus:

Case 10. T devises land "to A for life, remainder to A's children for their lives, remainder in fee to B." B (or his estate) is certain to acquire permanent possession of the property in the future. However, he will not acquire possession until the death of A's children, who may not be living at T's death. His remainder therefore may vest in possession too remotely. Under orthodox doctrine it is nonetheless valid under the Rule against Perpetuities because it is indefeasibly vested in interest.

Is a remainder which will vest in interest indefeasibly within the period, though perhaps in possession beyond, valid in Kentucky? The answer is uncertain. The cases point both ways. Two

[39] Ludwig v. Combs, 58 Ky. (1 Met.) 128 (1858). *But see* Davis v. Wood, 56 Ky. (17 B. Mon.) 86 (1856) (James Harlan arguing for the slaves), holding a devise of freedom to all Beck's children and grandchildren living twenty-six years after testator's death did not create a perpetuity.

cases have held an indefeasibly vested remainder to be valid, but each is also explicable on another ground. The first is *Ligget v. Fidelity & Columbia Trust Co.*[40] There John Taggart by will created a trust for his daughter Anna for life, remainder as she by will appointed, and in default of appointment to her issue. Anna appointed to her only son Robert for life, then to Robert's children for their lives, with remainder in fee to Robert's grandchildren. Only Robert was in being at testator's death, and the court held the appointment to Robert's grandchildren void. Under Taggart's will, the corpus passed in default of appointment to Robert, whose remainder vested indefeasibly at Anna's death though not in possession until the death of Robert's children. The court held this remainder valid, although it almost certainly would not vest in possession within Robert's own life (the life in being). It should be noted, however, that Robert, as reversioner, would be entitled to the corpus at the death of his children if his remainder were held void. Therefore the classification of Robert's interest as an indefeasibly vested remainder, and validating it as such, was unnecessary to the decision. He was entitled to the corpus in any event.

The other case holding valid an indefeasibly vested remainder is *Goodloe's Trustee v. Goodloe.*[41] The devise was to A for life, remainder in fee to A's children who reach twenty-one. A was given a power to appoint the property to any widow he might leave for her life. A exercised the power by appointing a life estate to his widow, who was in fact in being at testator's death. The remainder in fee would vest in interest indefeasibly within twenty-one years of A's death, but if A left a widow unborn at testator's death, it might vest in possession too remotely. The court held the remainder valid because it would vest in interest indefeasibly in due time. The case is also explicable on the ground that the remainder is to be treated as a remainder in default of appointment, that a "second look" is taken at A's death to see if his widow is a life in being, and that as she was in being at testator's death, the remainder will in fact vest in possession within twenty-one years of lives in being. The *Ligget* case is the only case which has held valid a remainder which would not in fact vest in possession within the period.

In addition to *Ligget* and *Goodloe*, there are strong dicta in

[40] 274 Ky. 387, 118 S.W.2d 720 (1938).
[41] 292 Ky. 494, 166 S.W.2d 836 (1942).

two cases that an indefeasibly vested remainder (but not a remainder subject to defeasance) will satisfy the Rule.[42] However, one cannot be certain of this in view of several decisions striking down what would commonly be classified as indefeasibly vested interests. Two of these cases require mention here. The others will be dealt with below under the discussion of "Vest in interest with possession postponed" and in a section of Chapter 3 entitled, "Is there a rule limiting the duration of trusts?"

The first of these is the well-known case of *Letcher's Trustee v. Letcher*.[43] The will of Dr. Letcher devised his extensive Ohio River farms to his son Gibney for life, then to a bank in trust to pay one-half the income to the children of his nephew Hugh and one-half to the First Presbyterian Church. Upon the death of Hugh's children the farms were to go to the church in trust forever, but if the church ceased to maintain the church house as a memorial to Dr. Letcher's wife, the farms were to go to the Presbyterian synod in fee. The remainder in fee to the church was, under orthodox classification, a remainder vested subject to divestment in favor of another charity. But since a gift over from one charity to another upon a remote condition is not subject to the perpetuity rule, the gift over could be ignored and the remainder to the church treated as if it were indefeasibly vested. The court, however, holding the gifts to church and synod both void, did not consider it important to determine whether the gift to the church was to be treated as indefeasibly vested. It implied the gift would be void whether classified as indefeasibly vested in interest or vested subject to divestment. The gift to the church was void, the court said, because of the "remoteness of time . . . before it passes to the Session of the Church in trust," and the gift to the synod void because it "postpones the vesting of the title for a remote and indefinite period."[44] This language appears to mean that the Rule requires vesting in possession.

The second case is *Thornton v. Kirtley*.[45] The facts were these. Testatrix created a fifty-year trust of bank stock and other assets

[42] Curtis v. Citizens Bank, 318 S.W.2d 33 (Ky. 1958); Fidelity & Columbia Trust Co. v. Tiffany, 202 Ky. 618, 260 S.W. 357 (1924).
[43] 302 Ky. 448, 194 S.W.2d 984 (1946).
[44] *Id.* at 456, 458, 194 S.W.2d at 989 (1946). The gift to the synod could have been invalidated as a remote gift over on a noncharitable contingency. The court also said the gifts violated the mortmain statute; as to this, see Note, 49 Ky. L.J. 552 (1961).
[45] 249 S.W.2d 803 (Ky. 1952).

23

for the benefit of her issue and to maintain cemetery lots. At the end of fifty years, five shares of bank stock were to be held in further trust to maintain cemetery lots; the remaining amount of principal was to be distributed to her issue then living. The five-share trust to commence after fifty years was, classified as either remainder or executory interest, an indefeasibly vested interest.[46] Nonetheless, it was held void, as was the gift of the remaining principal. The reason: "A future charitable trust must vest or become established within the time allowed by the perpetuity rule" (citing *Letcher*).[47]

It is possible to distinguish *Letcher* and *Thornton* from *Ligget* and *Goodloe* on the ground that vesting in possession is required only of gifts to charities, but this would be a peculiar reversal of the law's usual favoritism. Moreover, other cases dealing with noncharities reflect this same notion that vesting in possession is required. It is also possible that in *Letcher* the court regarded tying up five hundred acres of rich farmland in a church potentially forever as against public policy; that in *Thornton* it saw practical difficulties in creating an interest in five shares of bank stock to spring up in fifty years; and that in both it found a convenient escape from its dilemma in ambiguous words not meant to guide the future. Analyzed in traditional terms, however, these two cases cannot be squared with *Ligget* and *Goodloe*, insofar as they held an indefeasibly vested remainder satisfied the Rule.

C. Vest in interest with possession postponed

The concept of vested in interest with possession and enjoyment postponed originated in cases where the issue was whether the donee had to survive to a specific age or to a specified date to be entitled to the gift. If the donee did not have to survive, his interest was said to be vested in interest with possession postponed. Taking this concept out of its original context and applying it in perpetuities cases, without evaluating its relation to perpetuities policy, cannot be justified. As a verbal device to mitigate the

---

[46] 6 Am. L. Prop. § 24.20; 4 Restatement of Property § 370, com. h, ill. 2; Simes & Smith § 1236.

[47] 249 S.W.2d at 806. *But cf.* Street v. Cave Hill Investment Co., 191 Ky. 422, 230 S.W. 536 (1921), upholding gift to churches after ninety-nine years, if then in existence; Board of Nat'l Missions v. Harrel's Trustee, 286 S.W.2d 905 (Ky. 1956), upholding forty-year trust for Presbyterian Church, then over to Board of Missions.

harsh applications of the Rule, it operates capriciously and uncertainly. And control of enjoyment by the dead hand beyond the perpetuity period seems clearly at war with the purposes of the Rule.

Although the Kentucky court has had several opportunities to save gifts by classifying them as vested with possession postponed, it has consistently refused to do so. In *Hussey v. Sargent*[48] testator devised a sum "to be equally divided and paid to and distributed among" the children of Frederick "when" his daughter Emily reached thirty-five or when she would have reached thirty-five had she lived. Emily was age two at testator's death. There are several constructional rules, applicable where the issue is requirement of survival to distribution, that point to a construction of vested with possession postponed. Yet the court not only rejected that construction; it held the gift violated the Rule *"because* it postpones the enjoyment of the income for a period of 33 years."[49]

In *Coleman v. Coleman*[50] there was a devise in trust to pay income to testator's children, and at the end of twenty-five years to distribute the corpus to the children then living, with the "heirs" of any deceased child taking his share. The gift of corpus to the children must become possessory within their own lives, if at all, and the substitutional limitations to their heirs ordinarily would be construed as vesting in interest at the death of each child. However, the court held the entire trust void, saying that nothing could "vest . . . until 25 years after his death, as it was provided that his estate should not be divided" until then.[51]

The most recent case is *Curtis v. Citizens Bank.*[52] There testator set up a trust to pay part of the income to his four minor children, accumulate the rest, and distribute to each his share of accumulated income and corpus upon his reaching age forty-five. "Should any of my said children die leaving lawful issue of his or her body," the testator further provided, "then I direct that said issue of said deceased child shall take equally among themselves the deceased parent's share, per stirpes, at such time as such

---

[48] 116 Ky. 53, 75 S.W. 211 (1903).
[49] *Id.* at 70, 75 S.W. at 215. (Emphasis added.) See also Martin v. Harris, 305 Ky. 235, 203 S.W.2d 78 (1947), where lower court held void a trust of Tennessee land for benefit of children of named nieces and nephews until youngest child reached thirty-five, but appellate court reversed for lack of jurisdiction.
[50] 23 Ky. L. Rep. 1476, 65 S.W. 832 (1901).
[51] *Id.* at 1477, 65 S.W. at 833.
[52] 318 S.W.2d 33 (Ky. 1958). The trust provisions for testator's children are abridged in the text.

deceased child of mine would have received any distribution under this will had he or she lived." In line with its prior cases rejecting rules of construction that would have vested the gift, the court took the position that nothing vested until time for distribution arrived. It held the gift over to issue void. Professor Sparks, noting this case in his annual survey article, commented: "a testamentary plan was apparently defeated by the court's misunderstanding of the word 'vested'. . . . The court did not give any satisfactory reason why the gifts to grandchildren did not vest upon the deaths of their respective parents with only their payment postponed."[53] Professor Sparks' analysis is of course correct if a remainder vested in interest satisfies the Rule and if there is a constructional preference for vested interests. However, the court's rejection of this preference, which smuggles in policy unexamined, seems not wholly without merit.[54]

It is not entirely clear what these cases really stand for. The least that can be said is that the court has reversed the preference for a vested construction when payment is postponed to an age or date and violation of the Rule against Perpetuities is claimed. Without attempting to apply standard rules of construction, the court has construed gifts to "children," "heirs," and "issue" of living persons to be paid at a specific age or date as not vesting under the Rule until time of payment. *Communis error facit jus.*

D. Vest in interest subject to open (or subject to partial divestment)

A *gift* to a class without words of condition ordinarily vests in interest subject to open when one member of the class is in existence and ascertained. It is subject to partial divestment by the birth or ascertainment of other members of the class. Thus:

Case 11. T devises property "to A for life, remainder in fee to A's children." At T's death A has one son B alive. The remainder vests in B subject to partial divestment by the birth of other children. If C is born to A, C takes a share of the remainder.

[53] Sparks, "Future Interests," 1959 Ann. Survey of Am. Law, 35 N.Y.U.L. Rev. 401, 410 (1960).
[54] See Schuyler, "Drafting, Tax and Other Consequences of the Rule of Early Vesting," 46 Ill. L. Rev. 407 (1951), criticizing the preference for vested construction.

Under orthodox doctrine and under Kentucky cases a remainder vested in interest subject to open is not vested for purposes of the Rule against Perpetuities.[55] The policy reason for this is that those members of the class in existence cannot, by joining, transfer complete ownership of the property. The property is still unmarketable even though the remainder is vested in interest.

E. Vest in interest subject to total divestment

Distinguishing a remainder vested subject to divestment from a contingent remainder is one of the knottiest and most unrewarding of tasks. The former concept was developed by courts to avoid two legal consequences of contingent remainders: destructibility and inalienability. In determining what was a condition precedent and what a condition subsequent, courts drew fine and vexatious verbal distinctions in language; and without regard to their purpose, these distinctions were often carried over to other problems. Since contingent remainders are indestructible and alienable today, the survival of this distinction between conditions precedent and subsequent needlessly complicates the law.

A person who has a remainder vested subject to divestment does not have any present certainty of ever acquiring possession or of retaining possession once acquired. In the sense that the remainder may never become possessory, it is contingent. Professor Freund, with his usual perspicacity, pointed this out half a century ago:

When a testator creates life estates with remainders, he does one of two things: he either gives property to a designated person or persons, subject to a life provision for some other person, or he makes a life provision and leaves it to be determined by circumstances existing at the end of the life where the property is to go. These two alternatives represent the real difference between vested and contingent remainders; "vested subject to be divested," when applied to an estate in expectancy, is in reality contingent; and the treating of such a remainder as vested subject to be divested for the purpose of avoiding certain restrictions or liabilities attached to contingent remainders, is a mere conventional mode of construction that should not mislead or confuse us.[56]

For perpetuity purposes, the Court of Appeals is seemingly in agreement with Professor Freund that the real difference between

---
[55] See pp. 31-35 *infra*.
[56] Freund, "Three Suggestions Concerning Future Interests," 33 Harv. L. Rev. 526, 527 (1920).

vested and contingent remainders is certainty of possession. In several cases it has declined to classify gifts as vested subject to divestment, though standard rules of construction would point in that direction.[57] In two cases it has uttered a strong dictum that an interest vested subject to divestment was not vested for purposes of the Rule.[58] While it has never ruled this meaning of "vest" out of the Rule against Perpetuities, it clearly looks on it with disfavor.

Of course this notion that vesting depends upon certainty of possession is contrary to orthodox doctrine. That doctrine holds a remainder vested subject to divestment is just as much a vested interest under the Rule as a remainder indefeasibly vested. Perhaps the reason underlying the orthodox view is this: Because any divesting interest is void if the divesting may take place beyond the period, the remainder vested subject to divestment must turn into an indefeasibly vested remainder or fail altogether within the perpetuity period. This reasoning assumes that the alternative gifts should be tested separately, and the one which comes last in the instrument should be tested first. (Compare gifts vested subject to partial divestment, where the validity of the divesting interest is not tested separately, and both the vested and the divesting parts of the gift stand or fall together. Is there any policy reason for treating gifts subject to total divestment any differently from gifts subject to partial divestment?)

Summary of the meaning of "vest" under the Rule against Perpetuities. A remainder in fee is valid if it will vest in possession, *i.e.*, become possessory, free of any trust within the perpetuity period. A remainder for life is valid if it will vest in possession within the period, either in trust or as a legal estate.[59] A remainder indefeasibly vested in interest, *i.e.*, a remainder in fee in ascertained persons *certain* to become entitled to permanent possession at some future date, may be vested for purposes of the Rule. The cases on this point, however, are conflicting and the matter cannot be regarded as settled. It is believed that a remainder vested subject to divest-

[57] Curtis v. Citizens Bank, 318 S.W.2d 33 (Ky. 1958); Letcher's Trustee v. Letcher, 302 Ky. 448, 194 S.W.2d 984 (1946); Fidelity & Columbia Trust Co. v. Tiffany, 202 Ky. 618, 260 S.W. 357 (1924); Stevens v. Stevens, 21 Ky. L. Rep. 1315, 54 S.W. 835 (1900); see also cases cited in notes 48 and 50 *supra*.

[58] Curtis v. Citizens Bank, *supra* note 57; Fidelity & Columbia Trust Co. v. Tiffany, *supra* note 57.

[59] The requirement that a fee, but not a life estate, must vest free of any trust is discussed at pp. 57-65 *infra*.

ment, *i.e.*, a vested remainder given to ascertained persons but *not certain* to become possessory, does not satisfy the Rule; but one cannot be completely certain of this because the court usually has had a choice of construing the interest as either contingent or vested subject to divestment, and it may have been merely construing against a vested interest. The court has also rejected rules of construction which lead to vested with possession postponed classification, and has construed as contingent for perpetuity purposes gifts to become possessory at a specified future date or upon attaining a specified age. Lastly, in Kentucky, as elsewhere, a remainder vested in interest subject to open is not vested for purposes of the Rule against Perpetuities.

In short, the only clear channel of meaning is: "vest" means "become possessory." Any other meaning one accepts at his peril.

The court's orientation has not been toward the subtleties and refinements of the feudal concept of vesting, nor toward the academic horsemanship inherent in it. On the contrary, the court has, taking the cases as a whole, shown a sound grasp of policy in defining "vest." In spite of contrary dicta, the sheer weight of results indicates the essential idea basing the decisions is that a rational policy against perpetuities requires a rule against remote possession and enjoyment.[60] This is the indispensable, though largely unacknowledged, premise of the perpetuities cases rejecting the vested with possession postponed construction. It also underlies the rejection of the vested subject to divestment construction. It was, appropriately enough, John Chipman Gray himself who first suggested this was desirable policy. "It seems that in the ideal system of law," wrote Gray, "no interests which did not vest in possession within the allotted period would be allowed. They are within the practical reason of a Rule against Remoteness."[61] More recently, Professors Simes and Schuyler have come to the same conclusion.[62] If, as it seems, this is the policy that moves the court,

---

[60] Only two cases, Ligget and Goodloe, are discordant notes in the policy song the court has apparently been singing for over a century. But there is plenty of irreverent obbligato in dicta. Two recent writers suggest other courts are also "groping toward a possessory test of validity." Lynn & Van Doren, "Applying the Rule against Perpetuities to Remainders and Executory Interests: Orthodox Doctrine and Modern Cases," 27 U. Chi. L. Rev. 436, 461 (1960).

[61] Gray § 972.

[62] Simes, Public Policy and the Dead Hand 80-82 (1955) (with reservations); Schuyler, "Should the Rule against Perpetuities Discard Its Vest?" 56 Mich. L. Rev. 683, 887 (1958).

the law would be greatly clarified by a clear-cut decision to that effect. A decision that remainders must vest in possession within the period would settle the vexing question of whether an indefeasibly vested remainder satisfies the Rule and would, for the most part, take care of trusts that may last too long. It is the only meaning of "vest" that can be applied intelligently and with predictable consistency.

2

APPLICATION OF THE RULE AGAINST PERPETUITIES TO VARIOUS INTERESTS

1
GIFTS TO CLASSES

UNDER the Rule against Perpetuities a class gift cannot be partly valid and partly void. It must be valid for all members of the class, or it is valid for none. If the interest of any member can possibly vest too remotely, the entire class gift is bad. This means that (a) every member of the class must be ascertained (the class must close), (b) the precise share of each member must be determined, and (c) if vesting in possession is required, each member's interest must vest in possession and enjoyment within the period. *Case 1* illustrates a common class gift which is void according to these principles.

Case 1. T devises property "to A for life, then to A's children for life, remainder to A's grandchildren in fee." The remainder to A's grandchildren is void because every member of the class will not be ascertained until the death of A's children, some of whom might not be in being at T's death.[1] If at T's death A has a grandchild, X, alive, X's gift is vested in interest subject to open up and let in afterborn grandchildren, but it is not vested for purposes of the Rule.

Class closing rule. Some gifts to a class may be saved through the operation of a rule which closes the class prior to the time it closes physiologically. Under the "rule of convenience" adhered to in most states the class will close when any member of the class is entitled to immediate possession and enjoyment. This rule is not followed in Kentucky when the gift is to children of a "near relative." In that case the class will not close until it becomes physically impossible for any more members of the class to be born. Thus:

Case 2. O deeds land "to my daughter A for life, then to my grandchildren in fee." At the time of the transfer O has one grandchild, G, alive. Under the rule of convenience G can demand possession of his share at A's death, closing the class and forcing distribution among the grandchildren then living. The gift thus would be valid. In Kentucky, however, the class is kept open until O's children (including any afterborn) are dead. Holding the class open for lives possibly not in being causes the gift to grandchildren to be void.[2]

The theory of the Court of Appeals is that when there is a gift to children of a near relative, the donor intends all the children, whenever born, to share in the gift. Carrying out this intention is more important than the convenience of early distribution in fixed shares. This may be a wise construction when the Rule against Perpetuities is not involved. But so to construe the gift when such construction would violate the Rule is highly questionable. It is to construe first, and then to apply the Rule "remorselessly"—a method esteemed by Gray, but condemned by modern authorities.[3]

[1] Taylor v. Dooley, 297 S.W.2d 905 (Ky. 1957); Thomas v. Utterback, 269 S.W.2d 251 (Ky. 1954); West v. Ashby, 217 Ky. 250, 289 S.W. 228 (1926); Tyler v. Fidelity & Columbia Trust Co., 158 Ky. 280, 164 S.W. 939 (1914); Lindner v. Ehrich, 147 Ky. 85, 143 S.W. 778 (1912); Maher v. Maher, 139 F. Supp. 294 (E.D. Ky. 1956).

[2] Bach v. Pace, 305 S.W.2d 528 (Ky. 1957); Laughlin v. Elliott, 202 Ky. 433, 259 S.W. 1031 (1924).

[3] See 6 Am. L. Prop. §§ 24.43-.46.

Nevertheless, or therefore—one cannot tell which—the Court of Appeals has, by refusing to close the class where the gift is to children of a near relative, invalidated gifts which would be perfectly valid in other states.

It does not necessarily follow from the closing of the class within the perpetuity period that the gift is valid. Every member of the class may be ascertained, but his exact share may not be; and this too is required. In other words, the ultimate number of takers in the class must be fixed so that it neither increases nor decreases. Thus:

Case 3. T devises property "to A for life, remainder in fee to such of A's children as reach twenty-five." The class will close physiologically at A's death (a life in being), but the exact share each child of A will take cannot be determined until all of A's children have passed twenty-five or have died under that age. Because a child might reach twenty-five more than twenty-one years after A's death, the gift is void.[4]

The doctrine of severed shares. Quite frequently testators attempt to tie up property for two generations with remainder in fee to the third generation, as in *Case 1*. If the will is phrased slightly differently from that set forth in *Case 1*, the devise may be valid at common law. The will must provide that upon the death of *each* of A's children (rather than upon the death of *all* of A's children), the share of such child dying shall vest in his issue. If it does, the issue of the children in being at testator's death can prove that their interests will vest in absolutely fixed shares at the death of their parent, a life in being. Their interests are valid. The issue of A's yet-unborn children cannot offer such proof, since their parents are not lives in being, and their interests are void. This is known as the doctrine of severed shares or the doctrine of *Cattlin v. Brown*.[5] Thus:

Case 4. T devises property in trust to pay the income "to A for life, then to A's children for life, and as each child of A dies to distribute the share of corpus on which he had been receiving the income to that child's issue then living per stirpes." A has child B, born before T's death, and child C, born after T's death. The gift to B's issue is valid

[4] Fidelity & Columbia Trust Co. v. Tiffany, 202 Ky. 618, 260 S.W. 357 (1924). Compare Johnson's Trustee v. Johnson, 25 Ky. L. Rep. 2119, 79 S.W. 293 (1904).
[5] From the English case of Cattlin v. Brown, 11 Hare 372 (Ch. 1855). See 6 Am. L. Prop. § 24.29; 4 Restatement of Property § 389; Simes & Smith § 1267.

because it must certainly vest in possession in fixed shares within the period. The gift to C's issue is void.

This rule has been expressly rejected in Kentucky. In *U. S. Fidelity & Guaranty Co. v. Douglas' Trustee*,[6] where the instrument read the same as in *Case 4*, the first life tenant (A) had five children alive when testator died. None was subsequently born to her. It was argued that the doctrine of severed shares saved the gift to A's grandchildren, but the court held to apply this rule and validate the gift to some grandchildren while holding it bad as to others would not carry out the testator's intent. This is hard to justify on the facts of the case, for the evidence was very strong that testator assumed A would have no more children, and at the time of decision A had died without having any more children and it was certain all A's grandchildren would take their shares within lives in being. If the court would not apply the doctrine of severed shares in this case, it is difficult to see any case in which it would.[7]

Separability. The orthodox view is that a class gift cannot be separated into good and bad parts and the good part upheld. Yet in a few cases the court has separated the valid part and allowed it to stand. In *Sandford's Administrator v. Sandford*[8] there was a devise in trust "for the benefit of my brothers and sisters, my nephews and nieces, and their heirs so long as any of them are in existence," then to the X charity. The court held the trust was valid for the lives of the brothers and sisters and nephews and nieces in being at testator's death, and at their death the corpus should be distributed to the "then" heirs of testator. It should be noted that the court did not close the class of takers at testator's death but only the measuring lives of the trust. In effect it accelerated the final distribution date from the time "the family as stated should become extinct" to the death of persons in being. This saved the gift for afterborn as well as for living persons who became entitled to the income within the valid period, and invalidated it with respect to those would become entitled to

---

[6] 134 Ky. 374, 121 S.W. 328 (1909).

[7] Compare Maher v. Maher, *supra* note 1; Thomas v. Utterback, *supra* note 1; Ligget v. Fidelity & Columbia Trust Co., 274 Ky. 387, 118 S.W.2d 720 (1938). In these cases the gift was to A's grandchildren *per stirpes*. Restatement of Property § 389, com. c, says the doctrine of severed shares applies to such a gift, but it was not argued.

[8] 230 Ky. 429, 20 S.W.2d 83 (1929). *But cf.* Smith v. Fowler, 301 Ky. 96, 190 S.W.2d 1015 (1945).

income beyond that period. Changing the measuring lives of a trust, and then ordering distribution to the heirs of testator ascertained at the termination of the trust, comes very close to being an exercise of cy pres.

In a case six years later,[9] testator devised land to A and B "and their heirs for life." Without giving any explanation, the court held "the phrase 'and their heirs' is effectually deleted by the statute against perpetuities." Apparently the court assumed "heirs" meant lineal descendants per stirpes from time to time living and not A's and B's heirs at law ascertained at death. By severing off the lineal descendants as members of the class of life tenants, the court saved the gift for A and B. This case differs from *Sandford's* case in that here the court closed the class of takers rather than the measuring lives of the life estate.

In two other cases of the same era the court saved gifts by construing them as gifts to a class which would close at the death of persons in being.[10] Although the court validated the gifts by construction, in both cases the court went on to say by dictum that the whole gift would not fail even had the gift included persons who might be born too remotely. The good part would be separable from the bad.

These four cases liberally separating class gifts into good and bad parts seem to mark a stillborn epoch in perpetuities development (1929-1939) and not a sustained shift in policy. More often (both before and after the 1930s) the court has construed instruments in favor of invalidity and applied the Rule remorselessly. Witness the rejection of standard devices for saving gifts: the doctrine of severed shares, the class closing rule, the vested with possession postponed construction; witness also the frequent application of infectious invalidity and the tendency to equate "vesting" and "possession." On balance, the Court of Appeals has not been liberal with putative transgressors. It has been unusually strict.

Separating class gifts into good and bad parts is one of the ways the court has dealt with limitations violating the Rule. The other ways are discussed in section 7 of this chapter. And, as will be seen, the four cases above are not altogether reliable precedents.

[9] Renaker v. Tanner, 260 Ky. 281, 83 S.W.2d 54 (1935).
[10] Tuttle v. Steele, 281 Ky. 218, 135 S.W.2d 436 (1939); Tillman v. Blackburn, 276 Ky. 550, 124 S.W.2d 755 (1939); *cf.* Emler v. Emler's Trustee, 269 Ky. 28, 106 S.W.2d 79 (1937). *But see* Thornton v. Kirtley, 249 S.W.2d 803 (Ky. 1952); Fidelity Trust Co. v. Lloyd, 25 Ky. L. Rep. 1827, 78 S.W. 896 (1904).

2
POWERS OF APPOINTMENT

General powers presently exercisable. In applying the Rule against Perpetuities to powers of appointment, it is necessary to separate powers into (a) general powers presently exercisable, and (b) general testamentary powers and all special powers. General powers presently exercisable are treated as absolute ownership for purposes of the Rule. Nothing stands between the donee and absolute ownership except a piece of paper which can be signed at any time; hence the property is not tied up. All that the Rule requires of a general inter vivos power is that it become exercisable within the period. When it becomes exercisable, the property becomes marketable and the policy of the Rule is not offended. Since the donee of a general power presently exercisable is treated as owner, the validity of an interest created by exercise of the power is determined on the same basis as if he owned the property in fee. The perpetuity period runs from the exercise of the power.[11]

An unconditional power to revoke in one person is treated like a general power presently exercisable when the holder can exercise the power to revoke for his own exclusive benefit.[12] The period runs from the termination of the power.

General testamentary powers and special powers. General testamentary powers and all special powers are treated differently from a general power presently exercisable. A person holding one of these powers does not have an absolute and unlimited present right to alienate the property, and consequently he is not treated as owner. In applying the Rule to these powers, two questions arise: (a) Is the power itself valid? (b) Are the interests created by the exercise of the power valid? These questions are discussed below.

The initial validity of testamentary or special powers. For a general testamentary or a special power to be valid, it must not be possible for it to be exercised beyond the perpetuity period. If it can possibly be exercised beyond the period, it is void *ab initio.*[13]

---

[11] 6 Am. L. Prop. §§ 24.30, 24.31, 24.33; 5 Powell ¶¶ 786, 787.
[12] 6 Am. L. Prop. § 24.59; 4 Restatement of Property § 373; Simes & Smith §§ 1250-52.
[13] 6 Am. L. Prop. § 24.32; 5 Powell ¶ 786; Simes & Smith § 1273.

A testamentary or special power cannot be given to an unborn person unless its exercise is limited to the perpetuity period.

A power may be void for a reason other than offending the Rule against Perpetuities, such as improper delegation. The Kentucky court has held, contrary to the weight of authority, that a person who holds a general testamentary power cannot create a further power in another person, unless there is express authorization in the instrument.[14] If there is express authorization, the further power is treated as an extension of the original power. And, like the original power, it is void if it can be exercised beyond the perpetuities period measured from the effective date of the original instrument.

The validity of interests created by exercise of a testamentary or special power. The donee of a testamentary or special power is regarded as the "agent" of the donor with power to fill in blanks in the donor's will. Any interest created by exercise of such power must vest within twenty-one years of some life in being at the date the power was created.[15] The exercise of the power is read back into the original instrument, taking into consideration facts existing on the date of exercise. This is known as the "second look" doctrine (a variation of wait-and-see). This means we wait and see how the donee actually appoints the property, and then we determine on the basis of facts existing at the date of the appointment whether the appointive interests will vest within the period (computed from date of creation of the power). Thus:

Case 5. T devises property "to A for life, remainder as A appoints by will." A appoints "to B for life, remainder in fee to B's children." If B was in being at T's death, the remainder in fee appointed to B's children is valid, since it will vest at the death of B, a life in being. If B was not in being at T's death, the remainder in fee is void.

The second look doctrine is applied in Kentucky as in most jurisdictions.[16] Some writers have suggested that it was rejected in the *Brown*[17] case decided some fifty years ago, but the invalidity of the appointed future interests in that case has since been

---

[14] DeCharette v. DeCharette, 264 Ky. 525, 94 S.W.2d 1018 (1936), criticized 5 Am. L. Prop. § 23.49.
[15] 6 Am. L. Prop. §§ 24.34, 24.35; 5 Powell ¶ 788; Simes & Smith § 1274.
[16] Ligget v. Fidelity & Columbia Trust Co., 274 Ky. 387, 118 S.W.2d 720 (1938); DeCharette v. DeCharette, *supra* note 14.
[17] Brown v. Columbia Finance & Trust Co., 123 Ky. 775, 97 S.W. 421 (1906).

explained on the ground that the donee was authorized to appoint only in fee.[18]

If a donee makes an invalid appointment, what are the consequences? If the power was a general one, the doctrine of capture may apply where it is found the donee intended to blend the appointive assets with his own assets; the appointive assets then pass to the donee's estate. Otherwise the property passes in default of appointment to the takers in default or, if none, to the donor or his heirs.[19]

Any remainder in default of appointment is, like an appointive interest, subject to the Rule against Perpetuities.[20] A remainder in default that will vest indefeasibly in interest within the period has been held valid in two cases[21]—the only instances in Kentucky where a remainder vested in interest has been held to satisfy the Rule. The result in one of them (*Goodloe*) could have been reached by holding to the possessory test of validity and applying the second look doctrine to the gift in default of appointment, for which there is some little authority elsewhere.[22] In *Goodloe* the devise was to A for life, remainder in fee to A's children who reach twenty-one. A was given the power to appoint a life estate to his widow, which he exercised. His widow was, on second look, a person in being at the creation of the power; therefore the remainder would *vest in possession*, if at all, within twenty-one years of the death of A and his widow (lives in being). The court, however, put the case on the more orthodox ground that the remainder would *vest in interest*, if at all, within twenty-one years of A's death, which was enough to satisfy the Rule. Therefore it did not matter whether A's widow was actually unborn or not. Under the 1960 act, wait-and-see is applied to gifts in default of appointment as well as to the appointive interests.

The 1960 Perpetuities Act applies "to appointments made after July 1, 1960, including appointments by inter vivos instrument or will under powers created before July 1, 1960."[23] The

---

[18] Barnes v. Graves, 259 Ky. 180, 82 S.W.2d 297 (1935).
[19] 6 Am. L. Prop. § 24.47, cases 74 and 75.
[20] Chenowith v. Bullitt, 224 Ky. 698, 6 S.W.2d 1061 (1928).
[21] Goodloe's Trustee v. Goodloe, 292 Ky. 494, 166 S.W.2d 836 (1942); Ligget v. Fidelity & Columbia Trust Co., *supra* note 16. See discussion of these cases at p. 22 *supra*.
[22] Sears v. Coolidge, 329 Mass. 340, 108 N.E.2d 563 (1952); see 6 Am. L. Prop. § 24.36.
[23] KRS 381.223.

adoption of wait-and-see does not substantially change the old law on validity of exercise of testamentary and special powers, inasmuch as the validity of interests created by exercise of such a power was judged by a similar principle—second look. The statute leaves in full force the practice of reading back into the original instrument the exercise of the power, and of requiring the measuring lives to be in being at the date of creation of the power.

3

OPTIONS

Options incident to a lease. An option in a lease enabling the lessee to purchase the fee or to renew the lease is not subject to the Rule against Perpetuities.[24] Such options are commercially useful and tend to increase the marketability and development of land. Hence they are not within the policy of the Rule.

Options to expand the scope of an easement. An option to extend the scope of an easement upon future payment of money is, like an option in a lease, not subject to the Rule against Perpetuities. This was decided in *Sorrell v. Tennessee Gas Transmission Company*,[25] where the company was granted an easement for pipelines with the right to lay additional lines upon payment of $2.85 per lineal rod. The court, citing the *Restatement of Property*, held this was a grant of a "present interest" not subject to the Rule. But as the chief reporter for the *Restatement* has subsequently pointed out, avoiding the Rule by calling the option a present interest is specious reasoning. The proper basis for the decision, in Professor Powell's opinion, is that these options have "social advantages which outweigh the policy basing the rule against perpetuities."[26]

Options to purchase not contained in a lease. An option to purchase in gross (that is, not conferred on a lessee) creates in the optionee an equitable future interest subject to the Rule. If it is possible for the option to be exercised beyond the period, it is

---

[24] Vokins v. McGaughey, 206 Ky. 42, 266 S.W. 907 (1924); 6 Am. L. Prop. § 24.57; 5 Powell ¶ 771; Simes & Smith § 1244.
[25] 314 S.W.2d 193 (Ky. 1958); *accord*, Texas Eastern Transm. Corp. v. Carman, 314 S.W.2d 684 (Ky. 1958).
[26] 5 Powell ¶ 771, at 601.

void.[27] The reason for application of the Rule to options in gross is that they fetter alienability of the property, especially when the optionee may purchase at a price less than market price.

The option may take the form of a preemptive option (giving the optionee the power to buy *if* the owner desires to sell) or an ordinary option (giving the optionee the power to buy whether or not the owner desires to sell). The Kentucky court has held both come within the Rule, and has invalidated both preemptive options[28] and ordinary options[29] if unlimited as to time. If the option is personal,[30] or if it cannot be exercised more than twenty-one years after some life in being at its creation,[31] it is of course valid under the Rule.[32]

It is sometimes difficult to distinguish an option from a right of entry for condition broken, which is not within the Rule against Perpetuities. In two cases where the court was required to make this distinction, it came to opposite conclusions. In *Bates v. Bates*,[33] one T. G. Bates conveyed one-half acre to school trustees for $15 in 1908. The deed provided, "T. G. Bates is to have the land at the same price when it ceases to be public property as school house property." The land ceased to be used for school purposes in 1947, after Bates' death. Bates' heirs sued to enforce the provision, claiming Bates had a reversionary interest. The court held Bates had an option which, if personal, ceased at his death or, if unlimited as to time, violated the Rule. Under either construction the heirs could not enforce it. The decision is sound if an analogy is drawn to a preemptive option to repurchase at the price paid. Yet it is not easy to explain why Bates should lose if the deed provides he has to pay $15 to retake the land and should win if the deed provides he can retake it free. In the latter case he would have a right of entry, exempt from the Rule.

[27] 6 Am. L. Prop. § 24.56; 5 Powell ¶ 771; Simes & Smith § 1244.
[28] Saulsberry v. Saulsberry, 290 Ky. 132, 160 S.W.2d 654 (1942) (preemptive option to buy at owner's own price); Maddox v. Keeler, 296 Ky. 440, 177 S.W.2d 568 (1944), noted 33 Ky. L.J. 118 (1945) (preemptive option to buy at $1,000).
[29] *Cf.* Robertson v. Simmons, 322 S.W.2d 476 (Ky. 1959).
[30] Campbell v. Campbell, 313 Ky. 249, 230 S.W.2d 918 (1950); Bates v. Bates, 314 Ky. 789, 236 S.W.2d 943 (1950); *cf.* Rice v. Hall, 19 Ky. L. Rep. 814, 42 S.W. 99 (1897).
[31] Gilbert v. Union College, 343 S.W.2d 829 (Ky. 1961) (applying the 1960 Perpetuities Act). See p. 89 *infra*.
[32] It may, however, violate the rule against unreasonable direct restraints on alienation. See pp. 127-31 *infra*.
[33] 314 Ky. 789, 236 S.W.2d 943 (1950).

In the same year in which the court decided *Bates*, it decided *Trosper v. Shoemaker*.[34] The facts were these. Shoemaker sold land to Trosper with a "restrictive covenant" providing in part: "In the event the said second party fails to buy his petroleum products from the said first party, to-wit: E. S. Shoemaker, then said first party is given the right to repay the consideration herein mentioned, to-wit: $3,000, and take possession of said property." There were further provisions that this "covenant" was binding on the heirs and assigns of both parties and "ran with the land." It is plain the quoted provision did not create a covenant (though other provisions might have). The remedies for breach of a covenant are damages or an injunction. The remedy here was forfeiture upon repayment of the purchase price. The court held this was a "conditional reversionary right" which did not violate the Rule. It is difficult, however, to distinguish this case from *Bates*. Both involved deeds restricting the use of land and providing for forfeiture upon cessation of the specified use and repayment of the purchase price. It is believed the decision, in upholding this assignable forfeiture provision, is unsound. The exemption of the right of entry is a historical anomaly, which cannot be justified in policy, and should not be extended to include interests which can reasonably be classified as options because they require the payment of money to retake the premises.[35]

Fortunately the distinction between an option and a right of entry is somewhat minimized by the 1960 Perpetuities Act. Under KRS 381.216, unlimited options to purchase are valid for twenty-one years and void thereafter. Under KRS 381.219, rights of entry are terminated after thirty years. Hence under either classification, the interest will ultimately be terminated.

4

GIFTS TO CHARITY

A GIFT of property to one charity with a gift over to another charity is not within the Rule against Perpetuities.[36] Thus a gift in trust to pay the income to Christ Church so long as it exists, then

[34] 312 Ky. 344, 227 S.W.2d 176 (1950).
[35] See 4 Restatement of Property § 394, coms. a and c.
[36] Board of Nat'l Missions v. Harrel's Trustee, 286 S.W.2d 905 (Ky. 1956). See generally 6 Am. L. Prop. §§ 24.37, 24.42; 5 Powell ¶ 770; 4 Restatement of Property §§ 396-98; Simes & Smith §§ 1278-87.

to St. Joseph's Hospital, is wholly valid, even though the gift to the hospital may not become possessory for centuries. The rationalization for this exemption is as follows. The policy in favor of supporting charities is stronger than the policy against perpetual fettering of property.[37] It allows a perpetual trust for charity.[38] Since a charitable trust may be perpetual, it does not matter that the income may shift from one charity to another.

This exemption does not apply where the gift to charity follows a gift to an individual. If, in the example in the preceding paragraph, the income were to be paid to the testator's descendants per stirpes so long as there are any in existence (rather than to the church), the gift over to St. Joseph's Hospital would be void because it might vest too remotely.[39] Nor does the exemption apply where there is a gift to a charity with a gift over to an individual other than the transferor or his heirs. The gift over is required to vest within the perpetuity period or fail.

Some testators have devised property to trustees to hold in trust for a charitable institution not then in existence and which may not be organized within the perpetuity period. Without discussing the perpetuities problems which these gifts raise, the Court of Appeals has validated them either by the use of cy pres[40] or on the theory that the trustees have a reasonable time in which to establish the charity.[41]

5

TRUSTS FOR EMPLOYEES

IN 1956, KRS 381.220 was amended to exempt trusts for employees from the Rule against Perpetuities. The amendment provided:

A trust created by an employer as part of a stock bonus plan, pension plan, disability or death benefit plan or profit-sharing plan, for the exclusive benefit of some or all of his employes, to which contribu-

---

[37] But query whether this policy preference holds where the subject matter of the gift is land. See Letcher's Trustee v. Letcher, 302 Ky. 448, 194 S.W.2d 984 (1946).

[38] Kasey v. Fidelity Trust Co., 131 Ky. 609, 115 S.W. 739 (1909); Pullins v. Bd. of Educ. of Methodist Church, 25 Ky. L. Rep. 1715, 78 S.W. 457 (1904). A trust to maintain cemetery lots is treated as a charitable trust. Epperson v. Clintonville Cemetery Co., 303 Ky. 852, 199 S.W.2d 628 (1947).

[39] Smith v. Fowler, 301 Ky. 96, 190 S.W.2d 1015 (1945); Sandford's Adm'r v. Sandford, 230 Ky. 429, 20 S.W.2d 83 (1929).

[40] Myers v. Davis, 311 Ky. 471, 224 S.W.2d 690 (1949).

[41] Searcy v. Lawrenceburg Nat'l Bank, 312 Ky. 610, 229 S.W.2d 312 (1950).

tions are made by such employer or employes, or both, for the purposes of distributing to such employes the earnings or the principal, or both earnings and principal, of the fund so held in trust, shall not be deemed to be invalid as violating the rule against perpetuities or invalid as a suspension of the power of alienation of title to property; but such a trust may continue for such time as may be necessary to accomplish the purposes for which it may be created.

It was feared that such trusts would be found to be noncharitable and subject to the Rule, though there was no previous authority to that effect. Similar statutes allowing permanent trusts for employees have been passed in more than half the states.

The 1956 amendment was incorporated in the 1960 Perpetuities Act and is now KRS 381.217. The language (including the irregular spelling of "employees") was not changed except for omission of the words "or invalid as a suspension of the power of alienation of title to property." Dean Matthews criticized the inclusion of these words in the 1956 amendment on the ground they might revive the rule against suspension of the power of alienation which the court had previously interpreted out of KRS 381.220.[42] In any case their deletion was required when that statute was repealed.

6

TRUSTS FOR ACCUMULATION

STRICTLY speaking, the Rule against Perpetuities is not concerned with trusts for accumulation. It is concerned only with the vesting of interests. There has developed, nonetheless, an analogous rule against accumulations, which is measured by the same period (lives in being plus twenty-one years) and is sometimes thought of as part of the Rule against Perpetuities.[43] Under the rule against accumulations, directions to accumulate income must be limited to lives in being and twenty-one years. If not so limited, the direction to accumulate is void.[44] There are no Kentucky cases applying this

[42] Matthews, "Comments on 1956 Kentucky Legislation: The Perpetuities Amendment," 45 Ky. L.J. 111, 123-26 (1956).
[43] 6 Am. L. Prop. § 24.65; 5 Powell ¶¶ 831, 837, 838; Simes & Smith §§ 1464-65.
[44] Stevens v. Stevens, 21 Ky. L. Rep. 1315, 54 S.W. 835 (1900) (dictum). There was a direction to accumulate income not necessary for support until testator's children reached twenty-one, and then pay it over to them. There was no direction to accumulate income beyond this period. Record on Appeal, p. 2.

rule and passing upon the effect of an invalid direction to accumulate.[45]

7

CONSEQUENCES OF VIOLATING THE RULE

ONCE IT has been determined that an interest is void, the question arises what the consequences will be. If no interest transferred (*i.e.*, in case of a trust, neither income nor remainder interest) will necessarily vest within the period, the entire transfer of course is void. The more usual case, however, is where there is only partial invalidity, where only one of several interests is void. The problem of partial invalidity has long plagued the court, and it has from time to time come to different, and sometimes conflicting, solutions. Aside from a handful of learned specialists who may be blessed with extraordinary powers of divination, few lawyers find it easy to say with certainty what the consequences will be in a given case. There are several rules (given below) which might be applicable, and practically every case requires a court decree to determine the most appropriate one on the particular facts. In any case the consequences will be severe. In all probability the intended beneficiary of the void interest will be wholly deprived of it, and in some cases testator's entire estate plan will be dismembered as a consequence.

A. *Preceding estates stand; invalid interest passes by intestacy*

The general rule set forth in the treatises is that the invalid limitation is stricken from the instrument, and the prior valid estates take effect just as if the invalid limitation were not in the instrument.[46] If the preceding estates are life estates, they remain standing. Striking out the invalid remainder leaves a reversion in the transferor which, if the instrument is a will, passes by statute to the testator's heirs and not to the residuary devisees.[47] Thus:

---

[45] *But cf.* Curtis v. Citizens Bank, 318 S.W.2d 33 (Ky. 1958); Hussey v. Sargent, 116 Ky. 53, 75 S.W. 211 (1903). For possible effects of wait-and-see on the rule against accumulations, see Cohen, "The Rule against Accumulations and 'Wait and See,'" 33 Temp. L.Q. 34 (1959).

[46] 6 Am. L. Prop. § 24.47; Gray § 248; 5 Powell ¶ 789; Simes & Smith § 1262.
[47] KRS 394.500.

Case 6. T devises property "to D for life, remainder to D's children for their lives, remainder in fee to D's grandchildren." The life estates in D and D's children are valid and take effect as written. The invalid gift to D's grandchildren passes by intestacy to T's heirs.[48]

If the preceding valid estate is a defeasible fee, either in possession or in remainder, the invalid divesting interest is stricken out, leaving the fee not subject to divestment. Thus:

Case 7. T devises property "to A for life, remainder to A's children, but if any child of A dies at any time without issue him surviving, his share shall go to X." A has no children at T's death. The gift over to X on failure of issue is too remote because it might vest after the death of persons not in being. It is stricken out and A's children (when and if born) have a remainder in fee simple absolute.[49]

The rule may be otherwise if the defeasible fee would only vest in interest within the period, and not necessarily in possession. In that case the defeasible fee itself may be void for vesting in possession too remotely.[50]

B. *Preceding estates stand; invalid interest passes to the last person(s) entitled to the income*

A *second* rule for dealing with invalid remainders after life estates, directly opposed to rule A, has been applied in some cases.[51] Under

---

[48] Bach v. Pace, 305 S.W.2d 528 (Ky. 1957); Chenowith v. Bullitt, 224 Ky. 698, 6 S.W.2d 1061 (1928). In Thomas v. Utterback, 269 S.W.2d 251 (Ky. 1954), noted 43 Ky. L.J. 559 (1955); Renaker v. Tanner, 260 Ky. 281, 83 S.W. 2d 54 (1935); and Laughlin v. Elliott, 202 Ky. 433, 259 S.W. 1031 (1924), the preceding life estates stood, but the court declined to say what happened to the invalid remainder.

Compare Sandford's Adm'r v. Sandford, 230 Ky. 429, 20 S.W.2d 83 (1929), where the court ordered the property to be distributed, when life estates terminated, to "the *then* heirs and next of kin of the testator."

[49] Holoway v. Crumbaugh, 275 Ky. 377, 121 S.W.2d 924 (1938); Beall v. Wilson, 146 Ky. 646, 143 S.W. 55 (1912); Brumley v. Brumley, 28 Ky. L. Rep. 231, 89 S.W. 182 (1905); *cf.* Miller v. Miller, 151 Ky. 563, 152 S.W. 542 (1913).

[50] Letcher's Trustee v. Letcher, 302 Ky. 448, 194 S.W.2d 984 (1946). *Compare* Curtis v. Citizens Bank, 318 S.W.2d 33 (Ky. 1958), *and* Fidelity & Columbia Trust Co. v. Tiffany, 202 Ky. 618, 260 S.W. 357 (1924), *with* 6 Am. L. Prop. § 24.47, case 72. See pp. 23-28 *supra.*

[51] Barnes v. Graves, 259 Ky. 180, 82 S.W.2d 297 (1935); Curd's Trustee v. Curd, 163 Ky. 472, 173 S.W. 1148 (1915); Tyler v. Fidelity & Columbia Trust Co., 158 Ky. 280, 164 S.W. 939 (1914); Lindner v. Ehrich, 147 Ky. 85, 143 S.W. 778 (1912); U.S. Fidelity & Guaranty Co. v. Douglas' Trustee, 134 Ky. 374, 121 S.W. 328 (1909). This rule has been adopted by statute in Pennsylvania and Georgia. Pa. Stat. Ann. tit. 20, § 301.5(c) (1950); Ga. Code Ann. § 85-707 (1955).

this rule the invalid interest passes to the takers of the last valid life estate rather than to the transferor or his heirs. Applied to *Case 6*, the remainder in fee would pass to D's children.

In *Ligget v. Fidelity & Columbia Trust Co.*,[52] the court took notice of this line of cases which is opposed to the orthodox rule. It attempted to reconcile them by pointing out that, "It has merely happened that the one who took the last valid life estate was also the one who would take the property under our statute of descent and distribution. Such taker would take it under the statute of descent and distribution and not because he happened to be the holder of the last valid life estate."[53] The court's attempted reconciliation does not stand close inspection, for in the *Barnes*, *Curd*, and *Lindner* cases[54] the last life tenants and the testator's heirs were not the same persons. The testator had other heirs besides the life tenants. The instruments all read essentially the same as in *Case 6* and T's heirs were D, E, and F and not merely D alone. The cases held the invalid remainder passed to D's children. Obviously that result could not have been reached solely through application of rule A. Nevertheless, even though the facts in the prior cases were inaccurately presented (perhaps unconsciously), rule B is probably no longer operative in the state courts.[55]

C. *Infectious invalidity; preceding valid estates fall with invalid remainder*

The rule of infectious invalidity[56] is exactly what its name implies. The invalidity of the remainder infects the valid preceding estates and causes them to fall. It is an exception to general rule A. It is applied where the invalid gift is thought to be an essential part of testator's scheme, and if it fails, the testator would prefer the entire devise to fail. Applying it to *Case 6* above, the life estates in D and D's children would be struck down with the invalid gift in fee.

The Court of Appeals has applied the principle of infectious invalidity in numerous cases. The leading case is *Taylor v.*

---

[52] 274 Ky. 387, 118 S.W.2d 720 (1938).
[53] *Id.* at 396, 118 S.W.2d at 725.
[54] Note 51 *supra*.
[55] It was applied by a federal court as late as 1956, however. Maher v. Maher, 139 F. Supp. 294 (E.D. Ky. 1956), noted 9 Okla. L. Rev. 440 (1956), criticized by Professor Sparks, 32 N.Y.U.L. Rev. 419, 429 (1957) ("it is clear that the rule applied is not the law in Kentucky").
[56] 6 Am. L. Prop. § 24.48; 5 Powell ¶ 789; Simes & Smith § 1262.

Dooley.⁵⁷ There testator devised one-half of his property in trust for his daughter Elizabeth for life, then to Elizabeth's children for their lives, remainder in fee to Elizabeth's grandchildren (same as *Case 6*). The other half he devised outright to his son Edwin. Elizabeth and Edwin were his only children and heirs. The court pointed out that testator's basic scheme was to treat his children equally, and the general rule A would result in inequality. If the invalid remainder which testator attempted to devise to Elizabeth's grandchildren passed to testator's heirs, Edwin would wind up with three-fourths of the property—his half and half of that devised to Elizabeth's line. Since this would clearly violate testator's intention, the court struck down the valid life estates given to Elizabeth and her children *and* the devise in another clause to Edwin, resulting in intestacy.⁵⁸ The court then salvaged something from this wholesale destruction by ordering Elizabeth's intestate share to be held in trust for her life under provisions of the will applicable to her testate share.⁵⁹ (Is there any authority for this last action except cy pres, which prior to July 1, 1960, was not thought to apply to invalid private trusts?)

The result is sound under standard doctrine which gives the court only two choices: passing the invalid interest to testator's heirs or using the principle of infectious invalidity. A third choice, strikingly appropriate in a case where the general rule A results in unintended inequality and the preceding life tenants are the parents of the bereft remaindermen, is rule B above. One year before *Taylor v. Dooley*, in a case involving almost parallel facts, Federal Judge Swinford applied rule B, and held the invalid remainder passed to the preceding life tenants.⁶⁰ (Shades of *Erie Railroad v. Tompkins!*) If this had been done in *Taylor v. Dooley*, Elizabeth's life estate in trust would have remained standing and

---

⁵⁷ 297 S.W.2d 905 (Ky. 1957). See also Fidelity & Columbia Trust Co. v. Tiffany, 202 Ky. 618, 260 S.W. 357 (1924).

⁵⁸ *Accord*, 6 Am. L. Prop. § 24.52; see *In Re* Morgan's Trust, 111 N.Y.S.2d 142, *aff'd*, 118 N.Y.S.2d 556 (1952), reaching the same result on substantially similar facts.

⁵⁹ This required judicial insertion in the will of the words set off in brackets in the following quotation. Article 6 of the will read: "I direct that all property which passes or may pass to my daughter Elizabeth D. Flynn under the terms of this will [or by intestacy] shall pass to Lewis B. Flynn, Jr. as trustee for said Elizabeth D. Flynn for and during her natural life." (Record, p. 8.)

⁶⁰ Maher v. Maher, *supra* note 55. Counsel for both sides argued that cy pres applied, and the court may thus have been influenced into thinking it could choose whichever rule best carried out testator's intent.

her children would have taken the remainder in fee. This would approximate most closely the average testator's intention, which is what these rules are designed for. It should be noted that by ordering the fee which Elizabeth took by intestacy to be held in trust for her life, the court came to a net result fairly close to that which would be reached by way of rule B. But in view of the language in the *Ligget* case disapproving rule B, the Court of Appeals will probably not apply that rule confessedly to instruments taking effect before July 1, 1960.

The crucial fact in *Taylor v. Dooley* was that, contrary to testator's intent, the children would take unequal portions if the valid estates stood. That fact has not been present in several cases where valid gifts were struck down, and in all of them the use of infectious invalidity is extremely difficult to justify. The most recent example of this destructive principle unchained is *Curtis v. Citizens Bank*.[61] There testator left property worth more than $400,000 in trust for his four minor children. The trustee was directed to pay each $100 a month and was given discretionary power to pay hospital, medical, and emergency expenses, to pay for a college education for each, and to purchase a home for each child upon marriage. The trustee was further directed to distribute to each child one-third of his share of the corpus and accumulated income at age forty, one-third at age forty-five, and one-third at age fifty. In case any child failed to live to distribution, there was a gift over to his surviving issue, such issue to take at the time the parent would have taken had he lived. The gift over to grandchildren was held void. And then with one brief sentence—"the general scheme of the testator would be frustrated by attempting to uphold the trust as to his children"—the court struck down the gifts to the children as well. Surely this is a harsh way to deal with testator's estate plan. His scheme was clear enough. His children were in the custody of his divorced wife, who had remarried, and the will gives every evidence that testator (a self-made man) wanted to keep the corpus out of the control of his ex-wife and out of the hands of his children until they reached middle age. His provisions with respect to income were not as liberal as they might have been, but they did not leave the children entirely destitute ($100 a month each, medical and college expenses

[61] 318 S.W.2d 33 (Ky. 1958). The facts stated in the text which do not appear in the opinion are taken from the Record on Appeal, pp. 4-5.

paid, and a house upon marriage). The court gave no reason why this scheme was frustrated by the failure of the gift over. If the general rule had been applied, giving the invalid interest to testator's children by intestacy, they would have held all interests in the trust. They could have terminated the trust when they all became of age unless termination would frustrate a material purpose of the testator. If the court was disturbed by the partial accumulation of income after majority, the proper course would have been to allow termination of the trust at majority or to strike down the accumulation provisions. There seems to be no reason at all for infectious invalidity to kill off the entire trust.

A result similar to that reached in *Curtis* has been reached in other cases.[62] As in *Curtis*, the consequence was testator's children received the property immediately free of trust, which testator did not intend, but at least his intent was carried out to the extent that some or all of his intended beneficiaries did receive the property. The same thing cannot be said of *Letcher's Trustee v. Letcher*,[63] where the intended beneficiaries were wholly deprived of the property. There testator gave his nephew Hugh's children a life estate, with remainder in trust for a church. The court, holding the remainder void, struck down the gift to Hugh's children as well, resulting in the property passing to testator's daughter-in-law.

The constructional rule of infectious invalidity is a wise one if limited to circumstances where the testator's intent would clearly be frustrated by upholding the valid gifts. The Kentucky court has not so limited it. The court has given it broad application, sometimes seemingly treating it as a rule of law. Under the 1960 Perpetuities Act the rule of infectious invalidity is severely limited, if not totally abolished, with respect to instruments effective after July 1, 1960. KRS 381.216 now provides that the court shall reform the *invalid interest* "to approximate most closely the intention of the creator of the interest." Reforming the invalid interest is a narrower power than destroying the entire limitation under the rule of infectious invalidity.

---

[62] Thornton v. Kirtley, 249 S.W.2d 803 (Ky. 1952); West v. Ashby, 217 Ky. 250, 289 S.W.2d 228 (1926); Fidelity Trust Co. v. Lloyd, 25 Ky. L. Rep. 1827, 78 S.W. 896 (1904); Coleman v. Coleman, 23 Ky. L. Rep. 1476, 65 S.W. 832 (1901); Stevens v. Stevens, 21 Ky. L. Rep. 1315, 54 S.W. 835 (1900). In Thornton v. Kirtley, *supra*, the invalid limitation also infected a subsequent gift as well as the preceding estates.

[63] 302 Ky. 448, 194 S.W.2d 984 (1946).

D. Reform of invalid interest by cy pres

The power of a court to reform gifts to carry out the general intent of the donor when his express language cannot be given effect is known as cy pres. The standard view is that cy pres applies to charitable gifts only, never to trusts for private beneficiaries. Courts supposedly have no power to reform private trusts to make their provisions conform to the Rule against Perpetuities. Nonetheless, private trusts have occasionally been reformed in Kentucky, although usually without any mention of the cy pres doctrine.

In two cases just after the turn of the century the court reformed the invalid gift, although in quite different ways. In *Hussey v. Sargent*,[64] the court had before it the will of a New Hampshire testator, creating a testamentary trust for the support of his grandchildren. The trust was to terminate and the corpus vest (a) when his granddaughter Emily reached thirty-five, or (b) if she died before reaching that age, when she would have reached thirty-five had she lived. Testator was survived by his son and his two-year-old granddaughter Emily. Under standard doctrine the contingencies upon which the gift of corpus will vest are tested separately, since testator has expressly separated them.[65] The gift on the first contingency (Emily's reaching thirty-five) is valid, as it must vest, if at all, during Emily's life. The gift on the second contingency is void since it may vest more than thirty years after the death of Emily and testator's son. The Court of Appeals did not treat the two contingencies separately, however. It treated them as one and held the gift of corpus might vest too remotely. But since the law of New Hampshire controlled, and cy pres was applied there, the court did not strike down the gift. Instead, it ordered the trust to be terminated and the corpus distributed twenty-one years after testator's death. (The New Hampshire court probably would have reformed the gift by cutting back the age contingency to twenty-one.)[66]

The next year, in *Johnson's Trustee v. Johnson*,[67] the court had before it a Kentucky testatrix's will containing a devise similar to

[64] 116 Ky. 53, 75 S.W. 211 (1903).
[65] Miller v. Miller, 151 Ky. 563, 152 S.W. 542 (1913); Beall v. Wilson, 146 Ky. 646, 143 S.W. 55 (1912); Armstrong v. Armstrong, 53 Ky. (14 B. Mon.) 269 (1850); 6 Am. L. Prop. § 24.54.
[66] See Edgerly v. Barker, 66 N.H. 434, 31 Atl. 900 (1891).
[67] 25 Ky. L. Rep. 2119, 79 S.W. 293 (1904).

that in *Hussey*. The will devised property in trust to pay income to testatrix's son for life, then to the son's children until the youngest child reached twenty-five, then to divide corpus among them. The court ordered the age limitation struck from the will and the property distributed among the children at the son's death; "the period of distribution fixed by the testatrix being void, the will will be construed as if no such conditions were contained in it."[68] The case is also explicable on the ground that the children had vested interests with payment postponed and only the provision for holding in trust violated the Rule.

In two other cases the court has reached unusual results which are difficult to explain under any theory except cy pres. In *Sandford's* case[69] the court severed off afterborn persons as the measuring lives of a trust, held it valid for the remaining lives in being, and ordered the corpus to be distributed to the heirs of testator ascertained at the termination of the trust. In *Taylor v. Dooley*[70] the court inserted "or by intestacy" in a will in order to hold in trust an intestate share resulting from an invalid gift. The justification given in both cases is testator's intent. Neither case cites any authority for such remodeling, and it is believed there is none except the doctrine of cy pres, which has long been thought to apply to charitable gifts only.

With respect to instruments effective after July 1, 1960, cy pres is the required method of dealing with void interests.

[68] *Id.* at 2121, 79 S.W. at 295.
[69] Sandford's Adm'r v. Sandford, 230 Ky. 429, 20 S.W.2d 83 (1929) (see text accompanying note 8 *supra*).
[70] 297 S.W.2d 905 (Ky. 1957) (see text accompanying note 59 *supra*).

3

THE TROUBLES CAUSED BY THE STATUTE PROHIBITING SUSPENSION OF THE POWER OF ALIENATION

1

THE MEANING OF KRS 381.220, PROHIBITING SUSPENSION OF THE POWER OF ALIENATION (APPLICABLE TO TRANSFERS THAT TOOK EFFECT PRIOR TO JULY 1, 1960)

IN THE Senate debate on the 1960 Perpetuities Act the distinguished chairman of the Judiciary Committee, Senator George Overbey, characterized Kentucky perpetuities law as "disorganized confusion." Tautological though it may be, a more telling description would be hard to come by. There are not just the usual knots and nonsense of perpetuities law found everywhere. In addition, Kentucky has—or, more accurately, before 1960 had—a statute which prevented the law from being put into any particular set of verbal containers, and kept there. This was the 1852 act commonly referred to as Kentucky's perpetuities statute. With the reviser's headnote, it reads:

> KRS 381.220. *Restraints on alienation; duration of; exceptions.* The absolute power of alienation shall not be suspended by any limitation or condition whatever, for a longer period than during the continuance of a life or lives in being at the creation of the estate, and twenty-one years and ten months thereafter.

What this statute meant has been in dispute ever since it was enacted. In interpreting it, the Court of Appeals spoke ambivalently, and many of the cases were in sharp disagreement with each other.

By its express words the statute enacted a rule prohibiting suspension of the power of alienation, which must be clearly distinguished from the rule against remote vesting.[1] The rule against remote vesting (the common law Rule against Perpetuities) is concerned solely with *contingent* interests which may remain contingent beyond lives in being plus twenty-one years. The policy underlying it is that all contingent interests, assignable and nonassignable, impair marketability. The rule prohibiting suspension of the power of alienation proceeds upon a different policy assumption. The power of alienation is suspended only when there are not persons in being who can convey an absolute fee. The rule assumes that *legally unassignable* interests make property unmarketable and should be struck down if they remain unassignable for more than the permitted period. Since all vested and contingent future interests are assignable or releasable if the holders thereof are ascertainable, only interests given to unborn or unascertainable persons (unassignable interests) suspend the power of alienation. To put it shortly, the rule against remote vesting applies to all contingent interests; the rule against suspension of the power of alienation applies only to interests that are contingent because the taker is unborn or unascertainable.

The rule against remoteness of vesting is the more inclusive. Any interest which will violate the suspension rule will necessarily violate the rule against remoteness, but the converse is not true. Thus:

---

[1] For a very clear explanation of the difference between these two rules, see Gulliver, Cases on Future Interests 79-81 (1959).

Case 1 (Contingent remainder after term of years). T devises property "to A for ninety-nine years, then in fee to Christ Church if it is then in existence." The power of alienation is never suspended since A, Christ Church, and T's heir (the reversioner) may join together and convey a fee simple. Under the suspension rule all interests are valid.[2] However, the gift to Christ Church is contingent on its being in existence after ninety-nine years, and this violates the rule against remote vesting. (If the gift over had been to A's issue whenever born living ninety-nine years from date, the gift over would be to unascertained persons and would have violated both rules.)

Case 2 (Shifting executory interest). O deeds land "to the Fort Spring Turnpike Co., but if it ceases to use the land as a toll house, then to X." The contingent interest in X may be conveyed, and thus does not suspend the power of alienation.[3] However, it is contingent on an event that may happen too remotely and is void under the rule against remote vesting.

Whether the 1852 revisers intended by this statute simply to enact the common law Rule against Perpetuities, whatever it was (or turned out to be), or intended to enact a rule against suspension of the power of alienation is doubtful. The statute was modeled upon section 15 of the New York Revised Statutes of 1830. At the time the New York revisers worked, it was not clear whether the common law Rule was against remote vesting or suspension of the power of alienation or both. The New York revisers added three sections to the New York statutes: one forbidding suspension of the power of alienation beyond the period set by law (section 15); another requiring a contingent remainder after a term of years to "vest in interest" within the period (section 20); and a third providing that an executory interest might be limited on a fee if such executory interest were certain to become possessory within the period (section 24).[4] These three sections, covering all known types of future interests held void for perpetuity under decisions prior to 1830, indicated that the revisers were attempting to restate the common law as it then existed. In Kentucky, however, section 20 (which would invalidate the gift to the church in *Case 1*) and section 24 (which would invalidate the gift to X in *Case 2*) were not adopted. Since

---

[2] Street v. Cave Hill Investment Co., 191 Ky. 442, 230 S.W. 536 (1921). Counsel failed to argue the gift to the church vested too remotely.

[3] Patterson v. Patterson, 135 Ky. 339, 122 S.W. 169 (1909). Court held the statute did not enact the rule against remote vesting.

[4] Subsequently codified as N.Y. Real Prop. Law §§ 42, 46, and 50, respectively.

these sections covering known types of perpetuities were omitted, it is arguable that the Kentucky revisers were not endeavoring to restate the common law but were framing a new rule against unassignable interests to supplant the common law.

Unfortunately, the New York and Kentucky revisers worked in this field before the time of John Chipman Gray, whose great treatise on the Rule against Perpetuities was first published in 1886. Gray insisted the Rule was against remote vesting alone and assignable contingent interests subject to it. Ultimately this view prevailed in England and in practically every court in this country, and today it is generally accepted that the common law Rule against Perpetuities is a rule against remote vesting. The states which had enacted statutes prohibiting suspension of the power of alienation were left with the problem of determining whether their statutes were declaratory of the common law, as Gray had later interpreted it, or were additions to or replacements of that law.

In more than one hundred years and one hundred cases this problem was never finally resolved in Kentucky. At one time or another the Court of Appeals interpreted the statute as forbidding (a) interests which vest too remotely, (b) interests which suspend the power of alienation, and (c) direct restraints on alienation.[5] The reviser of statutes, by his heading supplied in 1894 and adhered to until the act was repealed in 1960, assumed it incorporated rule (c).[6] The express words of the statute enacted rule (b). Yet the court in recent years favored the view that it embodied rule (a). In 1956 the court, noting the confusion in interpretation, stated:

> The proper view is that the statute, as embodying the rule against perpetuities, is concerned with the remote vesting of estates rather than restraints on alienation of vested estates despite the language of the statute. . . . However, it is unnecessary to decide that the statute may not be applied to restraints on alienation.[7]

Three years later, in 1959, the court again dealt with the "unfortunate confusion" caused by the statute. Admitting that in recent

[5] See Roberts, "Kentucky's Statute against Perpetuities," 16 Ky. L.J. 97 (1928).

[6] The reviser confused the rule against suspension of the power of alienation with the rule against direct restraints on alienation, with which it has no logical connection. Direct restraints do not ordinarily suspend the power of alienation. See pp. 114-17 *infra*.

[7] Taylor v. Dooley, 297 S.W.2d 905, 907-08 (Ky. 1956).

cases the statute had been construed as prohibiting remote vesting, the court nonetheless concluded that "the common law rule against suspension of the power of alienation has existed in the common law of this state regardless of the troublesome statute."[8] Now here is an odd twist: to read the express language out of the statute, and then to bring the express language back in as a common law rule (which Gray said it never was). While there is an authoritative ring to this statement of the court, it cannot be taken at face value. Quite clearly the court did not mean to refer to the rule against suspension of the power of alienation at all, but to the rule against direct restraints on alienation, with which it has frequently been confused and which is discussed in Chapter 6.

As there never was an authoritative construction adhered to by the court, no one can really say what the statute meant. Only one thing is reasonably clear. The common law rule against remote vesting was in force prior to the statute and was repeatedly declared to be in force while the statute was on the books.[9] Whatever else the statute did, it did not change that rule, except possibly to extend the common law period by ten months.

The common law perpetuity period is "lives in being plus twenty-one years" (plus any actual periods of gestation). It will be noted that the 1852 revisers added "and ten months" to this period. Why they did this is unknown. A historian might find some connection with the 1807 act prohibiting reading or treating as authority in Kentucky courts any English post-Revolutionary cases.[10] This chauvinistic piece of legislation would have prevented anyone from considering as authority *Cadell v. Palmer*,[11] an 1833 English case which finally settled the period of the Rule. Before this case, it was not clear that the perpetuity period included only

---

[8] Robertson v. Simmons, 322 S.W.2d 476, 483 (Ky. 1959).

[9] Page v. Frazier's Ex'rs, 77 Ky. (14 Bush) 205 (1878); U.S. Fidelity & Guaranty Co. v. Douglas' Trustee, 134 Ky. 374, 120 S.W. 328 (1909); Cammack v. Allen, 199 Ky. 268, 250 S.W. 963 (1923); Curtis v. Citizens Bank, 318 S.W.2d 33 (Ky. 1958); Robertson v. Simmons, *supra* note 8. For pre-1852 cases, see note 12 *infra*.

[10] Ky. Acts 1807, c. 7. This was a compromise bill offered by Henry Clay. The original bill prohibited reading English cases of any date. It is not without irony that the Great Compromiser became one of the first victims of his own patriotic version of book burning. Less than three months after the act was approved, Clay attempted to read in court from an 1802 opinion of Lord Ellenborough summarizing cases before 1776, which were not available in their original reports. The chief justice stopped him and ruled: "The book must not be used at all in court." Hickman v. Boffman, 3 Ky. (Hardin) 356, 373 (1808). The act was repealed in 1852.

[11] 1 Cl. & Fin. 372 (1833).

actual periods of gestation after twenty-one years rather than nine or ten months in gross. *Cadell v. Palmer* decided only actual periods of gestation could be allowed. The revisers, in fixing the period at "lives in being at the creation of the estate, and twenty-one years and ten months thereafter," may not have considered *Cadell v. Palmer* as authority.[12] Indeed, if they adhered to the statute, they may not even have read it. Whether "and ten months" meant "ten lunar months," an old-fashioned way of referring to the period of gestation, or a further period in gross has never been decided by the Court of Appeals. And, since the statute has been repealed,[13] it probably never will be.

2

IS THERE A RULE LIMITING THE DURATION OF TRUSTS?

ONE REPEATEDLY finds in Kentucky cases references to "the Kentucky law of perpetuities which limits the duration of a trust."[14] Under the common law a trust does not have to conform to the perpetuity period and may extend beyond it. The Rule against Perpetuities is concerned only with the time interests vest, not with trust duration. The question arises, then, whether the Kentucky court is laying down a rule requiring trusts to conform to the perpetuity period or whether the court is merely saying the perpetuity rule *indirectly* limits the duration of a trust.

The cases which raise this question can be telescoped into two fact situations:

[12] The Kentucky cases fixing the period were ambiguous. Before 1852 the court referred to the period as follows: "life, or lives in being, and twenty-one years and a few months," Moore's Trustees v. Howe's Heirs, 20 Ky. (4 T.B. Mon.) 199, 201 (1826); "a life in being and twenty-one years and nine months," Brashear v. Macey, 26 Ky. (3 J.J.M.) 89, 91 (1829); "a life in being and 21 years," Luke v. Marshall, 28 Ky. (5 J.J.M.) 353, 355 (1831); "a life or lives in being and twenty-one years, and the period of gestation," Birney v. Richardson, 35 Ky. (5 Dana) 424, 427 (1837); "a life in being and twenty-one years thereafter," Atty. Gen. v. Wallace's Devisees, 46 Ky. (7 B. Mon.) 611, 616 (1847).

[13] The repeal was prospective only, however. KRS 381.220 remains applicable to inter vivos instruments and wills that took effect before July 1, 1960. Ky. Acts 1960, c. 167, § 9; KRS 381.223.

[14] Board of Nat'l Missions v. Harrel's Trustee, 286 S.W.2d 905, 907 (Ky. 1956) (Stanley, J.); see Farmers Nat'l Bank v. McKenney, 264 S.W.2d 881 (Ky. 1954); Sandford's Adm'r v. Sandford, 230 Ky. 429, 20 S.W.2d 83 (1929); Clay v. Anderson, 203 Ky. 384, 262 S.W. 604 (1924); Russell v. Meyers, 202 Ky. 593, 260 S.W. 377 (1924); Tyler v. Fidelity & Columbia Trust Co., 158 Ky. 280, 164 S.W. 939 (1914). See also cases cited notes 15 and 16 *infra*.

Case 3. T devises property in trust for twenty-five years "to pay the income to my children, and at the end of twenty-five years to distribute the corpus to my children then living, with the children of any deceased child taking his share." The gift of corpus will indefeasibly vest in interest at the death of all T's children (lives in being), but it may not become possessory until beyond the period. The gift of corpus has been held void under the Rule because it might not be distributed within the period,[15] often bringing down the entire trust as a consequence.

Case 4. T devises property in trust "to pay income to A for life, then to B's children for their lives, then to the First Presbyterian Church forever." A and B and three children of B survive T. The church has a remainder indefeasibly vested in interest, but it will not become possessory until A and B's children (including any afterborn ones) are dead. The gift to the church has been held void because it does not vest within the period of the Rule.[16] (The secondary life estate in B's children was also held void, either because it might last for lives not in being or because of infectious invalidity. The opinion is unclear.[17])

The *Restatement of Property* takes the position that when "these cases are examined carefully it appears that the Kentucky law on trust duration is in no way different from the common law."[18] Exactly how these cases are "examined carefully" to make them fit the common law is not revealed and remains *in pectore doctorum*. It is plain the cases do one of two things. Either they hold trusts invalid because of their duration, or they hold remainders invalid because they may vest in possession beyond the period

---

[15] Coleman v. Coleman, 23 Ky. L. Rep. 1476, 1477, 65 S.W. 832, 833 (1901) ("The testator, John Coleman, evidently intended that his children should not be vested with a fee simple title in his estate until 25 years after his death, as it was provided that his estate should not be divided among them until the end of the period named"); Stevens v. Stevens, 21 Ky. L. Rep. 1315, 54 S.W. 835 (1900); *cf.* Thornton v. Kirtley, 249 S.W.2d 803 (Ky. 1952); Ford v. Yost, 299 Ky. 682, 186 S.W.2d 896 (1944); Fidelity Trust Co. v. Lloyd, 25 Ky. L. Rep. 1827, 78 S.W. 896 (1904). *Contra*, 4 Restatement of Property § 386, com. j, ill. 7.

[16] Letcher's Trustee v. Letcher, 302 Ky. 448, 194 S.W.2d 984 (1946). *Contra*, 4 Restatement of Property § 378, ill. 1.

[17] *Compare* 302 Ky. at 456, 194 S.W.2d at 989, *with id.* at 458, 194 S.W.2d at 990.

[18] 4 Restatement of Property, app. B, ¶ 48. No change was made in the 1948 Supplement to the Restatement, which was published after Letcher's case came down. Inexplicably, Letcher's case is cited by the 1948 Supplement at 546 as a case "allowing a trust to continue for the lives of persons not in being when the creating instrument spoke." The case held the trust entirely void; it could not even begin, much less continue. See also 6 Am. L. Prop. § 25.87, where Letcher's case is cited as holding that a remainder is void if it will not vest within the period. The author does not note that under his meaning of "vest," the remainder held void is vested.

(and income interests invalid by reason of infectious invalidity). If the *Restatement* denies the first interpretation, which it does, it must affirm the second. Yet it does not. It assumes without discussion that a remainder vested in interest satisfies the Rule in Kentucky. If so, then these cases directly limit the duration of trusts. Fitting the cases into both the *Restatement's* position on trust duration and its position on the meaning of "vest" is impossible.

The chief reporter for the *Restatement*, Professor Richard R. Powell of Columbia, abandons the *Restatement's* position in his recent treatise. He explains away several decisions that say the duration of a trust is limited by pointing out the results could have been reached on orthodox grounds. "Despite these explanations applicable to many cases," he continues, "there are cases not thus explicable, which hold trusts invalid because of their duration. These results are difficult to reconcile with the language in other Kentucky opinions."[19] Although Professor Powell's analysis goes deeper into the cases than any other, he does not squarely face up to the dilemma posed by them. He—like the *Restatement*—assumes the court means by "vest" and "suspension of the power of alienation" what he himself would mean, and thus he assumes the answer to the fundamental question.

It is this assumption about the meaning of words which causes all the difficulty. It makes the cases irreconcilable. There is good reason to believe the court is using language in a different way. For, as we shall see, all the cases are reconcilable on a contrary assumption about the meaning of "vest": that "vest" means "vest in possession." At any rate, this assumption needs some looking into.

The material which we have to examine here is difficult and recalcitrant. The reasoning in most of these cases on trust duration is sketchy and preoccupied with the result, and the language used does not readily yield up any precise meaning. To narrow our examination to the exact question, it will be helpful first to state what rules are *not* involved in these cases.

The court is not applying a rule limiting the indestructibility of private trusts. Acording to the treatises, there may be a rule

[19] 5 Powell ¶ 816, at 785.

prohibiting any private trust from remaining indestructible beyond lives in being plus twenty-one years.[20] The rule is violated when there is a possibility the trust will remain indestructible beyond the period; the consequence is that the trust becomes destructible by the beneficiaries. Violation of this rule does not invalidate the trust or any interest therein.

The application of this rule can be illustrated with reference to *Case 4*. The trust there cannot be terminated during B's lifetime, because all parties who have a beneficial interest in the trust are not ascertained. Hence the trust is indestructible during this period. At B's death, however, all beneficiaries are known, and within twenty-one years all will reach the age of consent. A, B's children, and the church ordinarily may terminate the trust when the children become *sui juris*;[21] therefore the trust cannot remain indestructible beyond lives in being plus twenty-one years, and the rule is not violated. If the trust could not be terminated during the lifetime of B's children, however, either because of an express provision in the trust or because continuance is necessary to carry out a material purpose of the testator,[22] the trust may remain indestructible beyond lives in being and twenty-one years. Under the rule limiting the indestructibility of private trusts, the trust is not invalidated but the provision for indestructibility is, and the trust may be terminated after B's death when his children become *sui juris*.

In two cases the court may have applied this rule, since it merely struck down the provision for holding in trust and did not invalidate any of the interests therein.[23] However, in at least five cases the court has gone further and declared the entire devise in trust void, even though some of the interests therein were (or would become within the perpetuity period) vested in interest.[24] This clearly is not the application of a rule making valid trusts destructible at the will of the beneficiaries.

---

[20] Simes & Smith §§ 1391-93; 1 Scott, Trusts § 62.10 (2d ed. 1956). The case authority for any such rule is quite slim.
[21] Keith v. First Nat'l Bank, 256 Ky. 88, 75 S.W.2d 747 (1934); 3 Scott, Trusts § 337 (2d ed. 1956).
[22] First Nat'l Bank v. Purcell, 244 S.W.2d 458 (Ky. 1951); Miller's Ex'rs v. Miller's Heirs, 172 Ky. 519, 189 S.W. 417 (1916).
[23] Ford v. Yost, 300 Ky. 764, 190 S.W.2d 21 (1945); Carter's Trustee v. Gettys, 138 Ky. 842, 129 S.W. 308 (1910). Compare Johnson's Trustee v. Johnson, 25 Ky. L. Rep. 2119, 79 S.W. 293 (1904), striking age limitation from will.
[24] See cases cited notes 15 and 16 *supra*.

The court is not applying the New York definition of what suspends the power of alienation. The idea that trust duration is somehow limited is directly traceable to the perpetuities statute which was, prior to 1960, phrased as a rule prohibiting suspension of the power of alienation. The court has often used loose language to the effect that a trust suspends the power of alienation, but it is not using those words in their technical (New York) sense. The New York Revised Statutes of 1830, from whence KRS 381.220 came, provided that "the absolute power of alienation is suspended when there are no persons in being by whom an absolute fee in possession can be conveyed."[25] Prior to that time the words, "suspension of the power of alienation," had no well-defined meaning, but since then the commentators have accepted this definition as authoritative.[26] This definition was not, however, incorporated into the Kentucky statute prohibiting suspension of the power of alienation and, so far as can be ascertained from the dim lights of the Kentucky cases, has not taken root here. In any event it seems not to have been applied in these cases involving trust duration, as the following paragraphs will show.

If we take the New York sense of when the power is suspended, when the beneficiaries of a trust can individually or jointly convey an absolute fee in possession, the power of alienation is not suspended. In Kentucky all interests in trust are alienable, absent an express restraint.[27] Hence the only type of interest that suspends the power is one where the ultimate takers are unborn or unascertained. Since remainders vested in interest are by definition in ascertained persons, such vested remainders can never cause suspension of the power of alienation.[28] In *Case 3* the power of alienation is suspended during the lives of T's children; in *Case 4*, during B's life. Neither period is in excess of the rule, and therefore the gifts are good under the rule against suspension of the power of alienation (accepting the New York definition of "suspension").

It does not matter that the interests are in trust. The trustee cannot prevent alienation or termination of the trust if all the beneficiaries are ascertained, are *sui juris*, and demand it. If the trust cannot be terminated, either because it is expressly so provided in the instrument or because a court finds a material

[25] N.Y. Real Prop. Law § 42.
[26] 5 Powell ¶ 767; 4 Restatement of Property § 370, com. i.
[27] Newsom v. Barnes, 282 Ky. 264, 138 S.W.2d 475 (1940).
[28] Except a vested remainder in a class subject to open.

purpose of the settlor would be frustrated by termination, it is arguable that the power of alienation is suspended. However, an express restraint on alienation for more than the perpetuity period will be struck down under the doctrine prohibiting unreasonable restraints, and thus no valid express restraint could suspend the power of alienation too long. If the prohibition is not express, but the court implies termination would frustrate settlor's purpose, the interests in trust are not invalid. Only the implied provision against termination is struck down; or, to put it another way, the court will not imply indestructibility for more than the perpetuity period. As a consequence of these rules allowing a trust to be terminated by the beneficiaries at or before the expiration of the perpetuity period, no trust *as such* can suspend the power of alienation too long.

Thus it seems reasonably clear that when the court talks about a trust suspending the power of alienation, it is rejecting the New York statutory definition of when the power of alienation is suspended.[29] This is confirmed by the option cases and the cases on restraints. An option does not suspend the power of alienation under the New York definition, as the owner and optionee may at any time join together and convey a fee. Nonetheless, options have been held by the court to suspend the power of alienation.[30] Likewise, forfeiture restraints on alienation may be released by the person holding the forfeiture right, and a fee conveyed; but forfeiture restraints have been held to suspend the power of alienation.[31]

Although it is rarely crystal-clear what the particular judge had in mind when he referred to "suspension of the power of alienation" (and fortunately it is no longer necessary to try to find it out), it appears that over the years the court has been groping for a practical meaning which will implement a policy against remote

---

[29] Professor Powell disagrees. He believes the court's language is based on (a) the New York definition of suspension, and (b) an assumption by the court that beneficial interests in trust are inalienable (thereby suspending the power of alienation). 5 Powell ¶ 816, at 786. By assuming (a), which he does not examine, Professor Powell is forced to hypothesize (b) to explain these cases. Both of his assumptions seem untenable. The court has rejected (a) in the option and restraint cases, and has rejected (b) in several cases allowing transfer of equitable interests or termination of trusts.

[30] Robertson v. Simmons, 322 S.W.2d 476 (Ky. 1959); Maddox v. Keeler, 296 Ky. 440, 177 S.W.2d 568 (1944); Saulsberry v. Saulsberry, 290 Ky. 132, 160 S.W.2d 654 (1942).

[31] See cases cited in Chapter 6, note 8 *infra*.

distribution. The cases recognize the need of making property alienable, and at the same time they reveal a practical concern for the dead hand's continuing control of a quantum of wealth even though the specific property is alienable. This doubly acute perception is apparent from the beginning.[32] Whenever indestructible future interests are created in a trust, the settlor has in a practical way deprived any person of uncontrolled possession and enjoyment of the quantum of wealth the corpus represents. Even though the remaindermen are ascertained and *sui juris* so that the trust can be terminated, there are practical impediments to termination. The life tenant and remaindermen must all agree that termination is desirable, and they must agree how to apportion the proceeds among their respective interests. Agreement on termination and valuation is hard to achieve. Because of this it is not probable that any of the beneficiaries will enjoy freely any part of the corpus until the trust terminates. In this practical way the creation of equitable future interests suspends the power of free and unrestricted alienation of a quantum of wealth.

If this is what the court had in mind when it talked about suspension of the power of alienation, then it should be noted that legal future interests lessen the probability of alienation in the same way. And the objection is really to the existence of future interests, not to the existence of a trust. It follows from this that future interests that can last beyond the perpetuity period are objectionable, even though they are vested in interest. If this practical meaning is ascribed to "suspension of the power of alienation," these cases on trust duration can all be explained as invalidating gifts because they vested in possession too remotely.

The question resumed: Is the court applying a rule directly invalidating any trust which may last beyond the perpetuity period? The evidence that there is no direct limit on trust duration is not overwhelming, but it is fairly solid. "The fact that the Kentucky courts do not regard the statutory rule against perpetuities as

---

[32] See Carter's Trustee v. Gettys, 138 Ky. 842, 846, 129 S.W. 308, 309 (1910) ("There is no practical difference between a devise restraining in express terms alienation beyond the time allowed by the statute, and a devise of property in trust by which the power of alienation is taken away from the beneficiaries for a similar length of time"); Ford v. Yost, 299 Ky. 682, 685, 186 S.W.2d 896, 898 (1944) ("Technical alienability or the power of a trustee to sell and convey the particular property for investment is not enough to escape the statute, for the proceeds wear the same fetters of restraint").

actually regulating the duration of private trusts, *as such*," says the *Restatement*, "is indicated by several holdings and is conclusively established by one decision[33] allowing a trust to continue for the lives of persons not in being when the creating instrument spoke."[34] In addition to that one decision cited, there has since been another which held a trust entirely valid even though it might have lasted during the life of an unborn widow.[35] Furthermore, if the duration of trusts were directly limited, then a secondary life estate in unborn persons in trust would be void, but such a life estate has been held valid in several cases, regardless of whether it is in trust or not.[36] It vests in possession within the perpetuity period, even though it may last too long. In its most recent expression of opinion on the question, the court reiterated that "the statute relates to the *vesting of the fee simple title*, and, except possibly by indirection, does not purport to fix the time for the continuance of the intermediate estates."[37]

This evidence would appear to be conclusive but for the cases noted at the beginning of this section. Under an analysis which assumes that "vest" means "vest in interest" and that "suspension of the power of alienation" means what it means in New York, these cases hold trusts invalid because of their duration. Under an analysis based on no preconceptions as to word meanings, the cases can be interpreted as holding the remainder in fee must vest in possession free of any trust within the perpetuity period. Only the latter interpretation is reconcilable with the evidence noted in the paragraph immediately preceding[38] or with the apparent meaning the court has given to "suspension of the power of alienation" in other cases. If reconcile and synthesize we must—*de rigueur* in a restatement—then the real significance of trust duration is that

---

[33] Ligget v. Fidelity & Columbia Trust Co., 274 Ky. 387, 118 S.W.2d 720 (1938) (Restatement footnote).

[34] 4 Restatement of Property, app. B, ¶ 48; *accord*, 6 Am. L. Prop. § 25.87; Simes & Smith § 1414; Matthews, "Comments on 1956 Kentucky Legislation: The Perpetuities Amendment," 45 Ky. L.J. 111, 123-26 (1956).

[35] Goodloe's Trustee v. Goodloe, 292 Ky. 494, 166 S.W.2d 836 (1942).

[36] Ligget v. Fidelity & Columbia Trust Co., *supra* note 33 (life estate in trust); Thomas v. Utterback, 269 S.W.2d 251 (Ky. 1954) (legal life estate); Chenowith v. Bullitt, 224 Ky. 698, 6 S.W.2d 1061 (1928) (legal life estate); *cf.* U.S. Fidelity & Guaranty Co. v. Douglas' Trustee, 134 Ky. 374, 120 S.W. 328 (1909); Taylor v. Dooley, 297 S.W.2d 905 (Ky. 1957). *But cf.* Renaker v. Tanner, 260 Ky. 281, 83 S.W.2d 54 (1935).

[37] Farmers Nat'l Bank v. McKenney, 264 S.W.2d 881, 882 (Ky. 1954).

[38] But it is reconcilable only by some bending of the Ligget and Goodloe cases. See p. 22 *supra*.

it determines when the remainder in fee vests for purposes of the perpetuity rule. Hence, to say the duration of a trust is limited is but to say the *remainder in fee must vest in possession free of any trust within the perpetuity period*. In this indirect way perpetuity law limits trust duration.

Coupled with the doctrine of infectious invalidity, this proposition—and only this proposition—will explain the results in every perpetuities case in Kentucky. It is consistent with the court's rejection of constructional rules pointing to a vested with possession postponed classification and with the rejection of the vested subject to divestment concept in perpetuities cases. The same policy mainspring underlying the meaning of "vest"—a policy against remote distribution and possession—is visible here. There are no cases holding squarely to the contrary.

There are, however, recurring statements in the cases that perpetuity law is not concerned with remoteness of possession. If these dicta be accepted, it is impossible to reconcile the holdings of many cases with any interpretation of the statute prohibiting suspension of the power of alienation or with any rule respecting the duration of trusts. Acceptance of these dicta prevents the cases from falling into any consistent pattern of rationalization. It therefore seems that the court may have discovered a simpler order within apparent complexity, while adhering to traditional language patterns. In such ways the law moves to sounder ground.

The above analysis, reconciling case holdings and sloughing off dicta, appears to be the most satisfactory in any purported restatement of the law. But in truth the cases must be brutally bent to fit any proposition. The real explanation of this continuing conflict between what the court does and what it says, noted earlier in treating the meaning of "vest,"[39] is a mystery as puzzling as the one Henry James cunningly wove into the figure in his celebrated carpet. Now that the statute prohibiting suspension of the power of alienation has been repealed, we can hope that this mystery will ultimately be solved.

[39] See pp. 14-30 *supra*.

4

REFORMS OF THE 1960 PERPETUITIES ACT

1

WHY REFORM?

THERE is widespread agreement today that some reform of the Rule against Perpetuities is necessary. This current wave of dissatisfaction originated in many sources, but the main force was Professor Barton Leach's hard-hitting attack on the Rule published in 1952.[1] Professor Leach, indicting the Rule as "a technicality-ridden legal nightmare," set forth a detailed bill of particulars. His criticisms centered on the requirement of absolute certainty that the interest will vest in due time; on the harsh consequences of violating the Rule; on the subjection of commercial options to the Rule; and on the exemption of possibilities of reverter and rights of entry. Following Mr. Leach's article came a rash of articles and comments in law reviews and books,[2] and studies and pamphlets published by eminent committees.[3] Although some of these learned writers were distinctly unenthusiastic about Mr. Leach's specific proposals for reform, practically all of them agreed with his criticisms, and Professor Daniel Schuyler added a further criticism of the use of the "vested in interest" concept in applying the Rule.[4]

The real question is thus not if the Rule needs reforming, but what direction reform should take. To a large extent what is the right reform will depend upon what one conceives to be wrong with the Rule; the disease may suggest the cure. With this in mind the author undertook an examination of all the Kentucky perpetuities cases, including briefs and records on appeal, to discover in what ways the Rule was working badly. The findings of this study showed perpetuity law in Kentucky had failed to give predictability, consistency, and clarity. It was, in the exact words of one of the Commonwealth's most distinguished lawyers, "disorganized confusion." In addition, and perhaps more important, the law had failed to achieve fairness of result.

It may be useful here to set forth the findings of this study, from which we came to the conclusion that the best remedy would be a statute which judges the validity of interests by actual events and reforms those interests that actually vest too remotely.[5]

[1] Leach, "Perpetuities in Perspective: Ending the Rule's Reign of Terror," 65 Harv. L. Rev. 721 (1952).

[2] Among the more significant are Leach & Tudor, The Rule against Perpetuities, apps. I-V and *passim* (1957); Simes, Public Policy and the Dead Hand 32-82 (1955); Bordwell, "Perpetuities from the Point of View of the Draughtsman," 11 Rutgers L. Rev. 429 (1956); Leach, "Perpetuities Legislation: Hail Pennsylvania!" 108 U. Pa. L. Rev. 1124 (1960); Lynn, "Reforming the Common Law Rule against Perpetuities," 28 U. Chi. L. Rev. 488 (1961); Mechem, "Further Thoughts on the Pennsylvania Perpetuities Legislation," 107 U. Pa. L. Rev. 965 (1959); Simes, "Is the Rule against Perpetuities Doomed? The Wait and See Doctrine," 52 Mich. L. Rev. 179 (1953); Sparks, "A Decade of Transition in Future Interests," 45 Va. L. Rev. 493 (1959); Tudor, "Absolute Certainty of Vesting under the Rule against Perpetuities—A Self-Discredited Relic," 34 B.U.L. Rev. 129 (1954); Waterbury, "Some Further Thoughts on Perpetuities Reform," 42 Minn. L. Rev. 41 (1957).

[3] British Law Reform Committee, Fourth Report (The Rule against Perpetuities), Cmd. No. 18 (1956); Committee on Rules against Perpetuities, Am. Bar Assn. Sec. of Real Prop., Prob. & Trust Law, Legislators' Handbook on Perpetuities (1958).

[4] Schuyler, "Should the Rule against Perpetuities Discard Its Vest?" 56 Mich. L. Rev. 683, 887 (1958). See also McDougal & Haber, Property, Wealth, Land 250-51 (1948).

[5] Rights of entry and possibilities of reverter are separately treated in Chapter 5.

A. *The Rule against Perpetuities is essentially incomprehensible*

The Rule can be stated with Delphic simplicity, but like the oracles of old it has a reputation for being excessively resistant to understanding. The briefs and opinions in Kentucky perpetuities cases indicate this reputation is well deserved. There have been seventy-one perpetuities cases since 1900, an average of more than one a year. Of these seventy-one cases, nineteen were wrongly decided according to orthodox doctrine[6] and sixteen are doubtful by the same standard.[7] Only thirty-six (51 percent) of the perpetuities cases were clearly decided correctly[8]—a surprising figure considering leading authorities are in large agreement on how the Rule applies. In practically all these "wrongly decided" cases the court maintained it was applying the common law Rule. Yet it serves no purpose to argue who is in error. That would get us into semantics. The point is: There has been a breakdown in communications between the learned writers and the learned judges.

Nor have lawyers in their briefs consistently demonstrated complete or even partial familiarity with the esoteric technicalities of the Rule. In a brief of thirty years ago the entire (and unsuccessful) argument that the devise did not violate the Rule ran as follows: "Is the time at which the fee becomes fixed so indefinite, or remote, that it does violence to section 2360 Kentucky Statutes, or to the common law rule against perpetuities? We think not."[9] Although there are few briefs so patently inadequate as that one, there are many where counsel wrongly concedes that the gift does or does not violate the Rule; where counsel does not see additional (and, under orthodox doctrine, compelling) technical arguments in his favor; where the line of argument keeps coming unglued; where the gift is so clearly valid that the argument is absurd. There are also cases where the perpetuities issue is not raised in a prior lawsuit, and which are relitigated to the Court of Appeals years later when some sharp-eyed title searcher has spotted the defect.[10]

[6] See Appendix 2, Table 2 *infra*.
[7] See Appendix 2, Table 3 *infra*.
[8] See Appendix 2, Table 1 *infra*. This figure must be further discounted by the fact that in many of these cases the perpetuities argument is a mere makeweight.
[9] Brief for Appellant, p. 2, West v. Ashby, 217 Ky. 250, 289 S.W.2d 228 (1926).
[10] See, *e.g.*, Laughlin v. Elliott, 202 Ky. 433, 259 S.W. 1031 (1924). Compare Thomas v. Utterback, 269 S.W.2d 251 (Ky. 1954).

This situation is not peculiar to Kentucky. Thus Professor Sparks, who makes an annual survey of perpetuities cases in all states, commented in 1957:

Paradoxically the year is also unique in the inexpert way in which simple [perpetuities] problems have been handled by both courts and counsel. . . . Cases in which only one decision is possible but which serve to illustrate the pathetic lack of understanding of the Rule against Perpetuities by both bench and bar are frequently before the courts.[11]

It is a regrettable, but nonetheless seemingly irreversible, fact that it is no longer a matter of professional decency to be fluent in perpetuities.

While it is necessary to point out the lack of understanding of the Rule in any study of its workings, it does not seem proper to chastise severely bench and bar for their lack of expertise. Even in the best treatises the Rule is marked by imprecise and enigmatic concepts, unexpected contradictions of human experience, trifling linguistic distinctions, and deceptive subtleties and refinements. There is far more complexity than is rationally required to deal with the problems. When the technicalities are so strange and artificial and not rationally connected to any policy basis the ordinary lawyer can understand, the level of professional expertise is, in these busy times with so much else to master, bound to decline.[12]

Law which lawyers cannot understand is a reproach to the bar. It inevitably leads to a cynical disrespect for the law and lawyers. It was clear to us that any reform must simplify the law, making it more easily understandable by the average lawyer. Four basic causes of complexity and confusion were the statutory language prohibiting suspension of the power of alienation, the remote possibili-

[11] Sparks, "Future Interests," 1956 Ann. Survey of Am. Law, 32 N.Y.U.L. Rev. 419, 429-30 (1957).

[12] Gray saw this years ago. Said Gray § 782: "A serious objection to the continuance of the old doctrines of real property in the jurisprudence of to-day is that, while the judges are thoroughly familiar with and move at ease among the general doctrines of contract and equity which govern the ordinary transactions of modern life, it is impossible (or if not impossible at least very unlikely) that they should have at their fingers' ends the fundamental distinctions of a highly artificial system, and they are in danger of being unduly governed by 'the *cantilena* [melody] of lawyers' and of losing opportunities for the simplification of the law."

See also Lucas v. Hamm, 15 Cal. Rep. 821 (1961), which held that because the Rule was so esoteric violation of it by an attorney-draftsman was not actionable negligence.

ties test, the unsettled and harsh law with respect to consequences of violating the Rule, and the concept of vesting. By removing the first three of these causes, the 1960 Perpetuities Act should simplify the law and cut down the frequency of litigation.

> B. *The statutory language in KRS 381.220 prohibiting suspension of the power of alienation confused both bench and bar*

The confusion caused by this statute has already been discussed in connection with the common law Rule against Perpetuities[13] and will be discussed again subsequently in connection with restraints on alienation.[14] Repeal was necessary to bring a beginning of order. It is interesting to note that in the same year Kentucky discarded its statute of New York parentage, New York itself returned to the period of the common law Rule, threw out the unborn widow and administrative contingencies, and adopted a cy pres provision for age contingencies.[15]

> C. *The remote possibilities test, in about three-quarters of the cases, deprived beneficiaries of gifts which in fact would have vested in due time; we concluded this was unfair and unjustifiable in policy*

Under the common law Rule, as it has developed, there must be no possibility that a gift will vest too remotely. This test has defeated reasonable dispositions by reasonable property owners, and usually merely because the draftsman overlooked some highly remote possibility which did not in fact happen. In the nineteenth century only one gift was held to violate the Rule—and that was, of all things, a gift of freedom to a slave which actually did vest in due time.[16] Since 1900 there have been thirty-one cases invalidating future interests (excluding nonfamily cases dealing with possibilities of reverter, rights of entry, and options). In twelve of these it was known at the time the case was decided that the interest would in fact vest in due time, and thus the possibility

---

[13] See pp. 52-57 *supra*.
[14] See pp. 114-18 *infra*.
[15] N.Y. Laws 1960, cc. 448-52.
[16] Ludwig v. Combs, 58 Ky. (1 Met.) 128 (1858).

that defeated the interest never came to pass.[17] In seven cases it was highly probable the interest would vest in due time, but at the time of decision there was a remote possibility that a person over fifty-five would produce children, which possibility defeated the gift.[18] In eight cases, it was possible the interest would vest in due time, but at the time of decision one could only guess what the probabilities were.[19] This leaves only four cases where it was not possible or was highly improbable that the interests would vest in due time.[20]

The instruments in at least three-fourths of these cases do not show any intention to create a family dynasty or to tie up wealth beyond lives in being plus twenty-one years. Practically all of the invalid interests could have been saved had the draftsman been more careful and made a slight change in language. But the draftsman unfortunately overlooked the fertile octogenarian in thirteen cases, the unborn widow in one, and other unlikely possibilities in most of the others. These cases offer rather convincing support for Lord Blanesburgh's observation four decades ago that the Rule usually is "a snare, useless so far as its legitimate purpose is concerned,"[21] and for Professor Leach's recent attack on the remote possibilities test as destructive of innocent and reasonable family dispositions which actually do vest in due time. These cases show why Mr. Leach has called it the "Might-Have-Been" Rule.

What can be said for a rule which strikes down gifts that actually vest in due time on the ground that they might not have done so? Is public policy offended by an interest which *might, but does not in fact*, tie up wealth beyond "lives in being plus twenty-one years"? Two arguments have been advanced that it is. One assumes that too much wealth is presently being tied up in trust, and that any rule which tends to untie it is desirable. The other is that the remote possibilities test promotes the early alienability of land by destroying future interests.

The answer to the first argument is obvious. Even if it can be assumed that a significant social evil exists because of too much wealth in trust (of which we have no evidence), such an evil can

---

[17] See Appendix 2, Table 5, fact patterns 1, 3, 4, 6 *infra*.
[18] See Appendix 2, Table 5, fact patterns 2, 5 *infra*.
[19] See Appendix 2, Table 6, fact patterns 1, 2, 4 *infra*.
[20] See Appendix 2, Table 6, fact pattern 3 *infra*.
[21] Ward v. Van der Loeff, [1924] A.C. 653, 678.

hardly be combated by merely penalizing the inexpert draftsman. The amount of wealth in trust might be effectively reduced by shortening the perpetuity period for certain types of transfers or across the board (which New York and some other states have tried, disastrously) or by eliminating tax incentives for creating life estates. But there is little social utility in a rule which can be easily evaded by any competent draftsman, especially where a competent draftsman is likely to be hired by the very people—the rich—at whom the rule is directed. The proportionate amount of total wealth in trust which is freed by the remote possibilities test must be infinitesimal.

The second argument—that the possibilities test promotes alienability of land—assumes that a good end justifies any means. It has been voiced before in support of other archaisms, such as destructibility of contingent remainders and the rule in Shelley's Case. Those two pillars of feudal law also made land alienable one generation earlier; and as readers of legal history know, they were pulled down midst similar cries of inalienability. It took almost a century to destroy those doctrines (and doubtless it will take as long to get rid of the remote possibilities test), but who would now wish them back? The point is: Rules that operate so blindly and capriciously as destructibility, Shelley's Case, and the possibilities test are not rational implementations of any policy favoring alienability of land.

Moreover, alienability is basically irrelevant to the issue, for two reasons. First, legal future interests are seldom created in land any more. Second, the easiest and the best way to make alienable all land subject to legal future interests is to provide a simple procedure for court appointment of a trustee for sale. In Kentucky all land subject to vested or contingent future interests can be sold or mortgaged under court order if the court finds it in the best interests of the parties.[22] The petition for sale may be initiated by the life tenant or the owners of an indefeasibly vested remainder or reversion. The power of a court to order sale for reinvestment extends to land held in trust as well as by legal estates, and can be exercised even though the instrument expressly provides the land cannot be sold.[23] The future interests are transferred to the proceeds of the sale, which are paid into court and reinvested under

[22] KRS 389.030-.040.
[23] See pp. 140-42 *infra*.

court order. This broad power of sale makes the land marketable while preserving the proceeds for the intended beneficiaries. Whatever may be the effect of wait-and-see on marketability in other jurisdictions, its effect in Kentucky will be negligible.

It is very difficult, if not impossible, to justify the remote possibilities test on the ground that it is a rational method of furthering alienability or limiting dead hand control. Its real justification lies elsewhere. It lies in the convenience inherent in being able to go to court at the outset and get a determination of the validity of the interests. (No competent lawyer, under the state of the Kentucky authorities, would have relied upon his own opinion of invalidity and its consequences.) Under the remote possibilities test it is not necessary for the court to wait and see if the interests vest in time. Indeed, the only objection to the reform act voiced on the floor of the Senate (other than one Senator's understandable complaint that "this is the most complex subject ever brought up in the legislature, and I'm not going to vote for something I don't understand") was that wait-and-see would prove inconvenient. There are several answers to this. Inasmuch as they have been fully set forth elsewhere,[24] it is only necessary to note them briefly here.

The first is that the assumed inconvenience of wait-and-see is largely hypothetical. In more than one-half of the Kentucky cases invalidating gifts it was known at the time of decision that the gift would vest in time. No more inconvenience would have resulted from sustaining these gifts than results from sustaining any contingent interest that will necessarily vest or fail within the period. In the others, it is hard to say whether inconvenience would have arisen or not. The suits were usually brought immediately after the instruments became effective simply to declare the rights of the parties. But it is pertinent to note that where valid life estates were involved, no question of possession or distribution could have arisen until the termination of the life estates.

In three cases the court itself saw no inconvenience in waiting to resolve uncertainties. In two of them, holding remainders void, the court refused to say what happened to the fee upon termination of the life estates.[25] "Sufficient unto the day is evil thereof,"

[24] See the books and articles by Leach, Tudor, and Waterbury, note 2 *supra*, and the British Law Reform Committee report, note 3 *supra*.
[25] Renaker v. Tanner, 260 Ky. 281, 83 S.W.2d 54 (1935); Laughlin v. Elliott, 202 Ky. 433, 259 S.W. 1031 (1924).

said the court, quoting advice Jesus gave in the Sermon on the Mount.[26] If the court found it not necessary to say who takes the invalid interest until termination of the life estates, of what advantage is it to know the interest is invalid? In another case involving the validity of an interest in coal to become possessory after 999 years, the court declined to pass upon its validity at all.[27] Said the court, "In the event the coal remains unmined 999 years after the date of the instrument, future generations may be called upon to deal with the problem."[28]

Nonetheless, the truth of the matter is we do not have enough facts to warrant a conclusion either way with respect to the inconvenience of wait-and-see. No one has been able to point out a single situation where serious inconvenience will result from a wait-and-see plus cy pres statute, but of course it is not possible to foresee all possible situations which may arise. We must assume, therefore, that some inconvenience may result from wait-and-see, which brings us to the basic issue.

The basic issue involved in choosing between the remote possibilities test and an actual events test is convenience versus fairness. And the basic answer to the convenience argument is simply that mere convenience cannot justify ignoring the transferor's intention and depriving the intended beneficiaries of the gift. In an analogous situation, where testator makes a bequest to children of a near relative and one child calls for distribution of his share before all possible children are born, the Court of Appeals has rejected the "rule of convenience" in favor of holding the class open until it is physiologically closed. There the court does not regard convenience to the living as sufficient justification for closing the class and depriving the unborn. The same choice underlies the wait-and-see test.

In view of the demonstrated unfairness of the remote possibilities test, prima facie the choice must be in favor of wait-and-see unless serious inconvenience can be shown. But the choice really need not rest on conjectures about future inconvenience. By coupling wait-and-see with a cy pres power to reform invalid interests, as is done in KRS 381.216, any possible inconvenience can be taken care of. If serious inconvenience does in fact result

---

[26] Laughlin v. Elliott, *supra* note 25, at 437, 259 S.W. at 1033.
[27] Johnson v. Pittsburgh Consol. Coal Co., 311 S.W.2d 537 (Ky. 1958).
[28] *Id.* at 539.

in some unusual case, the court may reform the instrument to vest the gift within the period, thereby preventing the inconvenience while at the same time carrying out the transferor's intent as far as possible.

It has been suggested that the fantastic possibilities which have invalidated gifts—the fertile octogenarian, the unborn widow, administrative and age contingencies, and such—could be eliminated without jettisoning entirely the remote possibilities test. This approach was considered and rejected for four reasons. (1) It is wrong to strike down any interest which in fact vests in due time merely because it might not have done so. It is wrong whether or not the contingency on which it might not have vested be regarded as probable, improbable, or fantastic. (2) Remedying specific defects would require a complicated statute, and even then would not cure fantastic possibilities as yet undreamed of. (3) Agreement could not be reached on what to do with the fertile octogenarian, who accounted for so many invalid gifts. There was objection to deeming Kentucky men over sixty incapable of having issue;[29] a further stumbling block was the fact that a person of any age may adopt a child who shares in any remainder given to the adoptor's children.[30] (4) A simple statute was the only kind of reform statute salable in the legislature.

In our view the proper course was to lay down the soundest rule, and leave exceptions to be carved in it as time might require. To have kept a rule unsound in policy and carve sound exceptions in it would have added more complications, and brought inadequate relief.

D. *The consequences of violating the Rule were harsh and unsettled*

What to do with invalid gifts has long plagued the Court of Appeals.[31] For many years two contrary rules existed side by side, one giving the invalid interest to the takers of the last valid interest, the other passing it to the donor or his heirs by way of

---

[29] With a handy example. Former Judge Edward C. O'Rear of the Court of Appeals was born in 1863, when his father was sixty-seven years old. Judge O'Rear died in 1961.

[30] Breckinridge v. Skillman's Trustee, 330 S.W.2d 726 (Ky. 1960); Bedinger v. Graybill's Ex'r, 302 S.W.2d 594 (Ky. 1957), noted 47 Ky. L.J. 149 (1958).

[31] See pp. 44-51 *supra*.

reversion. In 1938 the cases supporting the former rule were brushed off, though not overruled, and the latter rule accepted as the true principle. In addition to this latter rule, there was the rule of infectious invalidity, under which both preceding valid estates and subsequent valid interests were struck down if the court believed the donor would have preferred total invalidity.

Neither of these rules proved to be satisfactory. The general rule of passing the void interest to testator's heirs often frustrated his scheme where he did not intend for his heirs to share equally or at all. Where he did intend equality among his children, the rule of infectious invalidity—applied to achieve equality—wrecked havoc with his plan for protecting his children from improvidence. And inasmuch as the Court of Appeals often gave the rule of infectious invalidity an unexpectedly broad application, most invalid limitations had to be litigated to that court to determine if that rule applied.

There appears to be no policy reason why a limitation which violates the Rule must be entirely struck down, often bringing down other gifts with it. If the testator cannot have all of what he wants, why cannot he have part? Most of the void gifts were merely the product of inept drafting and could be cured by the addition or deletion of a few words. If the question could be put to the average testator whether he would prefer the gift to be totally void or would prefer the gift to be suitably remodeled so as to vest at an earlier time, very likely he would say the latter.

Although giving a court cy pres power to reform invalid limitations is not altogether free from objection, we came to the conclusion that it is better than either of the alternatives a court presently has. It is a lesser power than the power to strike down other interests through infectious invalidity. It is a power to deal with the invalid interest only, leaving the valid gifts standing. Since cy pres is not resorted to if the interest does in fact vest in due time, on the basis of past Kentucky cases very few instruments should require reformation.

E. Confusion surrounds the meaning of "vest"

Somerset Maugham once observed that too much sincerity in society is like an iron girder in a house of cards. This metaphor conveniently fits the common belief, sincerely held by many, in an all-embracing definition of "vest" under which all the protean arrangements of words and parties and claims can be classified, and judgments rendered, without regard for community policies or the purposes of particular rules in which "vest" is used. As our analysis of Kentucky cases showed, this belief is an illusion. "Vest" has many meanings—at least as many as there are rules.

In the context of the Rule against Perpetuities, it is not clear under what circumstances a remainder is vested.[32] Only two things are certain. A remainder is vested when it vests indefeasibly in possession. A class gift commonly classified for purposes of survivorship and destructibility problems as vested in interest subject to partial divestment is not vested under the Rule. But one cannot say whether a remainder classified for most purposes as vested in interest indefeasibly or vested in interest subject to total divestment satisfies the Rule. The cases point both ways. At the very least they show an unorthodox preference for a contingent construction when the interest is alleged to create a perpetuity.

The concept of a remainder vested in interest developed out of the problem of destructibility, which no longer exists today. The transplanting of this confusing concept into the perpetuities field was unfortunate, both because it brought excessive disorder and because remainders vested in interest are as much within the reasons of the Rule as contingent remainders. Both vested and contingent remainders seriously lessen the probability of alienation, though neither type necessarily makes the property wholly inalienable. Hence it is arguable that any reform should extirpate the concept of vested in interest and require remainders to vest in possession within the period.

Professor Daniel Schuyler is the leading exponent of this reform, and has presented his views in a persuasive article.[33] This author agrees with Mr. Schuyler, and had the Kentucky reform act been left entirely to him, he would have incorporated relevant portions of the statute Mr. Schuyler has drafted.[34] But others believed such a statute would be too complex for the legislature to buy. It finally was decided to leave the problem of the meaning of "vest" with the court.

[32] See discussion at pp. 14-30 *supra*.
[33] Schuyler, "Should the Rule against Perpetuities Discard Its Vest?" 56 Mich. L. Rev. 887 (1958).
[34] *Id.* at 949.

As the analysis in Chapter 1 revealed, it is possible that the court has already eliminated the feudal concept of vest in interest in applying the perpetuity rule and that remainders must vest in possession within the period. If it has not done so (and only the future can tell us that), it could do so without overruling a single case. The author believes that a well-prepared argument, based on the existing Kentucky authorities and stressing the importance of policy and of substance over form, might well succeed in persuading the Court of Appeals to cut away its dicta about vesting in interest and to substitute order for confusion. In any event the difference between remainders vested in interest and remainders vested in possession is bound to become less and less significant under the wait-and-see test. The confusion surrounding the meaning of "vest" will be avoided to the extent the court does not have to determine, before the remainder becomes possessory, whether the remainder is vested or not.

2

ADOPTION OF THE COMMON LAW
RULE AGAINST PERPETUITIES

KRS 381.215 (section 1 of the 1960 Perpetuities Act) reads:

No interest in real or personal property shall be good unless it must vest, if at all, not later than twenty-one years after some life in being at the creation of the interest. It is the purpose of this section to enact the common law rule against perpetuities, except as hereinafter modified by KRS 381.215 to 381.223.

The section sets forth the common law Rule against Perpetuities, using the language of John Chipman Gray. Only the words "in real or personal property" are added to Gray's classic statement of the Rule. As the Court of Appeals long ago adopted the common law Rule by decision, the section is declaratory of existing law, set forth in Chapters 1 and 2, except as the law is modified by subsequent sections of the 1960 act. The effect of enacting this section and repealing KRS 381.220 is that the Rule is stated to be against remoteness of vesting rather than against "suspension of the power of alienation," which language has caused so much trouble. The rule against unreasonable restraints on alienation, discussed in Chapter 6, remains unchanged.

It should be noted that the 1960 Perpetuities Act expressly provides that this section and KRS 381.216 "apply only to inter vivos instruments and wills taking effect after July 1, 1960."[35] The reviser of statutes, in compiling the act, has stated that the act became "effective June 16, 1960." This is confusing. Laws become effective ninety days after adjournment of the legislature (which would be June 16, 1960), unless a later date is especially provided, as was the case here.[36] The reviser's advancement of the effective date of this act by fourteen days appears to be the result of inadvertence.

3

THE WAIT-AND-SEE DOCTRINE AND CY PRES

KRS 381.216 (section 2 of the 1960 Perpetuities Act) reads:

In determining whether an interest would violate the rule against perpetuities the period of perpetuities shall be measured by actual rather than possible events; provided, however, the period shall not be measured by any lives whose continuance does not have a causal relationship to the vesting or failure of the interest. Any interest which would violate said rule as thus modified shall be reformed, within the limits of that rule, to approximate most closely the intention of the creator of the interest.

The first sentence of the section adopts the wait-and-see doctrine. The second sentence, providing for reform of invalid interests, adopts cy pres.

A. *The wait-and-see doctrine*

The common law measured the validity of an interest by determining at the date of the instrument whether there was any possibility it would vest too remotely. Under this section validity is measured by actual events. We wait and see whether or not the interest actually vests in due time. If it does, it is valid; if it does not, it is void. The wait-and-see principle has been adopted in Pennsyl-

---

[35] KRS 381.223.
[36] Compare the treatment of the Uniform Commercial Code, which the reviser properly states became "effective July 1, 1960."

vania,[37] Vermont,[38] and Washington,[39] and in a modified form in Connecticut, Maine, Maryland, and Massachusetts.[40] It has also been adopted by the New Hampshire court, and possibly by the Florida court.[41] And in 1956 the distinguished English Law Reform Committee unanimously recommended it for adoption in the country where the Rule was born and grew up.[42] The reasons for adoption of wait-and-see in Kentucky were discussed in section 1 of this chapter.

In the great bulk of cases this principle will be of easy application and will save many gifts formerly held void.[43] These cases will usually involve life estates, with remainder over, and at the death of the first life tenant it will be known that the remainder will vest in due time. In other cases it may not be obvious who are the measuring lives or how long we wait before determining validity. The problems that might be raised by these cases are discussed below.

Who can be the measuring lives? The language *"provided, however, the period shall not be measured by any lives whose continuance does not have a causal relationship to the vesting or failure of the interest"* is original with the Kentucky statute. It is not contained in any of the other statutes. Its purpose is to cure the problem of what lives it is permissible to wait out. If wait-and-see is taken literally, it is possible to contend that an interest is valid if it actually vests within twenty-one years after the death of any person in the world who was alive when the instrument took effect. Obviously this result would be impractical, not to say absurd. Although probably no court would ever so hold, this provision clearly prevents such a result by limiting the permissible

---

[37] Pa. Stat. Ann. tit. 20, § 301.4 (1950).
[38] Vt. Stat. Ann. tit. 27, § 501 (1959). The Vermont statute served as a model for KRS 381.216.
[39] Wash. Rev. Code §§ 11.98.010-.030 (1959 supp.) (applicable to trusts only).
[40] Conn. Gen. Stat. Rev. § 45-95 (1958); Me. Rev. Stat. Ann. c. 160, § 27 (1959 supp.); Md. Ann. Code, art. 16, § 197A (1960 supp.); Mass. Ann. Laws, c. 184a, § 1 (1958).
[41] Merchants Nat'l Bank v. Curtis, 98 N.H. 225, 97 A.2d 207 (1953); Story v. First Nat'l Bank, 115 Fla. 436, 156 So. 101 (1934).
[42] See British Law Reform Committee, Fourth Report (The Rule against Perpetuities), Cmd. No. 18 (1956), discussed in Leach, "Perpetuities Reform by Legislation: England," 70 Harv. L. Rev. 1411 (1957).
[43] See Appendix 2, Table 5 *infra*.

measuring lives to lives causally related to the vesting or failure of the interest.[44]

What does the requirement that a measuring life have a "causal relationship to the vesting or failure of the interest" mean? In a sense it is simply declaratory of the measuring lives at common law, which, as the court said in *Bach v. Pace*,[45] "may be any lives which play a part in the ultimate disposition of the property." However, there is this difference. At common law the measuring lives had to have a causal relationship to vesting which *insured* vesting within the period.[46] Under wait-and-see, absolute certainty *ab initio* is not required, and hence the permissible measuring lives are those in being at the beginning of the period whose continuance *may* cause vesting. These are lives which "play a part in the ultimate disposition of the property"; these are lives with a causal relationship to vesting.

In practically all cases the measuring lives will be one or more of the following as fits the particular facts: (a) the preceding life tenant, (b) the taker(s) of the interest, (c) a parent of the takers of the interest, (d) a person designated as a measuring life in the instrument, and (e) some other person whose actions or death can expressly or by implication cause the interest to vest or fail. Though it seems obvious, perhaps it should be pointed out that this section does not at all narrow the lives usable at common law. Any gift good under the common law remote possibilities test is valid under KRS 381.216.

How long do we wait and see? Under wait-and-see the validity of an interest which might vest too remotely is not determined at the date of the creation of the interest. We wait and see if it actually vests in due time. The question thus arises: How long do we wait before determining the validity of the interest? The common law Rule, as modified by the "provided, however" clause discussed above, sets the maximum permissible period at (a) lives of persons in being at the beginning of the period which (i) can cause vesting or failure of the interest, and (ii) are neither so numerous nor so situated as to make it impossible or unreasonably difficult to

---

[44] A provision of this sort is recommended by Waterbury, "Some Further Thoughts on Perpetuities Reform," 42 Minn. L. Rev. 41, 66 n.96 (1957).
[45] 305 S.W.2d 528, 529 (Ky. 1957).
[46] See pp. 7-8 *supra*.

ascertain their termination, plus (b) twenty-one years, plus (c) any actual periods of gestation. Do we wait for the entire duration of the perpetuity period as thus set forth, or for some shorter period?

The answer is: We wait either for lives in being causally related to the gift *or* for twenty-one years, but not both. This answer follows from two rules which implement the wait-and-see principle. These rules interpreting the statute are part of the statute's legislative history,[47] and therefore it is assumed that they will be applied. They are easily workable and will cover practically every case where a remainder or executory interest is involved. They are:

(1) Where an interest is limited to take effect at or after the termination of one or more life estates in, or lives of, persons in being at the beginning of the period, the validity of the interest is determined at, and on the basis of facts existing at, the termination of such one or more life estates or lives.[48] If it is then found that the interest may still vest too remotely, it is then reformed to vest within the period.

(2) Where the vesting of an interest is not causally related to the continuance of any life in being, we wait for twenty-one years to see if the interest vests. If it actually vests within twenty-one years, it is valid. If it does not do so, it is void.

The reason why, under rule (1), we wait only during lives in being, and not for the full period, is that serious inconvenience may result if we cannot determine the validity of the remainder at the expiration of the prior life estates or lives. Suppose a gift to A for life, remainder to such of his children as reach the age of thirty. If A dies, leaving a child B under nine years of age, we know at A's death that it is possible for the remainder to vest more than

[47] Both indirectly through the legislative history of the parent Vermont statute and directly through its own legislative history. Professor Leach assumes these rules will be applicable in his memorandum explaining the Vermont statute's operation, which is part of the legislative history of that statute. Leach & Tudor, The Rule against Perpetuities 224-30 (1957). The author prepared a memorandum in support of the 1960 Kentucky Perpetuities Act which was submitted to the sponsors of the act, the Senate Judiciary Committee, the House Rules Committee, and lawyer members of the legislature. This memorandum stated the two rules at p. 10 thereof. It also included five examples of how the act would operate, reproduced in the text of this chapter as *Cases 1, 2, 3, 4,* and *5*. These examples are based on the assumption these two rules will be applied.

[48] This rule is adopted by statute in Massachusetts, Maine, Connecticut, and Maryland. For a very clear explanation of its meaning, see Leach, "Perpetuities Legislation—Massachusetts Style," 67 Harv. L. Rev. 1349, 1357-60 (1954).

twenty-one years later. Were we to wait for twenty-one more years only to find B still alive (and, of course, still under age thirty), the gift would have to be reformed by cutting down the age limitation. It will rid us of uncertainty and several possible difficulties if the age limitation is reduced at A's death.

Why were not these rules expressly written into the statute? Because of the difficulty of evolving a detailed statutory scheme to implement the wait-and-see principle which, without being too complex to be practicable, would cover all the various types of dispositions man can devise. These two rules solve the problem of how long we wait and see in every perpetuities case that has so far come to the Court of Appeals. If other cases arise which these rules do not fit, the court will have to work out interpretive rules to implement the wait-and-see principle, bearing in mind that it can reform the gift to vest within the period when serious inconvenience would result from waiting longer.

B. *Reformation by cy pres*

The second sentence of KRS 381.216 provides: *"Any interest which would violate said rule as thus modified shall be reformed, within the limits of that rule, to approximate most closely the intention of the creator of the interest."* It is copied from the Vermont statute. This sentence applies to invalid private dispositions the doctrine of cy pres, which has heretofore been applied to charitable gifts only.[49] (The term "cy pres," pronounced SEE-PRAY, comes from Law French and means "so nearly" as possible.) Applying cy pres to private dispositions was first suggested in 1904 by Judge James Quarles of the Chancery Court in Louisville,[50] who earlier had been successful in persuading the Court of Appeals to apply cy pres in *Hussey v. Sargent*.[51] Professors Simes and Leach, among others, have subsequently advocated it, and New Hampshire, Vermont,

---

[49] See Citizens Fidelity Bank v. Bernheim Fdn., 305 Ky. 802, 205 S.W.2d 1003 (1947); Moore's Heirs v. Moore's Devisees, 34 Ky. (4 Dana) 354 (1836).

[50] Quarles, "The Cy Pres Doctrine, with Reference to the Rule against Perpetuities—An Advocation of Its Adoption in All Jurisdictions," 38 Am. L. Rev. 683 (1904); revised and republished as Quarles, "The Cy Pres Doctrine: Its Application to Cases Involving the Rule against Perpetuities and Trusts for Accumulation," 21 N.Y.U.L. Rev. 384 (1946). Professors Simes and Leach both refer to the latter article as the pioneering piece, but it appears Quarles was on top of the problem years before as a result of some successful lawyering.

[51] 116 Ky. 53, 75 S.W. 211 (1903) (applying New Hampshire law).

Washington, and possibly Idaho have adopted it.[52] The object of applying cy pres to violations of the Rule against Perpetuities is, in the felicitous words of the Mikado, "to let the punishment fit the crime."

Without cy pres, the wait-and-see doctrine would create some serious difficulties in connection with how long we wait and with the application of infectious invalidity. Cy pres by itself would create uncertainty, though perhaps no more than presently exists if the law in practice is examined realistically. But joined together, these two doctrines offer the most workable solution to perpetuities problems yet devised.

The adoption of cy pres requires the court to reform the invalid interest only, leaving standing the preceding valid estates, which under prior law were frequently and dubiously struck down through the application of infectious invalidity. Exactly how an instrument will be reformed depends on what is suitable on the particular facts. The next section illustrates how the power may be exercised in some common cases.

4

ILLUSTRATIONS OF HOW KRS 381.216 APPLIES

Remainder after life estates of persons in being. Where there is a life estate, or a series of life estates, created in persons in being, it is usually not necessary for a court to pass upon the validity of the remainder until the preceding estates have expired. No issue of possession of land, nor of who takes the trust corpus, can arise until that time. Therefore, we wait until the expiration of life estates of persons in being and see what the facts are at that time. If it is then necessary, the gift is reformed to comply with the Rule.

Case 1 (Age contingency).[53] T devises property "to A for life, remainder to A's children who reach twenty-five." T's heirs are A, B, and C. Under former law the gift to A's children was void, and on A's death the property passed to B, C, and A's estate in equal shares (unless

---

[52] Edgerly v. Barker, 66 N.H. 434, 31 Atl. 900 (1891); Vt. Stat. Ann. tit. 27, § 501 (1959); Wash. Rev. Code §§ 11.98.010-.030 (1959 supp.) (applicable to trusts only); Idaho Code Ann. §§ 55-111 (1957) (applicable to trusts only; vague statute).

[53] *Cases* 1 and 2 are borrowed from Mr. Leach's explanation of the Vermont statute, on which KRS 381.216 was modeled. See Leach & Tudor, The Rule against Perpetuities 229-30 (1957).

infectious invalidity applied and A's life estate fell too). Under KRS 381.216, the validity of the remainder is not determined until A's death. If at that time it is found that all of A's children were born before T's death or if all of them are then over four years old, the remainder is certain to vest within the period. It is valid and no reformation is required. If, however, at A's death there is a child of A under four who was born after the testator's death, the will is reformed to give the property to such of A's children as reach twenty-one.[54] The justification is that testator obviously would prefer earlier vesting to total invalidity if the point could be put to him.

Remainder after successive life estates, the first of which is in a person in being, the second possibly in a person not in being. Where there is a secondary life estate given to a person who may or may not be in being at the date of creation of the interest, we wait until the death of the first life tenant to determine validity of the remainders. If it appears at that time that the secondary life tenant was in being at the date of creation of the interest, the remainder is valid and need not be reformed. If it appears at that time that the secondary life tenant was not in being at the date of creation of the interest, the remainder is reformed to approximate most closely the donor's intention.

Case 2 (Unborn widow). T devises property in trust "to pay the income to A for life, then to pay the income to A's widow for life, and then to pay the principal to A's issue per stirpes who are living at the death of the survivor of A and his widow." Under prior law the remainder to A's issue was void because it was possible that "A's widow" would be a person not in being at T's death. Under KRS 381.216 the validity of the remainder is not determined until A's death, when it will doubtless appear that his widow was in being at T's death and the gift to issue is valid. However, in the extraordinary case where A's widow was not in being at T's death, the gift to A's issue is reformed to read: "to the issue of A per stirpes who are living at the death of the survivor of A and his widow, provided that, if A leaves a widow who was unborn at my death, the interest given to A's issue shall indefeasibly vest not later than twenty-one years after A's death."[55] Thus reformed, the

[54] Reformation by reduction of age contingency to twenty-one is provided for by statute in some jurisdictions. English Law of Prop. Act (1925) § 163; Conn. Gen. Stat. Rev. § 45-96 (1958); Me. Rev. Stat. Ann. c. 160, § 28 (1959 supp.); Md. Ann. Code, art. 16, § 197A (1960 supp.); Mass. Ann. Laws, c. 184a, § 2 (1958); N.Y. Real Prop. Law § 42-b; N.Y. Pers. Prop. Law § 11-a. See also Hussey v. Sargent, 116 Ky. 53, 75 S.W. 211 (1903).

[55] Compare Goodloe's Trustee v. Goodloe, 292 Ky. 494, 166 S.W.2d 836 (1942), where a possible unborn widow was disposed of by construing the remainder to vest in interest indefeasibly twenty-one years after A's death. See also Gilbert v. Union College, 343 S.W.2d 829 (Ky. 1961), discussed at p. 89 *infra*.

gift is valid no matter what happens. If A's widow lives more than twenty-one years after his death, A's issue living twenty-one years after his death will take an indefeasibly vested remainder, not subject to surviving beyond that time. This would approximate most closely T's intent. (If, however, an indefeasibly vested remainder does not satisfy the Rule and vesting in possession is required, as some Kentucky cases seem to indicate, the reformation would require a different wording.)

Case 3 (The presumption of fertility). T has two children, a son and a daughter. T devises one-half of his estate to his son in fee. T devises the other one-half in trust "to pay income to D for life, then to pay income to D's children for their lives, then to pay the principal to D's grandchildren." Under prior law the gift to D's grandchildren was void, and the court had the choice of (a) letting it pass to T's heirs by intestacy (resulting in the son's family ultimately receiving three-fourths of T's property and the daughter's only one-fourth), or (b) striking down the entire trust *and* the gift to the son (resulting in total intestacy but equal distribution). Obviously either course does violence to T's intention. Under KRS 381.216, the validity of the remainder in fee is not determined until D's death. There are three possible states of facts that might be existing at that time:

(A) D had no children surviving her who were born after T's death. If such is the case—and prior Kentucky cases indicate it usually will be—the gift to grandchildren is incapable of vesting beyond the period. Therefore it can be declared valid.

(B) All of D's surviving children were born after T's death. Here we know the ultimate remainder cannot vest within lives in being. The will is thus reformed to read: "to D's grandchildren, provided that, if D is survived only by children who were unborn at my death, the interest to D's grandchildren shall indefeasibly vest not later than twenty-one years after D's death." This means the class of takers would close twenty-one years after D's death, if not before. Thus reformed, the testator's intent is carried out to the greatest possible extent. (If vesting in possession is required, or if D's surviving children were all very young so that closing the class twenty-one years later might exclude some grandchildren, the will might be reformed to read: "if the trust does not terminate under the instrument within twenty-one years after D's death, it shall then be terminated and the principal distributed to D's issue then living per stirpes.")

(C) Some of D's surviving children were born before T's death, and some after. In this case we cannot determine the validity of the gift to grandchildren at D's death, since it is still possible for the interest to prove either valid or void by actual events. We must wait until the death of D's children in being at T's death. There should be no inconvenience in waiting further, because D's children are still entitled to possession or income from the property. If the last surviving child of D turns out to be a person in being at T's death, the remainder will actually vest in time and will be valid. On the other hand, if all D's children in being at T's death die, survived by a child of D not in being, it will then be known that the remainder is incapable of vesting within lives in being. The will is then reformed, in a manner similar to (B) above, to vest the gift within twenty-one years of the death of D's children in being at T's death.

Trusts measured solely by a period of years. Frequently testators set up trusts not measured by any lives in being but for a gross period of years, such as forty. The Rule against Perpetuities is not concerned with the duration of the trust as such. Rather it is concerned with the vesting of interests in the trust. If the vesting of the interests is not causally related to any life in being, under KRS 381.216 the trust will last for twenty-one years and then terminate. If, as will more often be the case, the interests are causally related to lives in being though the trust is for a term of years in gross, the trust can last for the relevant lives plus twenty-one years,[56] which may or may not be longer than the specified duration. Thus:

Case 4 (Trust for years). T devises property in trust "for forty years to pay income to my issue per stirpes from time to time living, and at the end of forty years to distribute the principal to my issue then living per stirpes." With respect to both the income and the principal interest, the class can increase or decrease in membership depending upon the life, death, and generative powers of T's issue living at his death (and of T's afterborn grandchildren as well, but they are excluded as measuring lives). They have a causal relationship to the vesting of the gifts. Hence the trust will be valid for the lives of T's issue living at his death plus twenty-one years thereafter, or for forty years, whichever period is shorter. If the trust terminates on the former event, the will is reformed to distribute the principal to T's issue per stirpes living at the date of distribution. If the trust terminates on the latter event no reformation is required.

The same result should follow in a discretionary as well as a mandatory trust. If in *Case 4* the trustee had discretion to pay so much of the income, and in such shares, as he should determine among testator's issue, and to accumulate and add to corpus any

---

[56] This is the result under the common law when the trust is for "as long as the law allows." 6 Am. L. Prop. § 24.13; Simes & Smith § 1227. Hence this statute turns any invalid trust for years into a valid trust for the specified years or for "as long as the law allows," whichever period is shorter.

balance of income, "and at the end of forty years etc.," the issue of testator living at his death are the "lives in being." Their generative powers and deaths can affect the persons who take, and therefore the vesting of, the principal.

Transfers upon a contingent event not related to any life. Some gifts are made on contingencies not related to lives. Examples are: $1,000 to A immediately upon probate of my will; $100,000 to my testamentary trustee to hold in trust under certain provisions; fifty-year lease to X Corporation if a certain building is built. The contingencies in these cases are, respectively, probate of a will, appointment of a trustee, and erecting a building. These events are not causally related to the continuance of any life in being. In such cases the interests are valid if the contingencies actually occur within twenty-one years. They are void if the contingencies occur thereafter.

Options. Under prior law an option that could not be exercised beyond lives in being plus twenty-one years was valid under the Rule against Perpetuities.[57] But an option unlimited in time was void. KRS 381.216 will save for twenty-one years options, previously held void, that are unlimited in time or are limited upon contingencies unrelated to any life in being. Thus:

Case 5 (Options). O grants "to A, his heirs and assigns an option to purchase Blackacre for $5,000." Under common law the grant created an equitable interest in A, subject to the condition precedent of exercise. It was void under the Rule against Perpetuities, since it was assignable and inheritable and might not be exercised within the perpetuity period. Because it may be assigned to *any* person, who may exercise it (cause it to vest), there are no lives in being which can be used as measuring lives.[58] Hence, under KRS 381.216 the option is valid if it is actually exercised within twenty-one years, which is to say it is valid for twenty-one years. It is void thereafter. (If the option is personal to A, and not assignable, A's life is causally related to its exercise. It was valid at common law, and it is valid under this statute).

[57] But it may have been (and may still be) invalid as an unreasonable restraint on alienation. See pp. 127-31 *infra*.

[58] Even though any person can exercise the option, all persons in being cannot be used as measuring lives. The common law Rule, adopted by KRS 381.215, requires the measuring lives to be reasonable in number. 6 Am. L. Prop. § 24.13; 5 Powell ¶ 766. All persons in the world plainly constitute an unreasonable number.

A case involving the validity of an option has already arisen under the 1960 Perpetuities Act. The case is *Gilbert v. Union College*.[59] On September 8, 1960, Union College in Barbourville contracted to sell a lot in its faculty housing development to Dr. Frank Gilbert, a professor of biology at the college. Gilbert was in turn to construct a house thereon. To prevent the house and lot from falling into the hands of persons not connected with the college, the college proposed to insert in its deed five repurchase options. The first three options were exercisable upon termination of employment or death, which events must necessarily happen before or at Gilbert's death. These options are valid under the common law Rule and are of course valid under KRS 381.216. The fifth option gave the college a preemption for 120 days if Gilbert and his present wife (the grantees) ever desired to sell. This preemption, limited to the lives of the grantees, does not violate the Rule against Perpetuities, and the court also held it was not an unreasonable direct restraint on alienation.

The fourth option involved the hypothetical unborn widow. If Dr. Gilbert left a widow who wished to occupy the house, the option became exercisable "any time within 90 days after she shall have ceased to so occupy it or shall have died *or of the lapse of a period of 20 years after his death,* whichever shall first occur." (Emphasis added.) Without the italicized language the option would be void at common law, since it might become exercisable ("vest") at the death of a widow not in being. But the addition of this language saves it by expressly providing that it cannot be exercised ("vest") more than twenty years and ninety days after Gilbert's death. Hence the option could be declared valid without waiting to see if Gilbert left a widow unborn at the creation of the option, and the court so held. It was not necessary to apply KRS 381.216 to save it. Had the draftsman omitted the italicized language, however, the new statute would have been applicable. In that case the option could be exercised too remotely if the widow actually turned out to be a woman not living at the creation of the option. So we wait until Dr. Gilbert's death and see. If, at that time, we find that this professor of biology by some endemic series of miracles has left an unborn widow, the deed is reformed to limit exercise of the option to a twenty-one-year period after the professor's death.

[59] 343 S.W.2d 829 (Ky. 1961).

Powers of appointment. This section brings no substantial change in the application of the Rule to interests created by exercise of special and testamentary powers, since under prior law it was standard practice to wait until the power was exercised and judge the validity of interests by facts existing at that time. Usually the power will be exercised in such a way as to bring it within the fact pattern of *Case 3*. The exercise will be read back into the original instrument creating the power, and what was said with respect to that case will be applicable to it. If the donee fails to exercise the power, the validity of the gift in default of appointment is determined on the basis of the same considerations as would be applicable had he exercised it.

Although the application of wait-and-see to the exercise of powers is not new, the cy pres provision is. The old law that an invalid gift passed in default of appointment will no longer be applied if the donee's intention can be approximated more closely by reformation.

With respect to the validity of powers, rather than the validity of their exercise, it may also be observed that this statute does change the common law. Testamentary and special powers which might be exercised beyond the period were void *ab initio* under the remote possibilities test. Under this statute such powers are valid for the period of the Rule, and at the end of that time they lapse. Hence a discretionary trust to allocate income is valid for the lives of the income beneficiaries in being at the beginning of the perpetuity period plus twenty-one years, at which time, if it has not already ceased under the terms of the instrument, it ceases and the principal is distributed (as in *Case 4*).[60]

Summary. Cases 1 through 5 cover the fact pattern of every perpetuities case decided by the Kentucky Court of Appeals in which an interest has been held void.[61] And, as we have seen, the reform statute can be applied to every one of them with little difficulty. This should dispel any notion that wait-and-see and cy pres may be difficult to apply in run-of-the-mine cases.

That all these cases—all three dozen of them—fall into five

---

[60] For treatment of discretionary trusts under the common law Rule, see 6 Am. L. Prop. § 24.32.

[61] See Appendix 2, Tables 5, 6, and 7 *infra*. The statement in the text does not include cases on rights of entry and possibilities of reverter, which are dealt with separately in Chapter 5.

well-defined fact patterns is revealing. It indicates that bizarre hypothetical cases which can be dreamed up to show the inconvenience of wait-and-see may be, like the fertile octogenarian and the unborn widow, theoretically possible but as a practical matter rarely happen. Any general rule of law properly must be drawn to fit common and reasonable dispositions, instead of being drawn in fear of highly improbable ones. If such exceptional cases do arise, the Court of Appeals cannot be expected to push a sound principle to its dryly logical extreme, resulting in great and serious inconvenience in the distribution of property. The ability of the court to reform the instrument to carry out testator's intent to the greatest extent possible should, and was designed to, prevent the wait-and-see doctrine from getting out of control in any such manner.

5

DRAFTING TO AVOID PERPETUITIES PROBLEMS

WHILE the wait-and-see doctrine will be of tremendous comfort to the draftsman who belatedly discovers some unintentional oversight, the careful draftsman will make certain that all interests vest in due time. No instrument is properly drafted if the draftsman must wait and see whether his disposition is valid.

Thus instruments should continue to be drafted on the assumption that the common law remote possibilities test is still in effect. We should be able to tell from the beginning that the interests are all clearly valid. There is another reason for this besides the unnecessary uncertainty which would result from intentionally waiting to see. The law of another state may be applicable to the disposition. If the client is so unfortunate as to die domiciled out of Kentucky, or if he owns real property in another state, or if he exercises a power of appointment over a trust governed by the law of a sister state, Kentucky law may not be applicable to the disposition at all. Insofar as it is practicable, an instrument should be drawn which is valid in every state. An instrument which satisfies the common law Rule against Perpetuities will be valid in every state except for interests created in *land* located in Arizona,[62]

---

[62] 5 Powell ¶ 810 (two lives plus twenty-one years).

Minnesota,[63] and Mississippi,[64] or in real or personal property in South Dakota.[65] Where the client does not own land in those four states, and is not expected to die domiciled in South Dakota, the only feasible drafting standard is the common law Rule against Perpetuities.

The traps which face the draftsman under that Rule are legendary, and no complete list can be given here. Nonetheless, there are four traps which account for the large majority of invalid interests, and against these the draftsman must constantly be on guard. The following precepts give the necessary warnings.

(1) Do not create a trust that can last for more than twenty-one years after lives in being at its creation. A trust that can last longer than the perpetuity period is wholly invalid in some states. In others, beneficial interests will frequently be found to offend the Rule by construction, and discretionary powers in the trustee that can be exercised too remotely also will be struck down. In those states that are "groping toward a possessory test of validity" of interests, such as Kentucky, the gift of principal of a trust that possibly might last beyond the allotted period may be struck down even though the gift may be indefeasibly vested in interest. The client's essential desires, if they are the slightest bit reasonable, can be carried out without creating a trust to extend beyond the perpetuity period. It should be remembered that the perpetuity period begins, in case of an irrevocable inter vivos trust, at the date of creation of the trust, not at the settlor's death. The reports are full of cases where the draftsman of an inter vivos trust copied a wills-book form providing for termination of the trust upon the death of "my issue living at my death," only to have a court declare the gift of principal void. For drafting purposes, it is wise to assume that the perpetuity period for a revocable trust also begins at the creation of the trust, just as it does with an irrevocable trust. The law in all states is not settled, and it is better to play it safe.

If the trust will be certain to end within the perpetuity period, all interests therein will necessarily be valid under the Rule against Perpetuities. To avoid some unconscious error in the dispositive

---

[63] *Id.* ¶ 819 (two lives plus restricted minority).
[64] *Id.* ¶ 820 (lives only; no twenty-one-year period).
[65] *Id.* ¶ 825 (lives plus restricted minority).

provisions, counsel may wish to include a special safety clause terminating the trust in all events not later than lives in being plus twenty-one years. Here is an example of such a provision which, because it names the measuring lives, can be used in both inter vivos and testamentary trusts.

Anything herein to the contrary not withstanding, any trust established by this instrument shall terminate, if it has not previously terminated, twenty-one (21) years after the death of the survivor of the following persons living on the date this instrument is executed:
[List here the names of the settlor and of all beneficiaries of the trust then living.]
The then remaining principal and undistributed income of such trust shall be paid to the persons then entitled to receive the income therefrom in the same shares or portions in which such income is then being paid to them.[66]

This provision must not be used blindly as a boilerplate. It is designed to be relied upon only in an emergency. But, adapted to the particular instrument, it is useful as a safeguard against some unwitting slip-up.

If for some reason the draftsman does not wish to name the measuring lives, the provision could read: ". . . (21) years after the death of the last survivor of the *beneficiaries* of such trust who shall be living on the date this instrument is executed" [or in case of a will, "who shall be living on the date of my death"]. Because it may be uncertain who the "beneficiaries" are, specifically naming the measuring lives is the safer course.

(2) Take particular care in exercising a special or testamentary power of appointment. Under standard doctrine the appointment is read back into the instrument creating the power, and the perpetuity period runs from the creation of the power. Thus the power should be exercised so that the appointed interests are sure to vest within twenty-one years after some life in being at the creation of the power. What this means as a practical matter is that a life estate should never be appointed to a person who was not in being at the creation of the power.

(3) Think twice, or three times, before making a gift contingent on reaching an age in excess of twenty-one or postponing possession

---

[66] This provision is adapted from paragraph SIXTH in the Black Irrevocable Trust, Casner, Estate Planning 1206 (3d ed. 1961).

beyond the age of twenty-one. The line between a provision which makes a given age a condition precedent and a provision which makes it only the point of enjoyment, and does not prevent earlier vesting, is quite indistinct. The use of one word or one phrase can put the provision on one side of the line or the other. Drawing valid gifts postponing possession beyond age twenty-one is possible, but great care must be used in the doing.

(4) Use the names of beneficiaries rather than a class designation in describing life tenants. A glance at Table 5 in Appendix 2 will show that the type of devise most frequently held void in Kentucky was a gift "to Maude for life, remainder to Maude's children for their lives, remainder in fee to Maude's grandchildren." Because Maude was deemed to be capable of having another child, the remainder in fee was held void. If Maude's children had been described by name, and the remainder given to their children, the remainder in fee would have been valid, whether Maude proved fertile or not. Thus: "to Maude for life, then to Tom, Dick, and Harry, children of Maude, for their lives, then to the children of Tom, Dick, and Harry in fee." The remainder in fee must vest, if at all, at the death of Maude, Tom, Dick, and Harry. (Of course this gift is still objectionable on grounds of ambiguity. After the death of Maude, and then Tom, who is entitled to Tom's share of the income? Do the grandchildren take per stirpes or per capita? Etc. But the perpetuities objection is overcome merely by describing the beneficiaries by name.) Where there cannot, as a practical matter, be any afterborn members of a class, or where testator does not wish them to take in any event, describe the beneficiaries by name.

Is a boilerplate clause to avoid all violations desirable? Because of the ease with which even experienced draftsmen can run afoul of the Rule, Professors Leach and Logan have suggested that every will should contain a saving clause to take care of any possible violation. They have drafted an appropriate clause, which is set forth in a recent issue of the *Harvard Law Review.*[67] Their method is, in their language, "to give to a disinterested corporate fiduciary a power to appoint the assets which are the subject matter of any

[67] Leach & Logan, "Perpetuities: A Standard Saving Clause to Avoid Violation of the Rule," 74 Harv. L. Rev. 1141 (1961).

challenged interest in such a manner as to approximate the intention of the person creating the interest within the limits permitted by the rule under which the interest is challenged."[68] Their clause is well drafted, but quite complex, covering three pages in the *Review*. In sum, they give a corporate trustee cy pres power to take care of any violation where a court does not have such power by statute.

It will be immediately seen that this saving clause has no effect if the instrument is governed by Kentucky law. For Kentucky courts have cy pres power under KRS 381.216. Nonetheless, Messrs. Leach and Logan recommend it be included in a Kentucky will because the testator may be domiciled in another state at death. Or he may be exercising a power created by an instrument governed by the law of some other state.

Kentucky lawyers are invited to consider including this clause in their wills and trusts. If they wish a boilerplate, here is one. Doubtless many of them will reject this clause, however, because of its complexity, or because reliance is placed on a saving clause limiting duration of a trust, or because they have every reason to believe their client will die happily domiciled in Kentucky not exercising powers "located" elsewhere.

While this saving clause is useful under the present state of the law in other jurisdictions, the real solution for perpetuities problems does not lie in cluttering up wills with more saving clauses. It lies in reforming the law to make such clauses unnecessary. If the only way to protect draftsmen from perpetuities errors is to create a cy pres power, how much simpler and better it is for that power to be in a court by statute. The one thing this saving clause shows is the need for cy pres statutes in other jurisdictions.

[68] *Ibid*.

5

ABOLITION OF POSSIBILITIES OF REVERTER AND TERMINATION OF RIGHTS OF ENTRY

1

THE PURPOSE OF THE STATUTE

POSSIBILITIES of reverter and rights of entry limited on a fee historically have been exempt from the Rule against Perpetuities.[1] These interests are just as objectionable as interests within the Rule, in that they tie up property for long periods of time, potentially forever. With passage of time and change of conditions they leave the owner of the fee in a straitjacket.

The need for legislation to terminate these forfeiture interests has been extensively discussed elsewhere[2] and need not be repeated here. Everyone agrees that these interests should be extinguished at some point in time, but not everyone is in agreement as to how this should be accomplished. Various solutions have been proposed. Among these are subjecting possibilities of reverter and rights of entry to the Rule against Perpetuities; terminating them after a fixed period of years; transforming them into equitable servitures, subject to termination by change of circumstances; terminating such of them as are limited on "merely nominal" conditions; and terminating such of them as serve to restrict the use of land. One or more of these solutions have been adopted in about a dozen states, with some states combining two approaches.

Which solution best fits the problem depends largely upon the purposes for which possibilities of reverter and rights of entry are created. If these are known, a suitable and reasonable period (or periods) of time for their accomplishment can be devised. There has been, however, no factual functional study of these interests published. Experienced conveyancers and draftsmen believe these interests are primarily used to restrict the use of land, but this is merely an informed guess based on experience. Doubtless the reason no factual study has been made is that the time required for reading all the recorded deeds and wills necessary to give such a study validity would be prohibitive. And moreover, access to unrecorded instruments transferring personal property would be impossible to attain.

Nonetheless, studies limited to one community for a short period are feasible and are not without value. To acquire some evidence of the purpose and frequency of creation of possibilities of reverter and rights of entry, the author undertook to read all the wills and deeds recorded in Fayette County (population 125,000) for the year 1957.[3] In this task he had the very valuable

---

[1] Holding these interests exempt: Fayette County v. Morton, 282 Ky. 481, 138 S.W.2d 953 (1940); Fayette County Bd. of Educ. v. Bryan, 263 Ky. 61, 91 S.W.2d 990 (1936); Bowling v. Grace, 219 Ky. 496, 293 S.W. 964 (1927); Jefferson County Bd. of Educ. v. Littrell, 173 Ky. 78, 190 S.W. 465 (1917). See 6 Am. L. Prop. § 24.62.

[2] See Simes & Taylor, The Improvement of Conveyancing by Legislation 201-17 (1960); Report of the Committee on the Improvement of Conveyancing and Recording Practices, Am. Bar Assn. Sec. of Real Prop., Prob. & Trust Law, Proceedings 73 (1957), and articles cited therein; Note, 46 Ky. L.J. 605 (1958).

[3] Mr. Dale Bryant ran the deeds in rural Wolfe County (population 6,500) for the same year. Out of 276 deeds, he found one providing for reverter upon cessation of school use. Ironically enough, that deed provided for reverter of the tract to "the owner of said farm that it was taken from," which provision creates an executory interest and is void for perpetuity. McGaughey v. Spencer County Bd. of Educ., 285 Ky. 769, 149 S.W.2d 519 (1941). Mr. Bryant found no restrictive covenants recorded in Wolfe County in 1957.

assistance of two students, Mr. William Logan and Mr. Robert Zweigart, both now of the Kentucky Bar. There were 323 wills probated, none of which created possibilities of reverter or rights of entry. Out of 4,333 recorded deeds, only six created these interests. The contingencies upon which the possibilities of reverter or rights of entry were limited were: (a) cessation of use as a public park (two deeds from real estate development corporation to Fayette County); (b) cessation within twenty years of use for educational purposes (two deeds from U. S. Department of Health, Education and Welfare to University of Kentucky and county board of education); (c) cessation of use for church purposes (Ohio grantor to local church); (d) cessation of use for street purposes (individual to city of Lexington).

In contrast to these few deeds creating forfeiture restrictions on land use, the great majority of deeds contained or referred to nonforfeiture restrictive covenants. There were 748 deeds containing new express covenants, 1,088 referring to covenants contained in a prior deed, and 1,642 referring to a plat which may or may not have had restrictions recorded on its face. Only 849 deeds contained no restrictions or reference to any restrictions in prior deeds or reference to a plat. (But two-thirds of these deeds did except "restrictions, if any, of record" from the general warranty.)

Although this study was limited to the deeds and wills in one county for one year, it tends to confirm what many take to be common knowledge: that rights of entry and possibilities of reverter are used almost exclusively for the purpose of restricting the use of land,[4] and even for that purpose are used infrequently in modern times. The restrictive covenant has replaced them.

From a functional viewpoint, then, the problem created by possibilities of reverter and rights of entry is basically one of forfeiture restrictions on the use of land. And the fundamental question for the legislative draftsman is whether these interests

[4] The only other uses of these interests found in reported cases in Kentucky are in mineral deeds (Johnson v. Pittsburgh Consol. Coal Co., 311 S.W.2d 537 (Ky. 1958)); in charitable trusts (Kasey v. Fidelity Trust Co., 131 Ky. 609, 115 S.W. 739 (1909); Pullins v. Bd. of Educ. of Methodist Church, 25 Ky. L. Rep. 1715, 78 S.W. 457 (1904)); in deeds creating a charge for support (Lawson v. Asberry, 283 Ky. 390, 141 S.W.2d 564 (1940)); and in wills devising property to a widow so long as she remains unmarried (Cuddy v. McIntyre, 312 Ky. 606, 229 S.W.2d 315 (1950)). The first three types of transfers (mineral deeds, charitable trusts, and charge for support) are exempt from the thirty-year termination rule under KRS 381.222.

should be dealt with functionally or conceptually; that is, should the statute be drafted to apply only to those possibilities of reverter and rights of entry (and executory interests) that restrict the use of land, or should it be drafted to apply to all possibilities of reverter and rights of entry? There is much to be said for a straightforward functional approach.[5] But we rejected it on two grounds. First, some possibilities of reverter and rights of entry not created to enforce land use restrictions are equally objectionable if they can endure forever. Second, a statute terminating "forfeiture restrictions on the use of land" might require a substantial amount of judicial construction.

Instead of directly adopting a functional approach, we decided to deal with the functional problem indirectly. The statute was drafted in conceptual terms to apply to all possibilities of reverter and rights of entry and executory interests after determinable fees. Then certain specific uses of these interests for purposes other than restricting land use were excepted. This blanket-with-holes approach should have approximately the same effect as a statute applying only to forfeiture restrictions on the use of land.

The basic scheme of sections 4 through 7 of the 1960 Perpetuities Act (KRS 381.218 through 381.222) is to reduce all types of interests created to enforce forfeiture restrictions on the use of land to one—the right of entry—and then to provide for the termination of rights of entry thirty years after date of creation. Existing rights of entry and possibilities of reverter are subjected to the thirty-year termination rule unless they are re-recorded before July 1, 1965. Detailed comment on these sections, and how they accomplish the basic scheme, follows.

2

GOOD RIDDANCE: THE DETERMINABLE FEE
AND POSSIBILITY OF REVERTER ABOLISHED

KRS 381.218 reads:

The estate known at common law as the fee simple determinable and the interest known as the possibility of reverter are abolished. Words

---

[5] See N.Y. Law Revision Comm'n Report, Legis. Doc. 65(B) (1958). New York is the only state to adopt a functional approach.

which at common law would create a fee simple determinable shall be construed to create a fee simple subject to a right of entry for condition broken. In any case where a person would have a possibility of reverter at common law, he shall have a right of entry.

The purpose of this section was to abolish the anachronistic distinction between (a) a fee simple determinable with a possibility of reverter and (b) a fee simple subject to a condition subsequent with a right of entry for condition broken. These two estates with their related future interests may be illustrated by the following cases.

Case 1. O deeds land "to Trinity Church so long as used for church purposes." Trinity Church has a fee simple determinable, and O has a possibility of reverter by operation of law, since he did not grant an absolute fee.[6] An express clause providing that the land revert back to O and his heirs is technically superfluous, but it is a wise addition as a practical matter to prevent litigation.

Case 2. O deeds land "to Trinity Church, but if the land is ever used for other than church purposes the grantor and his heirs may enter and terminate the estate hereby transferred." Trinity Church has a fee simple subject to condition subsequent. O has a right of entry for condition broken (called a "power of termination" in the *Restatement of Property*).

Whether the grantor creates a determinable fee with a possibility of reverter or a fee simple subject to a right of entry supposedly depends upon the language used. The former is said to be created by such words as "so long as," "during," "until." The latter is alleged to be created by words granting a fee and then adding, "provided that," "on condition that," "but" if a specified event happens the grantor may reenter. It is notoriously difficult, however, to classify instruments by resort to such tenuous verbal distinctions. Few actual instruments fall neatly and clearly into one, and only one, category. Where classification leads to

[6] Devine v. Isham, 284 Ky. 587, 145 S.W.2d 529 (1940); Fayette County Bd. of Educ. v. Bryan, *supra* note 1. The dispositive language in *Case 1* should be compared with a grant "for church purposes only, and for no other purpose," which conveys a fee simple absolute. Scott County Bd. of Educ. v. Pepper, 311 S.W.2d 189 (Ky. 1958); Williams v. Johnson, 284 Ky. 23, 143 S.W.2d 730 (1940). It is not clear that a possibility of reverter would arise by operation of law in Kentucky where the grantee pays valuable consideration for the property. See Board of Educ. of Taylor County v. Bd. of Educ. of Campbellsville, 292 Ky. 261, 166 S.W.2d 295 (1942).

different legal consequences, it is necessary to litigate any given phrasing to determine what interpretation will be put upon it.[7]

The treatises set forth several differences in legal consequences between a possibility of reverter and a right of entry. One primary difference is that the former is more frequently held alienable. Indeed, it has been held in some few states that the mere attempt to alienate a right of entry destroyed it. This difference does not prevail in Kentucky, where by statute "the owner may convey any interest in real property not in adverse possession of another."[8] This statute has been interpreted as making alienable "every conceivable interest in or claim to real estate, whether present or future, vested or contingent,"[9] including possibilities of reverter and rights of entry.[10]

The other primary difference between a possibility of reverter and a right of entry is that the former by legal fiction becomes possessory *"automatically,"* while the exercise of the right of entry is *optional*. Several consequences are alleged to flow from this distinction,[11] though many of them seem to be more fanciful than

[7] Compare with *Cases 1* and *2* a deed "to Trinity Church, but if the land ceases to be used for church purposes it is to revert to the grantor or his heirs." "But if" points to a right of entry; "revert" points to a possibility of reverter. Held: grantor has right of entry—Ohm v. Clear Creek Drainage District, 153 Neb. 428, 45 N.W.2d 117 (1950); Sanford v. Sims, 192 Va. 644, 66 S.E.2d 495 (1951). Held: grantor has possibility of reverter—Baptist Church v. Wagner, 193 Tenn. 625, 249 S.W.2d 875 (1952); County School Bd. v. Dowell, 190 Va. 676, 58 S.E.2d 38 (1950). Held: church has fee simple absolute—Savannah School District v. McLeod, 137 Cal. App. 2d 491, 290 P.2d 593 (1955); Second Church v. Le Prevost, 67 Ohio App. 101, 35 N.E.2d 1015 (1941).

[8] KRS 382.010. See also KRS 381.210.

[9] Austin v. Calvert, 262 S.W.2d 825, 826 (Ky. 1953), holding possibility of reverter alienable. Contrary dictum in some prior cases was expressly disapproved. *But see* Dep't of Revenue v. Kentucky Trust Co., 313 S.W.2d 401 (Ky. 1958), ignoring the Austin case and referring to old dictum with approval.

[10] Austin v. Calvert, *supra* note 9; Webster County Bd. of Educ. v. Wynn, 303 Ky. 110, 196 S.W.2d 983 (1946); Fayette County Bd. of Educ. v. Bryan, 263 Ky. 61, 91 S.W.2d 990 (1936); Fulton v. Teager, 183 Ky. 381, 209 S.W. 535 (1919); Nutter v. Russell, 60 Ky. (3 Met.) 163 (1860); Kentucky Coal Lands Co. v. Mineral Dev. Co., 295 F. 255 (6th Cir. 1925); *cf.* Kenner v. American Contract Co., 72 Ky. (9 Bush) 202 (1872). Similar statutes in Virginia—from which KRS 382.010 was taken—and Mississippi have been interpreted as making alienable the possibility of reverter and right of entry. Sanford v. Sims, 192 Va. 644, 66 S.E.2d 495 (1951); Hamilton v. Jackson, 157 Miss. 284, 127 So. 302 (1930). See also 1 Am. L. Prop. § 4.68 and 2 Powell ¶ 282, stating these interests are alienable in Kentucky.

[11] See 1 Powell ¶ 191; Williams, "Restrictions on the Use of Land," 27 Tex. L. Rev. 158 (1948). See also Charlotte Park & Recreation Comm'n v. Barringer, 242 N.C. 311, 88 S.E.2d 114 (1955). In view of the Charlotte Park case, *supra*, one opponent of the reform act suggested this section might be civil rights legislation in disguise!

real.[12] The Kentucky cases do not treat the interests differently except in one situation, but in that situation the distinction between automatic and optional termination has led to striking results. The situation is where the holder of the determinable fee has lost actual possession and control of the property after the terminating event happens. For example, a school board holding a determinable fee closes the school and boards up the windows; the neighboring landowner then proceeds to fence in the school lot. It has been held that the school board cannot oust the possessor, irrespective of who he is or whether he has a valid claim of title, because the board's title has terminated.[13] This result, insofar as it gives the law's protection to someone who, without a better claim of title, ousts a prior peaceful possessor, is unsound. Even though the board's "title" has terminated, the board, as the last person peacefully in possession, should be entitled to remain in possession until the true owner appears. And, by eliminating automatic termination, KRS 381.218 so provides.

The distinction between automatic and optional termination of the fee serves no useful purpose today. Functionally the determinable fee with possibility of reverter and the fee simple with right of entry are equivalents. The grantor exhibits the same objective, describes the same persons who have a right to possession, and refers to the same event for shifting the possessory estate. The categorization will in most cases depend upon chance language used. Community policy respecting these interests should be the same regardless of the verbal form.

Abolition of this anachronism with its unfortunate contemporary consequences is the first step in the statutory scheme to bring to book the right of entry and the possibility of reverter, which are exempt from the common law Rule against Perpetuities. Conversion of the determinable fee with possibility of reverter into a fee simple subject to a right of entry for condition broken, rather than the converse, was desirable because it abolished the automatic nature of the reverter. An optional forfeiture is less objectionable than an automatic one. The sounder policy requires that the fee owner be left in possession until the transferor elects

---

[12] See Dunham, "Possibility of Reverter and Power of Termination—Fraternal or Identical Twins?" 20 U. Chi. L. Rev. 215 (1953).
[13] Barren County Bd. of Educ. v. Jordan, 249 S.W.2d 814 (Ky. 1952); Webster County Bd. of Educ. v. Gentry, 233 Ky. 35, 24 S.W.2d 910 (1930).

to declare a forfeiture. That this is desirable is confirmed by the abolition of automatic reverter on breach of a land use restriction by the New York legislature in 1958 and by the comprehensive study supporting that legislation.[14] Therefore the determinable fee was done away with.[15]

This act would have brought joy to the heart of John Chipman Gray, who labored hard to rid the law of the determinable fee. Gray attempted to prove that determinable fees were impossible to create after the Statute *Quia Emptores* in 1290, but his ingenious effort remained a tour de force without consequences.

What defeasible fees may now be created. The effect of this section is that it is now possible to create only two types of defeasible fees: (a) the fee simple subject to a right of entry for condition broken; and (b) the fee simple subject to an executory limitation. (The latter is commonly referred to in Kentucky as *the* defeasible fee, but technically the fee subject to a right of entry is also a defeasible fee.) The technical difference between these fees is that the former is subject to a power to terminate the fee *in the transferor or his heirs*, while the latter is subject to automatic divestment by an executory interest *in a third party*, which is treated for all practical purposes the same as a remainder. The functional difference is much wider, however. The fee subject to a right of entry, like the determinable fee, is almost always used to restrict the use of land. The fee subject to an executory limitation is rarely used to restrict the use of land; its common use is in instruments disposing of wealth within the family. Thus:

Case 3. T devises land "to A and his heirs, but if A at any time dies without issue surviving him then to B and his heirs." A has a defeasible fee, more narrowly described as a fee subject to an executory

[14] N.Y. Real Prop. Law § 347; N.Y. Law Revision Comm'n Report, Legis. Doc. 65(B) (1958). The New York statute abolishes both the automatic reverter and the right of entry, substituting therefor a cause of action in equity to compel a reconveyance of the land upon breach of the restriction. The action is subject to any equitable defense which might be interposed to prevent enforcement of a covenant, and forfeiture can be declared by the court only to protect a substantial interest in enforcement of the restriction. This is a more drastic curtailment of forfeiture restrictions on the use of land than is provided in KRS 381.218 and 381.219.

[15] The fee simple determinable is sometimes called a fee simple on a special limitation (meaning duration limited to a period shorter than normal duration), a qualified fee (meaning qualified in duration) or a base fee (meaning inferior). It was the purpose of the statute to abolish the estate by whatever name it is called.

limitation.[16] B has an executory interest. B's rights are identical with those of a contingent remainderman.[17] Only for historic reasons does his interest bear a different label.

The fee simple subject to divestment by an executory interest is not affected by KRS 381.218 or KRS 381.219. It is not used to restrict the use of land and is not within the reasons for these sections. The executory interest remains subject to the common law Rule against Perpetuities as modified by KRS 381.216. However, what would have been at common law a determinable fee *followed* by a subsequent but *nondivesting* executory limitation is, for reasons subsequently noted, treated under KRS 381.219 as a fee subject to a right of entry.

The section does not apply to reversions. Reversions have sometimes been confused with possibilities of reverter, and to forestall any questions about the applicability of the act to reversions, it may be just as well to point out the distinction between these two interests and why KRS 381.218 does not apply to reversions. In the words of Professor Lewis Simes, "A reversion is the interest remaining in the grantor, or in the successor in interest of a testator, who transfers a vested estate of a lesser quantum than that of the vested estate which he has."[18] Under the common law theory of estates a fee simple is a greater estate than a life estate, and a life estate is a greater estate than a term of years. Hence, whenever the owner of a fee simple transfers a life estate or a term of years, *not followed by a vested remainder in fee*, he has a reversion. He may transfer a life estate followed by one or more contingent remainders in fee, but he still retains a reversion, since he has not transferred away a vested remainder in a fee.

However, there can be no reversion where the owner of a fee simple has transferred a vested fee simple of any type (fee simple absolute, fee simple determinable, or fee simple subject to condition subsequent) either in possession or in remainder. Why not? Because—to put it shortly and ignore a lot of history, fiction, and

---

[16] Malone v. Jamison, 312 Ky. 249, 227 S.W.2d 179 (1950). In addition to death without issue, other events on which a defeasible fee may be limited include remarriage of testator's widow (Ramsey v. Holder, 291 S.W.2d 556 (Ky. 1956)); return of a long-lost son (Commonwealth v. Pollitt, 25 Ky. L. Rep. 790, 76 S.W. 412 (1903)); attachment by son's creditors (Scott v. Ratliff, 179 Ky. 267, 200 S.W. 462 (1918)).

[17] See Dukeminier, "Contingent Remainders and Executory Interests: A Requiem for the Distinction," 43 Minn. L. Rev. 13 (1958).

[18] 1 Am. L. Prop. § 4.16. See 2 Powell ¶ 271.

dubious logic—all fees simple are of the same "quantum."[19] It follows from this peculiar assumption of the law of estates that any interest remaining in the owner of a fee simple after he transfers a vested fee simple cannot, under the standard definition of a reversion, be called a reversion. If a grantor transfers a fee simple determinable, any interest retained by him is called a possibility of reverter. If he transfers a fee simple on condition subsequent, his interest is called a right of entry.

Certainty of possession has nothing to do with the classification of these interests. Although there is no certainty a possibility of reverter will become possessory in the future, this uncertainty does not make the interest a possibility of reverter. It is given that label solely because it follows a determinable fee. Indeed, many reversions are likewise uncertain to become possessory, such as one retained by an instrument creating a contingent remainder. But that uncertainty does not change the reversion, which is a conceptual interest retained when no vested fee has been transferred, into a possibility of reverter. Thus:

Case 4. A, owner of a fee simple, conveys "to B for life, remainder in fee to such of B's children as survive B." B has a life estate, B's children have a contingent remainder, and A has a reversion.[20] The reversion will be extinguished if B leaves children surviving him. While it may never become possessory, A's interest is a reversion (not a possibility of reverter) because he has not transferred a vested remainder in fee.

Sometimes when courts have had before them instruments retaining reversions which may not become possessory, they have spoken of "a possibility of reversion," referring ambiguously both to the legal interest known as a reversion and to the factual possibility that this reversion may not become possessory in the future. It has then been easy for them to slip from this factual reference into the legal concept, "possibility of reverter," although that interest has not been involved.[21] The conversion of a possibility of reverter into a right of entry by KRS 381.218 should make it less likely that a court will unwittingly fall into this fallacy. "Reversion" and "right of entry" have no verbal similarity.

Although the technical distinction between a reversion and a

---

[19] See Simes & Smith § 92.
[20] Thurman v. Hudson, 280 S.W.2d 507 (Ky. 1955).
[21] See, *e.g.*, Dep't of Revenue v. Kentucky Trust Co., 313 S.W.2d 401 (Ky. 1958).

possibility of reverter turns upon whether the transferor conveyed a vested fee simple, either in possession or remainder, these two interests are usually retained for quite different purposes. Outside of the landlord-tenant situation, a reversion is ordinarily retained in a disposition of family wealth, where its purpose or effect is to provide who shall take the property when the disposition is incomplete. Rarely does one find a possibility of reverter in a will or a private trust, for its common use is in imposing land use restrictions upon a grantee.

3

TERMINATION OF RIGHTS OF ENTRY AFTER THIRTY YEARS

KRS 381.219 reads:

A fee simple subject to a right of entry for condition broken shall become a fee simple absolute if the specified contingency does not occur within thirty years from the effective date of the instrument creating such fee simple subject to a right of entry. If such contingency occurs within said thirty years the right of entry, which may be created in a person other than the person creating the interest or his heirs, shall become exercisable notwithstanding the rule against perpetuities. This section shall not apply to rights of entry created prior to July 1, 1960.

Rights of entry and possibilities of reverter, being exempt from the Rule against Perpetuities, tie up property very seriously. Title held subject to one of these interests is not marketable, and frequently the property is not improvable because a mortgage cannot be obtained upon it. The land may remain undeveloped or limited to uneconomic uses, and the restriction cannot be released because of the difficulty in ascertaining who holds the right of entry or possibility of reverter created by a long-dead grantor. Because of their adverse effect upon the marketability of land, KRS 381.219 terminates all rights of entry (including under that designation what formerly would be called possibilities of reverter) that do not become exercisable within thirty years of creation.

Although the exemption of the right of entry (and the now-abolished possibility of reverter) from the Rule against Perpetuities was the loophole in the law allowing forfeiture restrictions to run on forever, it was decided that the best solution to the problem was not to subject rights of entry to that Rule. "Lives in being" have no functional relation to the proper duration of land use restrictions. The common law perpetuity period evolved naturally as a period covering ordinary dispositions of family wealth thought reasonable. A truly functional approach to these interests requires that each right of entry be evaluated separately and that it be terminated when it is of no actual and substantial benefit to the party holding it, when it unreasonably limits the use and development of land, or when the purpose of the restriction cannot be accomplished because of a change of conditions. New York has adopted this approach. The objection to it, however, is that a separate lawsuit is required to determine when each right of entry becomes unenforceable.

From the standpoint of certainty of land titles, it is preferable to fix the maximum duration by a period of years, after which it is certain from the record alone that the right of entry is void. Other states have terminated rights of entry after a fixed period ranging from twenty to forty years, with thirty years being the most common period.[22] Thirty years was selected here because in most cases it is a reasonable period of time for the restriction to run, after which the restriction will tend to become obsolete. It is also the minimum period of title search required by the statutes of limitation in Kentucky. Any valid recorded right of entry created after July 1, 1960, will come to the eye of the title searcher who makes a thirty-year search,[23] although by going back no further he still takes the risk that a right of entry created more than thirty years previously, which became exercisable upon breach of condition within thirty years of its creation, remains exercisable.[24]

[22] Twenty years—R.I. Gen. Laws §§ 34-4-19 to -21 (1956). Twenty-one years —Fla. Stat. Ann. § 689.18 (1959). Thirty years—Conn. Gen. Stat. Rev. § 45-97 (1958); Me. Rev. Stat. c. 160, § 29 (1959 supp.); Mass. Ann. Laws, c. 184A, § 3 (1955); Minn. Stat. Ann. § 500.20(2); Neb. Rev. Stat. § 76-2102 (1959); N.Y. Real Prop. Law § 345. Forty years—Ill. Rev. Stat. c. 30, § 37e (1959).

[23] The Massachusetts act, on which this section was based, starts the thirty-year period running from the date the fee subject to a right of entry becomes possessory, rather than from the date of creation. It also provides for the alternative application of the Rule against Perpetuities. To give the title searcher more protection from a thirty-year search, these provisions were rejected. See also the model act drafted by Simes & Taylor, The Improvement of Conveyancing by Legislation 214-17 (1960), rejecting these features of the Massachusetts act.

[24] This risk is minimized by the requirement that a right of entry be exercised within a reasonable time after breach. Hale v. Elkhorn Coal Corp., 206 Ky. 629, 268 S.W. 304 (1925), sixteen years unreasonable; Kenner v. American Contract Co., 72 Ky. (9 Bush) 202 (1873), three years unreasonable; Kentland Coal & Coke Co. v. Keen, 168 Ky. 836, 183 S.W. 247 (1916) (dictum). A short statute of limitations applicable to rights of entry is still needed for more complete protection.

The second sentence of KRS 381.219 provides that the right of entry *"may be created in a person other than the person creating the interest or his heirs."* This language means that where there is a transfer of what would have been a determinable fee at common law, followed by a nondivesting executory interest in a third person, such executory interest shall be treated as a right of entry and validated for thirty years.[25] It was required by the conversion of the determinable fee into a fee subject to a right of entry and was designed to cure the anomaly illustrated by the following case:

Case 5. O conveys land "to Trinity Church so long as used for church purposes, and when it ceases to be used for church purposes the land is to revert to the owners of the farm from which the land is taken." The Court of Appeals has held that "the owners of the farm" have an executory interest void under the Rule against Perpetuities.[26]

---

[25] The meaning of this language, taken from the Massachusetts act, is explained by Leach, "Perpetuities Legislation—Massachusetts Style," 67 Harv. L. Rev. 1349, 1364 (1954), and by Simes & Taylor, The Improvement of Conveyancing by Legislation 209-10 (1960).

If an instrument transfers a fee subject to a divesting executory interest, rather than what would have been at common law a determinable fee followed by an executory interest, this section does not apply. For example, take a conveyance of land "to X Church, but if it ceases to be used for church purposes then to A." If this language would give the church a determinable fee at common law (see note 7 *supra*), then A's executory interest is valid for thirty years under KRS 381.219. If (as most texts state) it would not, then A's executory interest is valid for twenty-one years under KRS 381.216. This small theoretical functional discrepancy is the result of choosing to subject rights of entry not to the Rule against Perpetuities, but to a thirty-year term.

Executory interests are of two main types functionally: (a) those used in family dispositions and the equivalent of remainders, and (b) those used in land use restrictions and the equivalent of rights of entry. Unless both remainders and rights of entry are subjected to the same restrictive period, there will be a functional discrepancy in subjecting all executory interests to either the Rule against Perpetuities or the thirty-year rule. We thought the advantages in a fixed duration for rights of entry (including possibilities of reverter and executory interests after determinable fees) outweighed the possible disadvantage of this discrepancy. It could have, as a practical matter, been eliminated, had we been willing to fix the period at twenty-one years rather than thirty, since land use restrictions are seldom causally related to a life in being and the executory interest would be valid for twenty-one years under both KRS 381.216 and 381.219. This solution appealed to the author. But some would have been unhappy with the shorter period. Others believed that it would be a very rare case where an executory interest *for breach of a land use restriction* did not follow a classical determinable fee, and an even rarer one where the court would not construe such an executory interest, however phrased, to come within this section; that the question would probably never be litigated anyway, because the owner of a fee subject to such an executory interest would comply with the condition for nine more years to be on the safe side; and that this was all an academic quibble.

[26] McGaughey v. Spencer County Bd. of Educ., 285 Ky. 769, 149 S.W.2d 519 (1941); Duncan v. Webster County Bd. of Educ., 205 Ky. 86, 265 S.W. 489 (1924); *cf.* Barren County Bd. of Educ. v. Jordan, 249 S.W.2d 814 (Ky. 1952).

Under wait-and-see the executory interest would be valid for twenty-one years, but because it follows what would have been a determinable fee at common law, under KRS 381.219 it is treated as a right of entry valid for thirty years.

There is no good reason why it should matter who reclaims the land upon cessation of church use—the grantor, his heirs, the owners of the farm, or any other person. Indeed, it may well be preferable from society's viewpoint for the forfeiture interest to be in the owners of the farm rather than the grantor's heirs, who may be numerous and difficult to locate. This provision carries through the basic scheme of the statute—to reduce forfeiture restrictions on land use to one interest, the right of entry, which may be held by any person and is terminated after thirty years.

4

TERMINATION AND PRESERVATION OF
POSSIBILITIES OF REVERTER AND RIGHTS
OF ENTRY CREATED PRIOR TO JULY 1, 1960

KRS 381.221(1) reads:

Every possibility of reverter and right of entry created prior to July 1, 1960, shall cease to be valid or enforceable at the expiration of thirty years after the effective date of the instrument creating it, unless before July 1, 1965, a declaration of intention to preserve it is filed for record with the county clerk of the county in which the real property is located.

This section aims to clear titles of old rights of entry and possibilities of reverter. Many of these are useless, and all of them impair the marketability of land and prevent its development or redevelopment under changed conditions. Such titles are not only in churches and schools. Every courthouse in Kentucky contains numerous deeds providing for forfeiture if liquor is ever sold on the premises. These ancient prohibitionist deeds utterly failed to dry up the flow of liquor in this state. Their only substantial effect today is to take the property out of the mortgage market, make it unimprovable, and hinder the efforts of private capital to rehabilitate a declining urban area. The undesirable social and economic consequences of these ancient forfeiture restrictions have been widely recognized. In 1953 the Court of Appeals called attention to this "troublesome and growing problem in real estate law as to what steps, if any, should be taken to clear titles . . . where an old express clause of forfeiture or reversion is involved,"[27] and suggested remedial legislation.

This section provides for termination of rights of entry and possibilities of reverter existing as such on July 1, 1960, unless a declaration of intention to preserve them is recorded before July 1, 1965.[28] Subsection (2) of KRS 381.221 sets forth what the declaration of intention must contain. If the declaration is filed, the interest will continue to exist unlimited in duration. Requiring continuous refiling every thirty years was rejected for two reasons: Very few of these interests are expected to be re-recorded; and requiring those which are re-recorded before 1965 to re-record every thirty years thereafter is, without a marketable title statute requiring continuous refiling of all claims, an unfair burden. Whether these reasons be persuasive, they controlled the matter.

If no declaration of intention is filed before July 1, 1965, with respect to a right of entry or possibility of reverter existing on July 1, 1960, and created before July 1, 1935, the interest will then cease to be valid or enforceable (a) if the contingency on which it was limited has not then happened, or (b) if the interest is a right of entry and the contingency happened before July 1, 1960, but the right remains unexercised.[29] If the contingency on which the interest is limited happens between July 1, 1960, and July 1, 1965, and the right of entry is exercised or the determinable fee automatically ends within thirty years of the creation of the interest, no declaration need be filed, since the forfeiture interest has become possessory within thirty years of creation. If, however, the contingency happens between 1960 and 1965 and the right of entry is exercised or the determinable fee ends more than thirty years after creation, a declaration is required to protect against the retroactive effect of the statute.

With respect to rights of entry or possibilities of reverter created after July 1, 1935, if no declaration of intention is filed

---

[27] Hoskins v. Walker, 255 S.W.2d 481, 482 (Ky. 1953).

[28] The original draft of KRS 381.221 was much more detailed, but caught between the hammer of simplification and the anvil of the legislature, all excess words (and some the author thought not excess) were struck out. Most of the provisions deleted covered expressly minor matters which are now covered by implication only.

[29] If the interest is a possibility of reverter and the contingency happened before July 1, 1960, the possibility of reverter automatically became a fee simple upon breach and is not an existing possibility of reverter on July 1, 1960.

before July 1, 1965, the interest will continue valid and enforceable until thirty years from the date of creation have expired.

Constitutionality of section. KRS 381.221 is the only section of the 1960 Perpetuities Act which is retroactive in effect, and a question of its constitutionality may be raised. It is believed that the section is constitutional. Five states have enacted legislation within the past decade terminating existing rights of entry and possibilities of reverter, with two of them providing for preservation of existing interests by re-recording within a given period.[30] In 1955 the Illinois Supreme Court upheld the Illinois Reverter Act terminating existing interests without the privilege of preservation by re-recording.[31] That act was more severe than KRS 381.221.

The inclusion of the provision for re-recording within five years should remove any question of constitutionality. There are many decisions upholding retroactive legislation of a similar nature where preservation by re-recording is provided. Closely analogous are statutes requiring owners of existing mortgages to re-record them to preserve them against bona fide purchasers and creditors,[32] and marketable title statutes requiring re-recording of interests which have been in existence for more than a specified number of years.[33]

5

EXCEPTIONS TO THE THIRTY-YEAR TERMINATION RULE

KRS 381.222 reads:

KRS 381.219 and 381.221 shall not apply to any possibility of reverter or right of entry contained in a deed, gift or grant from the

[30] Ill. Rev. Stat. c. 30, § 37e (1959); Neb. Rev. Stat. § 76-2102 (1959); Mass. Ann. Laws c. 260, § 31A (1959 supp.), preserved if re-recorded within ten years of act; N.Y. Real Prop. Law § 345, preserved if re-recorded within three years of act or within thirty years of date of creation; see Fla. Stat. Ann. § 689.18 (1959), no provision for re-recording—retroactive application declared unconstitutional in Biltmore Village v. Royal, 71 So. 2d 727 (Fla. 1954). See also the model act in Simes & Taylor, The Improvement of Conveyancing by Legislation 215-16 (1960), providing for preservation by re-recording within two years of act or within thirty years of date of creation.
[31] Trustees of Schools v. Batforf, 6 Ill. 2d 486, 130 N.E.2d 111 (1955).
[32] Upheld in Vance v. Vance, 108 U.S. 514 (1883); Opinion of the Justices, 101 N.H. 515, 131 A.2d 49 (1957); Livingston v. Meyers, 6 Ill. 2d 325, 129 N.E.2d 12 (1955).
[33] Upheld in Wichelman v. Messner, 250 Minn. 88, 83 N.W.2d 800 (1957), holding owner of possibility of reverter or right of entry lost it by failure to re-record; Tesdell v. Hanes, 248 Iowa 742, 82 N.W.2d 119 (1957).

Commonwealth or any political subdivision thereof; nor shall they apply where both the fee simple determinable and the succeeding interest, or both the fee simple subject to a right of entry and the right of entry, are for public, charitable or religious purposes; nor shall they affect any lease present or future or any easement, right of way, mortgage or trust, or any communication, transmission, or transportation lines, or any public highway, right to take minerals, or charge for support during the life of a person or persons, or any restrictive covenant without right of entry or reverter.

The first two clauses of this section exempt certain rights of entry and possibilities of reverter which are within the statute's ambit but which were exempted because of other overriding considerations. Forfeiture interests held by the Commonwealth or its political subdivisions were excluded because it was believed the power of determining when these interests become inimical to the public interest should rest with the public bodies holding them. The clause exempting a gift over from one charity to another charity carries on the present exemption of this kind of gift from the Rule against Perpetuities.

The last clause, taken from the Uniform Act Relating to Reverter of Realty,[34] exempts from the thirty-year termination rule certain rights of entry and possibilities of reverter not within the primary purpose of the statute, which is to clear titles of forfeiture restrictions on land use. Such exemptions include mineral interests,[35] easements and rights of way, and rights of entry incident to a lease. Restrictive covenants enforceable only by injunction or damages were exempted because an arbitrary thirty-year termination date would cut off many useful covenants increasing the marketability of the property. They may presently be terminated by a court when they have outlived their usefulness.[36]

[34] Handbook of the Nat'l Conference of Commissioners on Uniform State Laws 315 (1946).

[35] Neither the thirty-year termination rule nor, it is believed, the Rule against Perpetuities applies to mineral interests. In three cases the court assumed perpetual royalty or mineral interests to be valid without mentioning the Rule against Perpetuities. Bonzo v. Nowlin, 285 S.W.2d 153 (Ky. 1955); Maynard v. Ratcliff, 297 Ky. 127, 179 S.W.2d 200 (1944); Texas Co. v. Bowen, 292 Ky. 676, 167 S.W.2d 822 (1943). In Johnson v. Pittsburgh Consol. Coal Co., 311 S.W.2d 537 (Ky. 1958), the court refused to say whether the Rule applied, but the reversionary interest retained by the grantor would have been valid in any event. As a matter of policy, mineral interests should not be subject to the Rule. See Williams & Meyers, Oil and Gas Law §§ 322-36 (1959).

[36] See Note, Covenants—Termination Resulting from a Change of Conditions, 45 Ky. L.J. 292 (1957).

Lastly, it should be noted that exemptions not specifically mentioned are excluded under the maxim *expressio unius est exclusio alterius*. Thus minors and others under legal disability holding an existing right of entry or possibility of reverter are not exempt from the re-recording requirement.

6

THE RULE AGAINST DIRECT RESTRAINTS ON ALIENATION

1
THE RULE AGAINST RESTRAINTS DISTINGUISHED
FROM THE RULE AGAINST PERPETUITIES AND THE RULE
AGAINST SUSPENSION OF THE POWER OF ALIENATION

THE RULE against restraints on alienation is an entirely different rule from the Rule against Perpetuities.[1] Nor is it to be confused with the rule prohibiting suspension of the power of alienation, which was the rule set forth in KRS 381.220 (now repealed). The rule against restraints is a rule against *direct* restraints on alienation, whereas these other two rules are against restraining the power of alienation *indirectly* by creating nonvested interests (the Rule against Perpetuities) or by creating interests in persons not in being or not ascertained (the rule against suspension of the power of alienation). Direct restraints are created by expressly providing that the grantee or devisee has no power to alienate the property. Commonly the grantee is ascertained and his interest is vested, but these are unimportant matters under this rule. The important question is whether or not he is expressly restrained from conveying the property.

While it is easy to see that this rule against direct restraints has nothing to do with the rule against remote vesting (the Rule against Perpetuities), it is not so easy to avoid confusing it with the rule against suspension of the power of alienation. Both rules have the same objective—alienability—and both are phrased as rules concerning "alienation."[2] This similar phrasing has invited confusion because it has not specified alienation of *what*. And in that specification lies the difference between the rules. The rule against suspension is a rule against suspension of the power of alienation of the specific *property* (land, stocks, bonds, or other resources). It is violated if, and only if,[3] a fee simple title to the specific property cannot be transferred. The rule against restraints, on the other hand, is a rule against inalienable *interests* in property (fee, life estate, remainder, etc.).

At first blush this seems to be only a distinction in words. If the grantee cannot convey his interest because it is subject to a direct restraint, a fee simple title to the property would appear to be not transferable. But this is not necessarily—indeed, is very seldom—true. The reason is that a direct restraint does not suspend the power of alienation if it can be released by persons in being. In Kentucky, all disabling restraints on legal interests carry with them forfeiture provisions. If there is not an express provision for forfeiture, the transferor or his heirs have a right of entry as a matter of law. If the person who holds the right to enforce forfeiture is ascertained, he may release his interest and a fee may be conveyed. In such case there is no suspension of the power of alienation. Perhaps this can best be seen by way of illustrations.

Case 1 (Disabling restraint). T devises land in fee "to A, provided however, A cannot sell the land for twenty years." As a matter of law,

---

[1] For comprehensive treatment of restraints on alienation, see 6 Am. L. Prop. §§ 26.1-.132 (by Professor Schnebly); 6 Powell ¶¶ 839-48; Simes & Smith §§ 1111-71.

[2] For comparison of the two rules, see 6 Am. L. Prop. § 24.6; Norvell, "The Power of Alienation: Direct Restraint vs. Suspension," 31 N.Y.U.L. Rev. 894 (1956).

[3] With a qualification respecting assets held in trust, to be noted later.

T's heir, H, has a right of entry for condition broken.[4] A and H may convey the fee; there is no suspension of the power of alienation.

Case 2 (Forfeiture restraint). T devises land in fee "to A, but if A sells the land within twenty years, to B." A and B can convey the fee at any time, and the power of alienation is not suspended.

Case 3 (Forfeiture restraint). T devises land in fee "to A, but if A sells the land within twenty years, to A's issue per stirpes living at the time of sale." The power of alienation is suspended, since the persons holding the executory interest over (A's issue living at time of sale) cannot be ascertained until a sale is made.[5] Obviously the suspension is merely technical, however, if A has issue living, for a purchaser could acquire a fee from A and his present issue at any time. Nonetheless, only in a case such as this does a direct restraint on a legal interest even technically suspend the power of alienation in Kentucky.

The above illustrations all deal with legal interests. Are they equally applicable to equitable interests? With respect to a trust, if the trustee has power to sell the trust assets, the power of alienation of the specific property is not suspended. Nonetheless, in those states which have statutory rules against suspension of the power of alienation, courts have held that a *quantum* of assets is made inalienable by the creation of an indestructible trust.[6] This is perhaps an illogical extension of the suspension rule, but it is justified by policy. The trustee cannot really invest the assets as freely as if he owned them absolutely, and he cannot use them to purchase consumers' goods or other forms of wealth. It is still the dead hand controlling property, albeit the control relates to a quantum of wealth rather than to specific property. Therefore whether a trust suspends the power of alienation depends not upon the trustee's power to sell the trust assets but upon the restraints put upon the equitable interests and upon the ability of the beneficiaries to terminate the trust. If no restraints are put on such interests,[7] and all interests are held by persons *sui juris* who may

---

[4] Kentland Coal & Coke Co. v. Keen, 168 Ky. 836, 183 S.W. 246 (1916). See cases cited note 48 *infra*.

[5] Duncan v. Webster County Bd. of Educ., 205 Ky. 86, 265 S.W. 489 (1924).

[6] Grand Rapids Trust Co. v. Herbst, 220 Mich. 231, 190 N.W. 250 (1922); Allen v. Allen, 149 N.Y. 280, 43 N.E. 626 (1896); Estate of Hinckley, 58 Cal. 457 (1881); *cf.* Ford v. Yost, 299 Ky. 682, 685, 186 S.W.2d 896, 898 (1944): "Technical alienability or the power of a trustee to sell and convey the particular property for investment is not enough to escape the statute, for the proceeds wear the same fetters of restraint." *Contra*, Will of Walker, 258 Wis. 65, 45 N.W.2d 94 (1950).

[7] See Newsom v. Barnes, 282 Ky. 264, 138 S.W.2d 475 (1940), holding equitable interests alienable unless expressly restrained; Keith v. First Nat'l Bank, 256 Ky. 88, 75 S.W.2d 747 (1934).

terminate the trust, the power of alienation is not suspended. If the trust cannot be terminated because of a restraint on alienation, then such restraint has caused the power to be suspended. (It is pertinent to note here, however, that no restraint for more than a life in being and twenty-one years is valid in Kentucky. It is "unreasonable" and void. Therefore no valid restraint on alienation in Kentucky could ever have violated the old statute, now repealed, prohibiting suspension of the power of alienation for more than that period.)

Failure to distinguish the rule against direct restraints from the rule against suspension of the power of alienation can lead only into a thicket of words prickly with ambiguity. The court has many times been caught in that thicket. The recent case of *Robertson v. Simmons*[8] will suffice as an example. In that case there was an agreement between Robertson and Stilley providing that if either became the successful bidder at an auction of a certain tract of land, the other would have an option to purchase a set portion of it at a fixed percentage of the auction price. Stilley bid in the property at the sale and soon thereafter died. Seven years after the sale, Robertson attempted to exercise the option. Stilley's heirs refused to sell, claiming the option was void. The option was construed as unlimited in time, and thus the question was raised whether the option violated the Rule against Perpetuities, the statutory rule against suspension of the power of alienation, or the rule against unreasonable direct restraints. It is clear that the option does not violate the rule against suspension, for Robertson and Stilley (or his heirs) can convey an absolute fee to a purchaser at any time. Hence the power of alienation is not suspended for even one minute by the option. It is equally clear that the option, if unlimited in duration as the court found, created an equitable future interest in Robertson which violated the Rule against Perpetuities. It was unnecessary to deal with the rule against direct restraints at all. That rule could apply only if it was decided the option was in substance, though not in form, a direct restraint.

After reviewing the "unfortunate confusion" in perpetuities

[8] 322 S.W.2d 476 (Ky. 1959). Other cases where the rules have been confused include Fox v. Burgher, 285 Ky. 470, 148 S.W.2d 342 (1941); Hite v. Barber, 284 Ky. 718, 145 S.W.2d 1058 (1940); West v. Ashby, 217 Ky. 250, 289 S.W. 228 (1926); Perry v. Metcalf, 216 Ky. 775, 288 S.W. 694 (1926); Saulsberry v. Saulsberry, 140 Ky. 608, 131 S.W. 491 (1910); Robsion v. Gray, 29 Ky. L. Rep. 1296, 97 S.W. 347 (1906).

law, largely caused by "the troublesome statute," the court got itself gorgeously entangled by treating the rule against suspension of the power of alienation and the rule against direct restraints as one and the same. It noted that KRS 381.220, while phrased as a rule prohibiting suspension of the power of alienation, had been held by the court in many cases to prohibit the remote vesting of interests. This view of the statute, said the court,

> perhaps caused us to indulge in the defective logic [in *Maddox v. Keeler*[9]] while reaching a desirable conclusion. If the court had based its decision on the theory that the option created an unreasonable suspension of the power to alienate, regardless of whether the estate was vested, it would have had ample authority for its position [*quaere*]. ... Perhaps the cases, which so carefully pointed out that KRS 381.220 had no bearing on direct restraints of vested estates, may be disposed of or at least reconciled by the acceptance and the recognition that the common law rule against suspension of the power of alienation has existed in the common law of this state regardless of the troublesome statute.[10] [According to Gray, the rule against suspension of the power of alienation was not a common law rule; it is purely statutory. The rule against direct restraints on alienation is a common law rule.]

This choice of language was unfortunate, for it is apparent upon close analysis that the court was not referring to some spurious "common law rule against suspension of the power of alienation" at all, but to the rule against restraints on alienation. The case, carefully examined, holds that the option is an unreasonable direct restraint on alienation, not an unreasonable suspension of the power of alienation. Why an option should be treated as a direct restraint on alienation (the heart of the matter under the court's analysis) is not discussed.[11]

The 1960 Perpetuities Act repealed the statute prohibiting suspension of the power of alienation. It is hoped that this action will rid the law of all the obfuscation of the rule against direct restraints it has caused. The court will be able to base its decision either on the Rule against Perpetuities or on the rule against unreasonable direct restraints on alienation, which are easily dif-

---

[9] 296 Ky. 440, 177 S.W.2d 568 (1944). In Maddox the court held an option violated the Rule against Perpetuities on the assumption that it was unlimited in time, and then, having held the option void, the court declined to say whether the option was unlimited in time.

[10] 322 S.W.2d at 481, 483 (1959). The case is criticized by Professor Sparks in "Future Interests," 1959 Ann. Survey of Am. Law, 35 N.Y.U.L. Rev. 401, 412 (1960).

[11] For discussion of options as restraints, see pp. 127-31 *infra*.

ferentiated one from the other. The new act has no effect upon the rule against restraints, except in the very minor way noted in section 6 below.

2
RESTRAINTS ON LEGAL LIFE ESTATES AND REMAINDERS

DIRECT restraints on alienation of legal interests may be divided into (a) restraints on a life estate and on a remainder, and (b) restraints on a possessory fee. The former types of restraints are much easier to justify and will be dealt with first.

It is settled in Kentucky that a restraint prohibiting voluntary alienation of a legal life estate for the entire duration of the estate is valid.[12] A fortiori a restraint on a life estate for a lesser period or permitting alienation only to a small number of persons is valid. This rule has several justifications. The purpose of a restraint upon a life estate is usually to protect the life tenant with an assured means of support or to preserve the property for the remainderman. The restraint may add materially to the remainderman's protection against waste, since it prevents the life tenant from substituting an irresponsible person in possession. These purposes are entirely legitimate and may require a restraint for the whole life of the life tenant for this accomplishment. Hence both the purposes of the restraint and the time necessary for fulfillment are reasonable.

A restraint on a remainder for the duration of the life estate does not add substantially to the practical inalienability which results from the creation of such interests. There are few buyers for a life estate or a remainder separately. The property cannot be sold without joinder of the life tenant and the remainderman, whose cooperation may be difficult to obtain. Because the restraint adds little practical inalienability, the Kentucky court has in several cases upheld a restraint forbidding transfer of a vested remainder during the life tenant's life.[13] In the relatively recent case of *Gray*

[12] Gray v. Gray, 300 Ky. 265, 188 S.W.2d 440 (1945); Anderson v. Simpson, 214 Ky. 375, 283 S.W. 941 (1926); Robsion v. Gray, 29 Ky. L. Rep. 1296, 97 S.W. 347 (1906); Morton's Guardian v. Morton, 120 Ky. 251, 85 S.W. 1188 (1905); *cf.* Howell v. Weisemuller, 299 S.W.2d 118 (Ky. 1957). *But see* West v. Ashby, 217 Ky. 250, 289 S.W. 228 (1926), holding restraint on life estate of a person not in being void.
[13] Hale v. Elkhorn Coal Corp., 206 Ky. 629, 268 S.W. 304 (1925); Polley v. Adkins, 145 Ky. 370, 140 S.W. 551 (1911); Frazier v. Combs, 140 Ky. 77, 130 S.W. 812 (1910); Lawson v. Lightfoot, 27 Ky. L. Rep. 217, 84 S.W. 739 (1905).

v. Gray,[14] however, the court cast doubt on these cases. It struck down a restraint on contingent remainders in fee measured by the lives of the life tenants. The life estates were also restrained, which restraints were upheld. The rationalization of this holding is not easy to come by inasmuch as the remainders were contingent upon the remaindermen surviving the life tenants. Such a remainder following an inalienable life estate is surely not marketable; the restraint adds little inalienability to what already exists. More perplexing is why the court would strike down the restraint on a contingent remainder and uphold a restraint on an indefeasibly vested remainder, which is the type of remainder involved in the prior cases. Under the common law, exactly the contrary conclusions would be probable.[15] Here the *Gray* case appears unsound.

While restraining transfer of the remainder during the period it remains nonpossessory may be reasonable, restraining it for a period after it becomes possessory is a horse of another color. The restraint then becomes a restraint on a fee in possession. The court has held restraints on remainders that continue beyond the time of possession are valid if they would be valid imposed on a possessory fee.[16] The rules respecting restraints on fees, discussed below, control.

3

RESTRAINTS ON A LEGAL FEE IN POSSESSION:
THE DOCTRINE OF REASONABLE RESTRAINTS

CONTRARY to the common law, Kentucky has long permitted reasonable restraints on a fee.[17] From more than six dozen cases stretching over a century the court has developed what is known as the Kentucky doctrine of reasonable restraints. Yet the court has never, in all these cases, laid down any general test of reasonableness; nor has it articulated any policy rationalization for its

[14] Note 12 *supra; cf.* Dills v. Deavors, 266 S.W.2d 788 (Ky. 1953).
[15] See 6 Am. L. Prop. § 26.54.
[16] Restraint on remainder for fifteen years after death of life tenant is valid: Speckman v. Meyer, 187 Ky. 687, 220 S.W. 529 (1920). Restraint for the remainderman's whole life is void: Cammack v. Allen, 199 Ky. 268, 250 S.W. 963 (1923); Ramey v. Ramey, 195 Ky. 673, 243 S.W. 934 (1922); Robsion v. Gray, *supra* note 12; West v. Ashby, *supra* note 12. Restraint until youngest remainderman reaches twenty-one is valid: Young v. Young, 20 Ky. L. Rep. 1741, 49 S.W. 1074 (1899).
[17] 6 Am. L. Prop. § 26.22; Simes & Smith § 1150; Note, 40 Ky. L.J. 337 (1952).

doctrine. The analysis below attempts to fill these gaps by providing an operational definition of reasonableness and a policy base. It must be admitted, however, that supplying policy rationalizations where the court has given none is like playing Sancho Panza to the court's Don Quixote. And so they should be read.

Importance of purpose. The cases indicate the court has been primarily concerned with the duration of the restraint, but it is believed this is not the sole test of reasonableness. The duration of the restraint should be related to a reasonable purpose as well. Restraints on life estates and leasehold interests were allowed at common law because they served a reasonable purpose. It was important for the remainderman or reversioner to have a responsible tenant in possession. If society's interest in the free alienability of property is to give way to a grantor's desire to project his control beyond the time of transfer, the grantor's purpose must be one that will benefit either himself during his life or the grantee during a reasonable period of time. If the restraint is capricious or merely to perpetuate the testator's memory, or if it cannot possibly benefit the transferees, or if it makes property unimprovable, or if its sole purpose is to concentrate wealth, there is no reason for society's interest in alienability to give way. Just as purpose was important to the limited common law relaxation of the rule against restraints, so it should be equally important to the more extensive relaxation permitted in Kentucky.

In the first case allowing a restraint on a fee (until the devisee reached the age of thirty-five), the court carefully pointed out that the restraint served a reasonable purpose. Said the court:

> The land is on a turnpike near the growing city of Louisville; and we presume that the principal motive for the restriction was that the value would increase rapidly. . . . [T]he locality of the land and circumstances of this case indicate [the testatrix's] prophetic wisdom in securing from waste as safe and growing an investment as probably could be made for her young daughter.[18]

The importance of reasonable purpose is also reflected in a few later cases,[19] but on the whole it has not been discussed. This can be explained either on the ground that reasonableness of purpose

---

[18] Stewart v. Brady, 66 Ky. (3 Bush) 623, 625 (1868).
[19] Cooper v. Knuckles, 212 Ky. 608, 279 S.W. 1084 (1926); Frazier v. Combs, 140 Ky. 77, 130 S.W. 812 (1910); Kean's Guardian v. Kean, 13 Ky. L. Rep. 956, 18 S.W. 1032 (1892).

is unimportant or on the ground that such discussion is unnecessary because of the stereotype facts of the case. The first explanation ignores the sound basis of the original judicial relaxation of the common law—appraisal of purpose. The second seems more realistic. Restraints upheld by the court have fallen into four fact patterns: restraints limited to twenty-one years or less, to a specified age, to the grantor's life, and to the life tenant's life. The purpose served by restraints so limited are, as will be seen below, much the same. Once it is established that a particular duration is reasonably related to a legitimate purpose, it is usually unnecessary to discuss the purpose of a restraint similarly limited. Thus, although the court has set outside limits beyond which no restraint for any purpose will be allowed, it is believed that a restraint within those limits would not necessarily be valid. It still must be a reasonable restraint under the particular circumstances of the particular case.[20]

Importance of duration. The court has frequently stressed the importance of duration in determining the validity of a restraint. The following rules (a) through (h) state the permissible duration of restraints, based on case holdings.

(a) *An absolute restraint on the fee unlimited in duration is unreasonable and void.*[21] The ordinary purpose of an unlimited restraint is, like a fee tail, to keep property in a family perpetually. Courts early invented means of docking the entail, principally by the fictitious lawsuit known as the common recovery. They subsequently dealt with unlimited restraints in a simpler manner—by invalidating the restraint *ab initio.*

(b) *An absolute restraint on the fee measured by a period of years more than twenty-one is unreasonable and void.*[22] The opinions indicate the court was influenced by the perpetuities statute

[20] Hutchinson v. Loomis, 244 S.W.2d 751, 752 (Ky. 1951): "As to what is a reasonable period, no invariable test has been prescribed and each case must be determined upon the facts and circumstances it presents."
[21] Winn v. William, 292 Ky. 44, 165 S.W.2d 961 (1942); Robsion v. Gray, 29 Ky. L. Rep. 1296, 97 S.W. 347 (1906); Ernst v. Shinkle, 95 Ky. 608, 26 S.W. 813 (1894); Henning v. Harrison, 76 Ky. (13 Bush) 723 (1878); *cf.* Saffold v. Wright, 228 Ky. 594, 15 S.W.2d 456 (1929), voiding provision that bank stock "shall not be sold or converted into money as long as said banks do business."
[22] Fox v. Burgher, 285 Ky. 470, 148 S.W.2d 342 (1941), fifty years; Hite v. Barber, 284 Ky. 718, 145 S.W.2d 1058 (1940), sixty years; Perry v. Metcalf, 216 Ky. 755, 288 S.W. 694 (1926), thirty years; Saulsberry v. Saulsberry, 140 Ky. 608, 131 S.W. 491 (1910), fifty-four years.

in striking down restraints for more than twenty-one years, but the perpetuity period is not the criterion of validity. That is made clear by the invalidation of restraints limited to the life of the grantee, a person in being. The twenty-one-year period of the Rule was, however, a handy analogy by which to set a maximum limit on restraints measured by years.

(c) *An absolute restraint on the fee measured by the life of the grantee is unreasonable and void.*[23] The grantee may be restrained from alienating the property for twenty-one years, until he reaches middle age, or during the life of the grantor, but he cannot be expressly restrained for his whole life. It is difficult to find any wholly satisfactory reasons for this rule in the cases. In several cases the court has said such a restraint is repugnant to the fee, but of course that explanation will not stand close inspection, as Professors Gray and Schnebly long ago pointed out.[24] Alienability is not an inseparable incident of the fee. In upholding restraints for a period shorter than the grantee's whole life, the court has necessarily conceded this. In two cases the court has said to give effect to the restraint would turn the fee into a life estate, which is simply a variation of the repugnancy argument. No other reasons have been advanced in the cases.

The crux of the difficulty is this. Since the law does not forbid an inalienable life estate, why should it forbid a fee inalienable for life? If it is reasonable to restrain a life estate, why is it not reasonable to restrain a fee for the same period? Three reasons for distinguishing between these two interests suggest themselves. First, by creating a life estate and remainder, the grantor makes the interests inalienable in a practical way during the life tenant's life. The life estate is not readily marketable by itself, and the life tenant and remainderman are not likely to agree upon a valuation of their respective interests. Unless both parties join, the property cannot be sold without going to court. Hence the restraint on the life estate does not cause much more practical inalienability of the life estate or of the property than would be the case without it. With respect to an absolute fee, which is readily marketable,

---

[23] Winn v. William, 292 Ky. 44, 165 S.W.2d 961 (1942); Lindsay v. Williams, 279 Ky. 749, 132 S.W.2d 65 (1939); Cammack v. Allen, 199 Ky. 268, 250 S.W. 963 (1923); Brock v. Conkwright, 179 Ky. 555, 200 S.W. 962 (1918); Cropper v. Bowles, 150 Ky. 393, 150 S.W. 380 (1912); Harkness v. Lisle, 132 Ky. 767, 117 S.W. 264 (1909).

[24] Gray, Restraints on Alienation § 21 (2d ed. 1895); 6 Am. L. Prop. § 26.19.

the restraint adds inalienability where none existed before. This rationalization may explain *Holt's Executor v. Deshon*,[25] though it was not referred to therein. In that case, testator devised land to two sisters in fee, defeasible upon death without issue, with a restraint on alienation for their lives. (Neither sister at that time had children, but being married and age twenty-eight and thirty-three respectively, it was possible for them to have them.)[26] The gift over in default of issue made the fee as inalienable as it would be were the sisters given life estates; the restraint added little practical inalienability. The court—giving no reason except the sisters did not hold an absolute fee—held the restraint valid. Under the analysis here suggested, treating a fee defeasible upon death without issue like a life estate is proper where under the facts the restraint does not add much inalienability.

Secondly, a restraint on a life estate has another purpose in addition to protecting the life tenant. It protects the remainderman by keeping a responsible person in possession. This purpose cannot be carried out unless the restraint is for the whole duration of the life estate. When the grantee is given the absolute fee, however, there is no purpose to protect against waste whoever may take the property at the grantee's death. The grantee can waste the property if he sees fit, as there is no one else who has an interest to be protected. Hence, the protection of the remainderman is an additional reason for upholding a restraint on a life estate which cannot be given for upholding a restraint on an absolute fee.

Lastly, it is arguable that the type of person whom the law would favor protecting includes the persons to whom a testator commonly would give only a life estate if he desired to protect them. Seldom would he give a fee to persons who are under some practical disability. In all the cases in Kentucky dealing with restraints on a fee limited for the life of the transferee, the restraint has been imposed by a testator devising his property to his issue. There is nothing to indicate the devisees were not (at least in the court's eyes) perfectly competent to deal with the property. The court has not been convinced that they needed protection, and it is arguable that this is substantiated by the testator's very act of giving them a fee rather than a life estate.

[25] 126 Ky. 310, 103 S.W. 281 (1907). *But cf.* Cammack v. Allen, *supra* note 23, voiding restraint on defeasible fee for devisee's whole life.

[26] Record, p. 26, Brief for Appellant, p. 7, Holt's Ex'r v. Deshon, *supra* note 25.

These reasons are not, of course, wholly satisfactory justifications for the rule forbidding restraints on a fee for the life of the grantee. Contrary arguments may be made: that the rule cannot be sustained logically if restraints for a lesser period are permitted; that it is mere juggling with labels which is not accompanied by any corresponding examination of special circumstances which might justify the restraint for the entire life of the fee tenant; and that the rule is easily evaded by a skilled draftsman and thus is of little social utility. The doctrine of reasonable restraints does not purport to be logical, however. The test of reasonableness is essentially pragmatic, and the limits drawn under it must be appraised pragmatically. While special circumstances might arise, the cases show no evidence that they have in fact. And although the rule may be circumvented by a skilled draftsman creating a life estate with general testamentary power, it seldom is. Good lawyers usually realize the importance of keeping property marketable and advise a trust or a life estate with power of sale. Unlimited restraints on the fee have appeared usually in homemade instruments or in deeds drafted by notaries or, in one case, an itinerant preacher.

(d) An absolute restraint on the fee measured by a period of years less than twenty-one is valid.[27] Restraints limited for less than twenty-one years usually have the purpose of protecting the grantee from improvidence until he reaches a more mature age or of keeping the family funds invested in property which the transferor regards as a good "short-term" investment. They may also be used, where alienation is allowed within the period with the grantor's consent, to protect a subdivider against undesirable persons buying in the subdivision prior to the sale of all the lots and recoupment of his investment. These are legitimate objectives, and twenty-one years is in most cases more than adequate for their accomplishment.

(e) An absolute restraint on the fee until the grantee reaches early middle age is valid.[28] The purpose of imposing a restraint of

[27] Auxier's Ex'x v. Theobald, 255 Ky. 583, 75 S.W.2d 39 (1934), five years; Johnson v. Dumeyer, 23 Ky. L. Rep. 2243, 66 S.W. 1025 (1902), twenty years; *cf.* cases cited note 32 *infra.*

[28] Howard's Adm'x v. Asher Coal Co., 215 Ky. 88, 284 S.W. 419 (1926), age twenty-one; Smith v. Isaacs, 25 Ky. L. Rep. 1727, 78 S.W. 434 (1904), age thirty-five; Wallace v. Smith, 113 Ky. 263, 68 S.W. 131 (1902), age thirty-five; Stewart v. Barrow, 70 Ky. (7 Bush) 368 (1870), age thirty-five; Stewart v. Brady, 66 Ky. (3 Bush) 623 (1868), age thirty-five; *cf.* Highfill v. Konnerman, 241 Ky. 282, 43 S.W.2d 657 (1931), restraint against partition until age twenty-one.

this type on a grantee is to protect him from indiscretion until he reaches maturity. The cases might be explained on the ground that the age specified would in fact be reached within twenty-one years after transfer, and thus the restraint was measurable by a period of years less than twenty-one. The opinions do not state how old the respective grantees were at time of transfer, however, so that such an explanation cannot be verified. It is believed the best explanation is legitimate purpose and reasonable duration.

(f) *An absolute restraint on the fee measured by the life of the grantor is valid.*[29] A person may wish to convey property to his children inter vivos, retaining a veto power over sale. This is the effect of a provision forbidding transfer during the grantor's life, for the grantor can release the restraint and join with the grantee in conveying the fee. Such a restraint may protect the grantor if there is a charge for support on the transferred property.[30] Or it may protect a subdivider until he recoups his investment. The court has held restraints for the grantor's lifetime reasonable.

(g) *A partial restraint on the fee permitting alienation only to members of a small group is void if unlimited in duration.*[31] The effect of a restraint narrowly qualified as to alienees is substantially the same as an absolute restraint or as an unlimited preemptive option at less-than-market price. The property is not likely to be sold. The dynastic purpose of a perpetual absolute restraint is usually also present in a restraint of this type.

(h) *A partial restraint on the fee permitting alienation only to members of a small group is valid if limited in duration to a period which would be valid for an absolute restraint.*[32] If a

---

[29] Hutchinson v. Loomis, 244 S.W.2d 751 (Ky. 1951); Turner v. Lewis, 189 Ky. 837, 226 S.W. 367 (1920); Kentland Coal & Coke Co. v. Keen, 168 Ky. 836, 183 S.W. 247 (1916); Pond Creek Coal Co. v. Runyon, 161 Ky. 64, 170 S.W. 501 (1914).

[30] Hutchinson v. Loomis, *supra* note 29; Pond Creek Coal Co. v. Runyon, *supra* note 29; Hale v. Elkhorn Coal Co., *supra* note 13; Polley v. Adkins, *supra* note 13; Frazier v. Combs, *supra* note 19.

[31] Courts v. Courts' Guardian, 230 Ky. 141, 18 S.W.2d 957 (1929), not to be sold "out of the name Courts"; *cf.* Saulsberry v. Saulsberry, 290 Ky. 132, 160 S.W.2d 654 (1942).

[32] Restraint *for twenty years* limiting alienation to issue of grantor or grantee, held valid: Cooper v. Knuckles, 212 Ky. 608, 279 S.W. 1084 (1926); Price v. Virginia Iron Co., 171 Ky. 523, 188 S.W. 658 (1916); Francis v. Big Sandy Co., 171 Ky. 209, 188 S.W. 345 (1916). Restraint *for grantee's life* limiting alienation to grantor's issue, held void: Hutchinson v. Loomis, 244 S.W.2d 751 (Ky. 1951); Carpenter v. Allen, 198 Ky. 252, 248 S.W. 523 (1923); Chappell v. Frick Co., 166 Ky. 311, 179 S.W. 203 (1915); Chappell v. Chappell, 119 S.W. 218 (Ky. 1909); *cf.* Dills v. Deavors, 266 S.W.2d 788 (Ky. 1953).

restraint forbidding alienation to anyone within a certain period is reasonable, a fortiori a less restrictive restraint for the same period —allowing alienation within a small group—is good. If the partial restraint is for a longer period than an absolute restraint is allowed, it should ordinarily be void.[33] Limiting alienation within a small class is only slightly less objectionable than an absolute restraint. The difference is too insubstantial to treat them differently.

4

RESTRAINTS UPON EQUITABLE INTERESTS

ANY RESTRAINT on voluntary alienation valid as to a legal interest is valid as to its equitable counterpart. Restraints on equitable life estates,[34] and on equitable fees until the grantee reached a certain age,[35] have been upheld. Moreover, the court has upheld restraints on equitable fees for the entire life of the grantee,[36] something it has declined to do with respect to legal interests. This is perhaps justifiable where the trust cannot be terminated because of the application of the Claflin doctrine. If the trustee can keep possession and control of the property, the equitable fee is not readily marketable. The restraint adds little additional inalienability.

5

OPTIONS TREATED AS DIRECT RESTRAINTS

BOTH ORDINARY options and preemptive options have been held subject to the Rule against Perpetuities in Kentucky.[37] They may also be subject to the rule against direct restraints. Although an

[33] *But cf.* Gilbert v. Union College, 343 S.W.2d 829 (Ky. 1961), discussed at pp. 129-30 *infra*, holding preemption for grantee's life reasonable restraint on alienation.
[34] Maher v. Maher, 207 Ky. 360, 269 S.W. 287 (1924); *cf.* Lane v. Taylor, 287 Ky. 116, 152 S.W.2d 271 (1941); Louisville v. Cooke, 135 Ky. 261, 122 S.W. 144 (1909).
[35] So. Nat'l Life Ins. Co. v. Ford's Adm'r, 151 Ky. 476, 152 S.W. 243 (1913), age twenty-five; Kean's Guardian v. Kean, 13 Ky. L. Rep. 956, 18 S.W. 1032 (1892), age twenty-eight.
[36] Muir's Ex'rs v. Howard, 178 Ky. 51, 198 S.W. 551 (1917).
[37] See pp. 39-41, 88-89 *supra*.

option is limited to lives in being plus twenty-one years or is given effect for that period under KRS 381.216, it is possible that the court may still hold it invalid as an unreasonable restraint on alienation.

Under standard doctrine, ordinary options are subject to the perpetuity rule but not to the rule against restraints.[38] The reason for this is that in practically all jurisdictions other than Kentucky, direct restraints on the fee are not permitted regardless of duration. To treat an option as a direct restraint would mean that options could not exist at all. Therefore in balancing the interest in alienability against the necessity and usefulness of options, the courts applied to options the Rule against Perpetuities rather than the rule against restraints. The practical effect was to strike down only options unlimited in time. In Kentucky, however, where restraints on the fee are permitted if reasonably limited in duration, there is no logical reason why the rule against direct restraints could not be applied to options.

Standard doctrine respecting preemptions is not so clear. (A preemption requires the owner of the property to offer it first to the holder of the preemption before conveying it to others. It is sometimes known as "a right of first refusal.") Some courts have held preemptions subject to the Rule against Perpetuities; others have dealt with them under the rule against direct restraints.[39] The reason for applying the latter rule is that some preemptions which would be void under the perpetuity rule, such as a preemption of unlimited duration to purchase at the offeror's own price or at the market price, do not seriously affect alienability. Other preemptions which would be valid under the perpetuity rule, such as a preemption limited to a life in being to purchase at a stipulated sum below market price, constitute serious impediments to alienability. Preemptions to purchase at less than market price are in substance, though not in form, direct restraints on alienation. If the owner must sell the property at less than market price if he sells it, the property is not likely to be sold.

Prior to *Robertson v. Simmons*[40] it was assumed that both ordinary options and preemptive options were not subject to the rule against unreasonable direct restraints. In four previous cases

[38] 6 Am. L. Prop. §§ 24.56, 26.66.
[39] 6 Am. L. Prop. § 26.67.
[40] 322 S.W.2d 476 (Ky. 1959).

preemptions were subjected to the Rule against Perpetuities.[41] In *Robertson* the court had before it an ordinary option to purchase at a stipulated portion of the price paid by the offeror. The contract did not state whether the option was personal to the offeree or was inheritable and unlimited in duration. The court found "the option was unlimited as to time," but it did not invalidate it under the perpetuity rule. Rather it held the option was a direct restraint on alienation and unreasonable "because even in his [the offeree's] lifetime it would be possible for the restraint to endure for too long a period."[42] No mention was made of *Campbell v. Campbell*,[43] which nine years earlier had upheld a preemption limited to the life of the offeree. On the question of duration, the cases are contrary. But they may be distinguished on the ground that *Campbell* involved a preemption at offeror's own price, whereas *Robertson* involved an option at a price below market.

The important holding in *Robertson* was that options are subject to the rule against direct restraints. If this case is followed, the court will have to decide if the rule against restraints applies to preemptions as well as to ordinary options and what formula, if any, is to be used to test the reasonableness of these commercial transactions. It is to be hoped, however, that *Robertson* will not be followed with respect to options created after the effective date of the 1960 Perpetuities Act. The court may well regard that case as based on the repealed statute prohibiting suspension of the power of alienation, with which the rule against direct restraints became curiously entangled.

That this is likely to happen is indicated by *Gilbert v. Union College*,[44] where the validity of options created after July 1, 1960, was at issue. In this case the court held valid under the Rule against Perpetuities several options to repurchase at market price which

---

[41] Saulsberry v. Saulsberry, 290 Ky. 132, 160 S.W.2d 654 (1942), holding void unlimited preemption to purchase at offeror's own price; Maddox v. Keeler, 296 Ky. 440, 177 S.W.2d 568 (1944), holding void unlimited preemption to purchase at sum below market price; Bates v. Bates, 314 Ky. 789, 236 S.W.2d 943 (1950), holding preemption to purchase at sum below market void if of unlimited duration; Campbell v. Campbell, 313 Ky. 249, 230 S.W.2d 918 (1950), holding preemption to purchase at offeror's own price, limited to life in being, valid; *cf.* Rice v. Hall, 19 Ky. L. Rep. 814, 42 S.W. 99 (1897), reforming deed to provide for preemption, limited to life in being, to purchase at stipulated sum.

[42] 322 S.W.2d at 483. For discussion of how the court arrived at this conclusion after a fearful entanglement with the law, see pp. 117-18 *supra*.

[43] 313 Ky. 249, 230 S.W.2d 918 (1950).

[44] 343 S.W.2d 829 (Ky. 1961). The application of the Rule against Perpetuities to this case is discussed at p. 89 *supra*.

were limited in duration by a life in being plus twenty years. In so doing, it remarked:

> The "unfortunate confusion" in this field, as commented upon by Judge Moreman in Robertson v. Simmons . . ., arising under former Section 381.220 governing restraints on alienation (now repealed), we believe will be avoided by new Section KRS 381.216.[45]

The court did not mention the rule against direct restraints in connection with these options, although the question of whether that rule applied was raised in the briefs. It appears from this that the court assumed *Robertson* was grounded on KRS 381.220 and that the rule against direct restraints does not now apply to ordinary options. However, in the *Union College* case there was also a preemption requiring the grantees to offer the property to the college first, should they desire to sell. To this preemption the rule against direct restraints was applied. In line with the *Campbell* case, this preemption at the offeror's own price was held to be reasonable.

On the basis of these cases it is impossible to state categorically whether, and in what circumstances, options are to be treated as direct restraints. Only one limited conclusion is warranted. Preemptions to purchase at the offeror's own price or market price are, and should be, valid if limited to the perpetuity period. Even if they are treated as direct restraints, it is reasonable for them to exist for that period, since they constitute no impediment to alienability. However, where a preemption at the offeror's own price is unlimited in time, it will be necessary for the court to decide whether or not both rules apply, and, if so, whether the Rule against Perpetuities or the rule against direct restraints applies first. If the former Rule, as modified by wait-and-see, is applied first, an unlimited preemption would be valid for twenty-one years, a reasonable period of time under the latter rule. On the other hand, if the reasonableness of the unlimited preemption is determined first, the preemption may be held to violate the rule against restraints because of unlimited duration, without ever reaching the application of the wait-and-see doctrine. Where the preemption is at offeror's own price and does not impede marketability, applying the Rule against Perpetuities first and saving the preemption for twenty-one years seems clearly preferable.

[45] *Id.* at 830.

Ordinary options and preemptions to purchase at less than market price do impede alienability, and strong arguments can be advanced for subjecting them to the rule against unreasonable direct restraints and limiting them to a period less than the perpetuity period. However, uncertainty will result from subjecting them to an "unreasonable" test unless the court lays down a fairly precise formula, something it has declined to do with respect to direct disabling and forfeiture restraints. Options, unlike such direct restraints, are commercially useful, and draftsmen should be able to create them with certainty of their validity. Unless an appropriate formula can be devised, it would seem better to leave all options and preemptions subject only to the Rule against Perpetuities as modified by KRS 381.216. Under that statute, options and preemptions are valid for twenty-one years and void thereafter unless their exercise is so limited that it must occur within the perpetuity period.

6

CONSEQUENCES OF VIOLATING A VALID RESTRAINT:
FORFEITURE AND DISABLING RESTRAINTS DISTINGUISHED

IN MANY jurisdictions a distinction is drawn between a disabling restraint and a forfeiture restraint. A disabling restraint simply withholds the power to sell from the transferee.[46] A forfeiture restraint provides for forfeiture of the interest upon alienation; there is a gift over upon alienation to a third party or a right of entry retained in the transferor or his heirs. Disabling restraints are more objectionable than forfeiture restraints, because there is no possible way they can be released. If enforced as such, the interest cannot be transferred during the period of restraint. A forfeiture restraint, on the contrary, can be released, and a fee title can be conveyed during the period of restraint if the persons who have the right to enforce forfeiture join in the conveyance.

In Kentucky, restraints against voluntary alienation of *legal interests*, whether in disabling or forfeiture form, are treated as forfeiture restraints. If there is no express provision for forfeiture in the instrument, the law implies one and creates a right of entry

[46] See *Case 1*, p. 115 *supra*.

in the transferor or his heirs. This was early established in *Kentland Coal & Coke Co. v. Keen*[47] and has been adhered to since.[48] It is a sound position. It obviates the difficulty of classifying ambiguous language as disabling or forfeiture. More important, by allowing the restraint to be released, it makes it possible for the property to be sold.[49] Construing all restraints on legal interests as forfeiture restraints renders the doctrine of reasonable restraints far less objectionable than it would otherwise be.

Where a person transfers his legal interest in property in violation of a valid restraint, the transfer is not void. It is only voidable within the period of the restraint by the person entitled to enforce forfeiture (either the transferor or his heirs,[50] holding a right of entry, or a third person designated in the instrument). If such person acts within a reasonable time after breach and within the period of restraint, he is entitled to the interest forfeited.[51] But he is barred from enforcing forfeiture after the period of restraint has run.[52]

The 1960 Perpetuities Act may have some small effect upon the time within which a forfeiture can be claimed. KRS 381.219 terminates rights of entry if the contingency upon which they are limited does not happen within thirty years from date of creation. This is applicable to rights of entry retained to enforce restraints on alienation. Where the restraint is measured by a period of years, this section can have no application, since a restraint for more than twenty-one years is void *ab initio*. Where, however, the

[47] 168 Ky. 836, 183 S.W. 246 (1916), overruling Pond Creek Coal Co. v. Runyon, 161 Ky. 64, 170 S.W. 501 (1914) and Frazier v. Combs, 140 Ky. 77, 130 S.W. 812 (1910).

[48] Auxier's Ex'x v. Theobald, 255 Ky. 583, 75 S.W.2d 39 (1934); Howard's Adm'x v. Asher Coal Co., 215 Ky. 88, 284 S.W. 419 (1926); Cooper v. Knuckles, 212 Ky. 608, 279 S.W. 1084 (1926); Hale v. Elkhorn Coal Corp., 206 Ky. 629, 268 S.W. 304 (1925); Pond Creek Coal Co. v. Day, 187 Ky. 820, 220 S.W. 1053 (1920); Price v. Virginia Iron Co., 171 Ky. 523, 188 S.W. 658 (1916); Francis v. Big Sandy Co., 171 Ky. 209, 188 S.W. 345 (1916); Gray v. Gray, 300 Ky. 265, 188 S.W.2d 440 (1945) (life estate).

[49] See England v. Davis, 273 Ky. 424, 116 S.W.2d 977 (1938); Francis v. Big Sandy Co., *supra* note 48.

[50] On who can enforce restraint when restrained devisees are testator's heirs, see Auxier's Ex'x v. Theobald, *supra* note 48; Cooper v. Knuckles, *supra* note 48. See also Gray v. Gray, *supra* note 48, as to who can enforce restraint on life estate.

[51] Turner v. Lewis, 189 Ky. 837, 226 S.W. 367 (1920); Hale v. Elkhorn Coal Corp., *supra* note 48 (sixteen years after breach unreasonable); Kenner v. American Contract Co., 72 Ky. (9 Bush) 202 (1872) (three years after breach unreasonable).

[52] Kentland Coal & Coke Co. v. Keen, *supra* note 47; Price v. Virginia Iron Co., *supra* note 48; Francis v. Big Sandy Co., *supra* note 48; Howard's Adm'x v. Asher Coal Co., *supra* note 48; Pond Creek Coal Co. v. Day, *supra* note 48.

restraint is measured by the grantor's life, or by the grantee's life, or is for some other reasonable period, KRS 381.219 will apply if the period of restraint does in fact run beyond thirty years. The right of entry will then be terminated, and the restraint can be ignored. This section does not, of course, have any effect upon the question of what restraints are valid. That remains to be determined under the reasonable restraints test. The section comes into play only after it has been decided the restraint is reasonable, and then only after the restraint has in fact run for more than thirty years.

Restraints *on equitable interests* may be in either disabling or forfeiture form. Whether they, like restraints on legal interests, are to be treated as forfeiture restraints regardless of form is not entirely clear. In *Southern National Life Insurance Company v. Ford's Administrator*[53] the question was presented whether a disabling restraint on an equitable interest would be enforced as such. Testator there devised property in trust to pay income to his son until he reached age twenty-five, then to distribute corpus to him. After he reached twenty-one, the son, "a wayward, profligate and extravagant" young man, undertook to raise money by giving a mortgage on his interest. The court implied a disabling restraint against voluntary alienation and held the mortgage void. The mortgagee, however, was allowed to recover as a creditor out of the beneficiary's interest.[54] It will be noted that at the time of this case, disabling restraints on legal interests were also enforced as such, and assignments in violation thereof were held void, not voidable.[55] It was not until three years later that *Kentland Coal* overruled the prior cases enforcing disabling restraints on legal interests and laid down the rule that disabling restraints on legal interests were to be construed as forfeiture restraints. Since no mention was made of *Ford's* case or of equitable restraints in the latter case, it is assumed *Ford's* case is still law.

In *Newsom v. Barnes*[56] plaintiff attempted to raise the question whether a disabling restraint on an equitable interest is to be treated as a forfeiture restraint, but she was unsuccessful. Testatrix had created a trust for the benefit of her son to last for four years

[53] 151 Ky. 476, 152 S.W. 243 (1913). See also Kean's Guardian v. Kean, 13 Ky. L. Rep. 956, 18 S.W. 1032 (1892).
[54] See Ford v. So. Nat'l Life Ins. Co., 160 Ky. 449, 169 S.W. 874 (1914).
[55] Pond Creek Coal Co. v. Runyon, 161 Ky. 64, 170 S.W. 501 (1914); Frazier v. Combs, 140 Ky. 77, 130 S.W. 812 (1910).
[56] 282 Ky. 264, 138 S.W.2d 475 (1940).

after her death. At the end of four years the trust was to terminate and the property pass to the son in fee. The son assigned his interest in the trust, whereupon testatrix's daughter claimed a forfeiture. There was no express restraint on alienation, however, and the court refused to imply one. Thus the court did not reach the question of whether an assignment in violation of a disabling restraint on an equitable interest is void or merely voidable.

If enforcement of a disabling restraint on an equitable interest is to be justified, whereas a disabling restraint on a legal interest is not, it must be on one of two grounds. First, if the trustee has a power of sale, the property composing the corpus is not made inalienable by the disabling restraint on the equitable interest. A disabling restraint on a legal life estate or fee necessarily makes the property itself unmarketable. Secondly, where the trust cannot be terminated, either because of application of the Claflin doctrine or because all interested parties have not consented, implying a right of entry in testator's heirs who can consent to alienation of the equitable interest would not make the interest much more marketable as a practical matter. Where these grounds do not exist—*i.e.*, where the trustee has no power of sale and the trust could be terminated if there were no restraint—it would seem that a disabling restraint on an equitable interest should be treated as a forfeiture restraint, just as is done with respect to restraints on legal interests.

7

CREDITORS' RIGHTS

So FAR we have been concerned with restraints against voluntary alienation, which are valid if reasonable. Restraints against voluntary alienation have the purpose of preventing a voluntary transfer (sale, gift, or mortgage) by the transferee. In addition, the donor may wish to impose a restraint against involuntary alienation to prevent a sale under court order to satisfy a debt or judgment. Restraints against involuntary alienation are expressly designed to prevent creditors from reaching the interest of the transferee.

Although Kentucky law is liberal in upholding restraints against voluntary alienation, it is stricter than the law of most other jurisdictions in validating restraints against creditors. In Kentucky, all restraints against voluntary alienation of legal[57] and equitable[58] interests are void against creditors. A spendthrift trust which would prevent the creditors from reaching the property is not recognized. Likewise, all disabling restraints against involuntary alienation of legal and equitable interests are void against creditors.[59] Thus:

Case 4 (Legal interest). O by deed transfers property "to A in fee, provided that A shall not have the power to convey this property until he reaches thirty years of age, and provided further that before A reaches the age of thirty this property shall not be subject to or liable for the claims of A's creditors." A is age twenty-one. The first restraint against voluntary alienation is reasonable and valid. The second restraint against involuntary alienation is void, even though reasonably limited in time. Any assignment by A before he reaches thirty is voidable by O, who can claim forfeiture, but A's creditors can reach his interest. However, since an assignment by A is not void but only voidable by O, A's creditors must secure a lien on the property prior to any assignment by A.

Case 5 (Equitable interest). T by will creates a trust "to pay income to A for life, and on A's death to distribute the corpus to A's issue then living per stirpes. A shall not have the power to alienate or assign his interest or anticipate income, and his interest shall in no event be subject to or liable for the claims of A's creditors." The restraint against voluntary alienation is valid; the restraint against involuntary alienation is void. A cannot make a valid assignment of his interest, but his creditors can reach it. If A purports to assign his equitable interest to B for a valuable consideration, the assignment is (probably) void, but B may subsequently reach the property as a creditor.[60] Oddly enough, creditors receive more protection when the restraint on voluntary alienation is treated as a disabling restraint than they do when it is treated as a forfeiture restraint.

[57] Anderson v. Blackburn, 297 S.W.2d 919 (Ky. 1956); Smith v. Smith, 115 Ky. 329, 73 S.W. 1028 (1903); Auxier's Ex'x v. Theobald, 255 Ky. 583, 75 S.W.2d 39 (1934) (dictum); cf. George v. George, 283 Ky. 381, 141 S.W.2d 558 (1940); KRS 426.190.

[58] Meade v. Rowe's Ex'r, 298 Ky. 111, 182 S.W.2d 30 (1944); Spilman v. Mercer County Nat'l Bank, 268 Ky. 761, 105 S.W.2d 1031 (1937); Ford v. Ford, 230 Ky. 56, 18 S.W.2d 859 (1929) (subject to children's claim for support); Dority v. W. E. Rogers Co., 223 Ky. 238, 3 S.W.2d 636 (1928); So. Nat'l Life Ins. Co. v. Ford's Adm'r, 151 Ky. 476, 152 S.W. 243 (1913); cf. First Owensboro Bank v. Central Trust Co., 275 Ky. 453, 121 S.W.2d 953 (1938); KRS 381.180.

[59] Meade v. Rowe's Ex'r, *supra* note 58; cf. Louisville v. Cooke, 135 Ky. 261, 122 S.W. 144 (1909); Bland's Adm'r v. Bland, 90 Ky. 400, 14 S.W. 423 (1890); Brock v. Brock, 168 Ky. 847, 183 S.W. 213 (1916).

[60] So. Nat'l Life Ins. Co. v. Ford's Adm'r, *supra* note 58.

There is one exception to the rule allowing creditors to reach inalienable interests. It rests upon such peculiar reasoning and is so objectionable as a matter of public policy that it must be dealt with at some length. It is this: An express forfeiture restraint against involuntary alienation of a legal[61] or equitable[62] interest will be given effect. If the donor provides that the donee's interest shall be forfeited if creditors levy execution on it, the interest will cease and the gift over will take effect upon execution. The creditors are left out in the cold with nothing to warm them but the doubtful satisfaction of punishing the debtor.

The reason given for upholding a forfeiture restraint against involuntary alienation is that as soon as the creditors subject the debtor's interest to their judgment, his interest ceases "instanter" and there is nothing for them to reach. This reasoning contains a double fallacy. In the first place, it begs the question by assuming that the interest does cease, which is the very question in issue. Secondly, it rests upon a further assumption that the interest ceases simultaneously with execution (unlike an interest subject to forfeiture for voluntary alienation, which does not cease until a forfeiture has been declared by the party entitled). But how can this interest cease simultaneously with execution? Can one have a valid execution and at the same time not have it? One could equally well assume there must be one moment of time between execution and forfeiture. On that assumption, since the forfeiture condition is not to become operative until execution, after execution it cannot become operative because the property is now subject to the order of the court. But in either assumption, property lawyers will recognize the ghost of Pimbe's Case[63] and the great sixteenth century controversy over scintilla juris and later momentous disputes over simultaneous seisin. In truth, the problem cannot be solved by giving a time sequence to purely conceptual events.

[61] Scott v. Ratliff, 179 Ky. 267, 200 S.W. 462 (1918); Phillips v. Big Sandy Co., 32 Ky. L. Rep. 1262, 108 S.W. 276 (1908).

[62] Bottom v. Fultz, 124 Ky. 302, 98 S.W. 1037 (1907); Bull v. Ky. Nat'l Bank, 90 Ky. 452, 14 S.W. 425 (1890); cf. Lane v. Taylor, 287 Ky. 116, 152 S.W.2d 271 (1941) (dictum that forfeiture restraint on settlor's life estate reserved was valid). But cf. Louisville v. Cooke, 135 Ky. 261, 122 S.W. 144 (1909), enforcing tax lien against life estate in spite of forfeiture restraint against involuntary alienation; Bland's Adm'r v. Bland, 90 Ky. 400, 14 S.W. 423 (1890), enforcing creditors' rights because debtor did not forfeit his entire interest in the property.

[63] Moore 196 (1585). For a translation, see Scott, Cases on Trusts 255 (4th ed. 1951).

At bottom the validity of an express forfeiture restraint against involuntary alienation is a question of public policy. It does not rest upon any supposed power of a donor of property to give it away upon such terms as he may choose to impose. For, of course, the donor has no such power. Any lawyer on very slight reflection can point to numerous dispositions the law will not allow. Looking solely within the law of restraints, we see the law will not allow the donor to impose unreasonable restraints on voluntary alienation or any disabling restraint against involuntary alienation; nor can the donor impose any restraint which would prevent a court sale for reinvestment. Hence, the question of validity of the restraint does not turn on what power the donor has, but on whether or not his attempted restraint offends public policy.

A forfeiture restraint against involuntary alienation is seriously objectionable as a matter of public policy for three reasons. In the first place, the legislature has provided in general terms that all legal interests and all equitable interests shall be subject to execution unless specifically exempt by statute.[64] It has declared a policy that "no man can hold as his own and enjoy property free from the claims of his creditors, but that all property not exempt from execution shall be subject to the payment of his debts."[65] It is difficult to understand why the court should carve a single exception in this policy in the case of a forfeiture restraint against involuntary alienation. The purpose of the statutes is to benefit creditors. It is not satisfied by penalizing the debtor, where that penalty does not benefit creditors.

Secondly, even if the legislative policy could be satisfied by penalizing debtors, as a practical matter they are seldom penalized or even seriously threatened by the existence of a forfeiture restraint against involuntary alienation. Such a restraint has a tendency to discourage creditors from attempting to collect debts, since the result of the attempt is to put the property beyond the creditors' reach and defeat any possibility that the debtor might use the income from the property to pay his debts. While it may be argued

[64] KRS 426.190: "Land to which the defendant has a legal or equitable title in fee, for life or for a term, whether in possession, reversion or remainder, or in which the defendant has a contingent interest or a contingent remainder or a defeasible fee, may be taken and sold under execution."
KRS 381.180: "Estates of every kind held or possessed in trust are subject to the debts and charges of the beneficiaries thereof the same as if the beneficiaries also owned the similar legal interest in the property."
[65] Anderson v. Blackburn, 297 S.W.2d 919, 921 (Ky. 1957).

that the creditor has some protection because he holds the whip hand, reflection leads to the conclusion that it is a very weak hand that wields the whip.

If the forfeiture restraint is against involuntary alienation only, the debtor may dispose of his interest voluntarily and defeat the creditors before execution. He may give it to his wife. Or he may transfer it in trust, giving the trustee absolute discretion over the income during the settlor's life, with any remainder interest to go on settlor's death to his children. In neither of these transfers would the debtor retain an interest subject to debts, but he could as a practical matter retain beneficial enjoyment. It is doubtful if either of these transfers could be set aside by creditors as fraudulent, since the only right creditors lose by the transfer is the right to an execution which avails nothing.[66] If the forfeiture restraint is against both voluntary and involuntary alienation, the debtor may arrange with the takers on forfeiture (usually his wife and children) for continuing indirect benefits. To best serve his interests, the debtor can play a cat-and-mouse game with the creditors and the takers on forfeiture.

The only real protection the creditors may have is to throw the debtor into involuntary bankruptcy. And this protection is available only where the debtor could have voluntarily transferred his interest, where the restraint is against involuntary alienation alone. In case of bankruptcy the trustee in bankruptcy succeeds to any interest of the bankrupt which he could have transferred voluntarily.[67] This leads to the peculiar result that the trustee in bankruptcy has greater rights than the creditors. He can subject the interest to debts, but the creditors cannot. Although some protection may result from a threat of throwing the debtor into bankruptcy, the creditors' hand is weakened by the exemption of farmers from involuntary bankruptcy and by the strict requirements for filing a petition. It is indeed hard to understand why, if the debtor has the means of discharging his obligations voluntarily, the creditors must take such a roundabout and hazardous route in an attempt to collect.

[66] See Glenn, Fraudulent Conveyances and Preferences § 186 (rev. ed. 1940).
[67] Section 70(a)(5) of the Federal Bankruptcy Act (11 U.S.C.A. § 110) gives the trustee in bankruptcy title to property which the bankrupt "could by any means have transferred." For its application to interests which the beneficiary may assign but creditors cannot reach, see Griswold, Spendthrift Trusts §§ 358-61 (2d ed. 1947).

The third reason enforcement of a forfeiture restraint against involuntary alienation is contrary to public policy is that it obstructs the court's process by rendering ineffective the order of execution. If the condition is valid and the property is levied upon, the only effect of the levy is to defeat the levy. A private condition which requires a court to pass upon a moot case or do a useless thing (*i.e.*, determine the interest is subject to debts) ought to be void as an interference with judicial administration. In view of this "trifling with the judicial process,"[68] it is remarkable that the Court of Appeals has held that "the right of the devisee ceased instanter upon the determination by a court of competent jurisdiction that the estate was subject to the debts of the devisee."[69]

Equitable interests beyond the reach of creditors. There are two equitable interests that creditors cannot reach in Kentucky, one the interest of a beneficiary of a discretionary trust, the other an inseparable equitable life estate in several beneficiaries. If the settlor, in creating a trust, provides that the trustee has absolute and complete discretion to determine whether the beneficiary shall receive anything at all, the Court of Appeals has held the beneficiary's interest is free from the claims of his creditors.[70] If, however, the beneficiary's interest does not lie in the complete discretion of the trustee and the interest is one that equity will enforce, creditors can reach his interest. Thus creditors can reach the interest of a beneficiary where the trustee is directed to pay the beneficiary as much as is needed for his maintenance and support.[71]

Where the settlor creates a trust for the benefit of several

[68] Commissioner v. Proctor, 142 F.2d 824, 827 (4th Cir. 1944). In this case the court held void as contrary to public policy a forfeiture condition on a gift of property, which was to take effect should the transfer be determined by a court to be subject to the federal gift tax. Is a condition against creditors' reaching the property less objectionable than a condition against the federal tax collector's reaching it?

[69] Bottom v. Fultz, 124 Ky. 302, 309, 98 S.W. 1037, 1039 (1907).

[70] Calloway v. Smith, 300 Ky. 55, 186 S.W.2d 642 (1945); Todd's Ex'rs v. Todd, 260 Ky. 611, 86 S.W.2d 168 (1935); Louisville Tobacco Warehouse Co. v. Thompson, 172 Ky. 350, 189 S.W. 245 (1916); Davidson's Ex'rs v. Kemper, 79 Ky. 5 (1880); see 6 Am. L. Prop. §§ 26.116-.118.

[71] Department of Public Welfare v. Meek, 264 Ky. 771, 95 S.W.2d 599 (1936); Ratliff's Ex'rs v. Commonwealth, 139 Ky. 533, 101 S.W. 978 (1907); Cecil's Trustee v. Robertson, 32 Ky. L. Rep. 357, 105 S.W. 926 (1907); *cf.* Huffman v. Chasteen, 307 Ky. 1, 209 S.W.2d 705 (1948); see 6 Am. L. Prop. § 26.113.

persons as a unit, such as a man and his family, and the trustee has power to determine the proportion which each shall receive, the court has held the beneficiary's interest cannot be reached by creditors if it is inseparable.[72] What facts are required in order to hold the interest inseparable is not entirely clear.[73]

Discretionary trusts may contain express restraints on alienation. Such restraints are surplusage, since the beneficiary cannot assign his interest anyway. There are no Kentucky cases, and few elsewhere, dealing with the question of voluntary assignment of an inseparable interest. Therefore, one cannot say whether express restraints on such interests would be surplusage.

8

SALE FOR REINVESTMENT UNDER COURT ORDER

MAY A COURT order sale of property and reinvestment of the proceeds where alienation of the property or some interest therein is expressly prohibited? The answer is yes. By statute, circuit courts are authorized to order sale of property held in trust or by legal estates, including property in which there are vested or contingent future interests, where the sale will benefit the parties interested in the property.[74] Prior to 1942, section 492 of the Civil Code of Practice provided that no sale could be ordered by a court for twenty years where forbidden by the deed or will. After twenty years the court could order a sale where a change of circumstances made a sale beneficial to the grantees or devisees. The Court of Appeals, interpreting this statutory ban on court sale narrowly, held it did not apply unless a sale by a *court* was expressly forbidden

---

[72] Harned v. Dorman, 252 Ky. 237, 67 S.W.2d 5 (1934); Russell v. Meyers, 202 Ky. 593, 260 S.W. 377 (1924); Bank of Taylorsville v. Vandyke, 159 Ky. 201, 166 S.W. 1024 (1914); Hackett v. Hackett, 146 Ky. 408, 142 S.W. 673 (1912) (very doubtful since income was to be distributed "equally"). Compare Ford v. Ford, 230 Ky. 56, 18 S.W.2d 859 (1929); Hubbard v. Hayes, 30 Ky. L. Rep. 406, 98 S.W. 1034 (1907).

[73] See generally Griswold, Spendthrift Trusts §§ 435-45 (2d ed. 1947).

[74] Legal fee may be sold in action brought by guardian (KRS 389.010); by legal life tenant (KRS 389.030); by trustee (KRS 389.035); by owner of any present or vested interest (KRS 389.040). See also KRS 353.300, authorizing court to appoint trustee to execute mineral lease; KRS 395.200(1)(d), authorizing sale of personal property even though forbidden by testator. See generally Rodes, Judicial Sales of Real Property 116-56 (1941).

by the instrument.[75] Nor did it apply where the court did not decree sale, but merely approved a sale entered into by a trustee.[76] The court restricted the section in several more technical ways, but since section 492 was repealed in 1942,[77] it is not necessary to go into them.

The purpose of repeal was to remove the twenty-year stay of the court's hand and allow court sale for reinvestment under the various statutory procedures even though sale is expressly prohibited in the instrument. So it was held in *Kelly v. Marr*.[78] In that case, testator's will provided that neither the trustee nor any of the life beneficiaries should have the power to sell the trust property during their lives. The court held the restraint on alienation could not prevent a sale of real property held in trust where a sale would benefit the beneficiaries. The court reasoned that a private restraint could not prevent the exercise of either the power conferred on a court by statute or the inherent supervisory powers courts have over trust investment.[79] In a subsequent case involving the same will, the court reiterated that a restraint must yield to any judicial sale authorized by statute.[80]

Apart from procedural requirements, there is only one definite statutory restriction on the court's wide discretion to order sale of trust assets. If the trustee is expressly given a power of sale, a court cannot order the property sold without the trustee's consent.[81] In sum, the settlor cannot prevent a court from ordering a sale of trust assets unless he gives the power of sale to the trustee. Some living person—either the trustee or the chancellor—must have power to sell the property to protect the beneficiaries of the trust.

Since the power of sale granted to courts by statute cannot be nullified by a private restraint on alienation, restraints on legal

[75] Latta v. Louisville Trust Co., 198 Ky. 45, 247 S.W. 1103 (1923); Gillespie v. Winston's Trustees, 170 Ky. 667, 186 S.W. 517 (1916); Sparrow v. Sparrow, 171 Ky. 101, 186 S.W. 904 (1916); Rousseau v. Page's Ex'x, 150 Ky. 812, 150 S.W. 983 (1912). See also Vittitow v. Keene, 265 Ky. 66, 95 S.W.2d 1083 (1936), holding will cannot prevent sale to pay debts of testator.

[76] Consolidated Realty Co. v. Norton's Trustees, 214 Ky. 586, 283 S.W. 969 (1926).

[77] Ky. Acts 1942, c. 137, § 4.

[78] 299 Ky. 447, 185 S.W.2d 945 (1945), noted 35 Ky. L.J. 147 (1947).

[79] Courts of equity have inherent power to order sale where sale is necessary to preserve the trust corpus. See 2 Scott, Trusts §§ 167, 190.4 (2d ed. 1956).

[80] Adams v. Security Trust Co., 302 Ky. 287, 194 S.W.2d 521 (1946). For further litigation over how the proceeds should be reinvested, see Security Trust Co. v. Mahoney, 307 Ky. 661, 212 S.W.2d 115 (1948).

[81] KRS 389.045(8).

interests are likewise ineffective to prevent court sale. In the recent case of *Groger v. Long*,[82] the testator created legal life estates and remainders in a tract of land. He expressly prohibited sale of the property for reinvestment.[83] The circuit court ordered sale on the ground that it would prove advantageous to the beneficiaries. The Court of Appeals affirmed.

Subjecting restrained land to court sale for reinvestment is sound public policy. Especially is this true in Kentucky, where restraints on the legal fee are permitted. If the purpose of allowing such restraints is to protect the beneficiary, they should become ineffective when, in the opinion of the chancellor, they no longer serve that purpose. Without intending in any way to disparage our many distinguished chancellors, one may agree with Professors Leach and Logan: "To regulate events in 1980 the judgment of a mediocre mind on the spot is incomparably preferable to the guess in 1960 of the greatest man who ever lived."[84]

9

CRITIQUE OF KENTUCKY DOCTRINE OF REASONABLE RESTRAINTS

THE UNIQUE Kentucky doctrine permitting reasonable restraints on the legal fee has never found much favor with the commentators or with courts in other jurisdictions. Is it then a socially undesirable doctrine? Professor Schnebly has noted the objections to all restraints: that they take the property out of commerce, discourage improvements, protect drones, work hardships on creditors, and allow the dead hand to control the one basic resource of the community, land.[85] On the other hand, restraints have often served quite useful purposes, such as protecting a child until maturity or a subdivider until he recoups his investment or a grantor who retains a charge for support. Whether the objectionable aspects of restraints reasonably limited in duration outweigh their useful-

---

[82] 269 S.W.2d 291 (Ky. 1954). See also Whisman v. McMullan's Ex'r, 312 Ky. 402, 227 S.W.2d 926 (1950).

[83] Brief for Appellee, p. 5, Groger v. Long, *supra* note 82.

[84] Leach & Logan, Cases and Text on Future Interests and Estate Planning 242 (1961).

[85] 6 Am. L. Prop. § 26.3. *But see* Bernhard, "The Minority Doctrine Concerning Direct Restraints on Alienation," 57 Mich. L. Rev. 1173 (1959), approving the Kentucky doctrine and concluding the majority rule overstresses alienability.

ness depends largely upon (1) the amount of property which is thereby made inalienable, and (2) local rules allowing restraints to be ignored under certain circumstances.

There is no evidence that any substantial amount of property has been made unmarketable or unimprovable by allowing reasonable restraints. Definitive data on the amount of land subject to restraints is of course impossible to obtain. But if the amount were substantial, it is likely there would have been some complaints from real estate dealers and developers, from lawyers, and from title insurance companies. The only evidence is the number of reported cases involving restraints. There were six in the last decade (of which only three involved restraints on the legal fee), compared with nineteen in the 1920s (of which nine involved restraints on the legal fee). Judging from these cases, it appears that effective restraints on alienation are steadily declining in number. Unless that trend sharply reverses itself, toleration of the few restraints indicated by the cases is not a significant social evil.

More important than this speculative evidence, however, is the fact that certain complementary rules in Kentucky make restraints far less objectionable than they appear to be at first blush. The Court of Appeals has laid down three rules which severely curtail their undesirable effects. (1) Every disabling restraint on a legal life estate or fee is construed as a forfeiture restraint, thus making it possible for all such restraints to be released.[86] (2) All restraints on legal and equitable interests are void against creditors except a forfeiture restraint against involuntary alienation. (3) Lastly, and most important, restraints may be overridden by a court sale for reinvestment when a sale would be advantageous to the beneficiaries. Although restraints are impediments to alienability, they do not operate as an absolute bar to transfer of the property. Nor do they, except in one instance, prevent creditors from reaching the debtor's interest. Taking into consideration the usefulness of restraints, the apparent infrequency of their imposition, and these

[86] No other jurisdiction treats disabling restraints on legal interests as forfeiture restraints as a matter of law. 6 Am. L. Prop. § 26.11 n.12. The rule got started in Kentucky by use of a remarkable (some would say illegitimate) judicial technique. In Kentland Coal & Coke Co. v. Keen, 168 Ky. 836, 183 S.W. 246 (1916), the court announced the new principle ex cathedra: "That this [disabling] clause creates what is known in the law of real estate conveyances as a *condition subsequent* there can be no doubt. This is so manifest as to be at once accepted without citation of authorities." Having thus established the law, the court then proceeded to overrule two Kentucky cases to the contrary!

ameliorative rules, from society's viewpoint the doctrine of reasonable restraints seems rather innocuous.

The most forceful criticism which can be directed at the doctrine is its vague and uncertain nature. Few restraints on a fee can reasonably be regarded as valid without a judicial determination. There is probably no cure for this except a rule voiding all restraints on the fee (the majority rule) or a rule validating them for a certain fixed period and voiding them thereafter. Whether either cure would not be worse than the disease is questionable.

It profits nothing to attempt to compare the majority rule and the doctrine of reasonable restraints with a view to determining which is preferable. There are too many unknown variables which a rational choice would require taking account of—the number, the purposes, and the duration of attempted restraints; whether the draftsman can, and, if so, how often he does, avoid either doctrine by creating inalienable life estates and interests in trust; local rules respecting the validity of restraints against creditors and judicial sales. Without more information than is presently available, any conclusion must necessarily be a statement of preference based upon conjectures. And in reality, neither doctrine can be appraised apart from the entire doctrinal structure respecting direct and indirect restraints on property.

Both the majority rule prohibiting all restraints on the legal fee and the Kentucky rule permitting reasonable restraints have the purpose of making land (and personal property) alienable. But in all jurisdictions there are countervailing doctrines which permit land to be made inalienable either directly by the imposition of restraints on lesser interests or indirectly by the creation of life estates and remainders. For example, a direction to a trustee not to sell property going into the trust is a valid restraint on the legal fee, even though it may last for the entire duration of the trust. A forfeiture restraint on a legal life estate is allowed in a majority of states, although it is no less objectionable than a restraint on a defeasible fee. And the mere creation of a legal life estate in land followed by a contingent remainder makes the land unmarketable. Where the policy against inalienable land is so easily avoided, of what efficacy is a doctrine against restraints on a fee?

Since the Kentucky court has held that restraints cannot prevent a judicial sale of land where a court finds it would be advantageous, it is quite possible that the Kentucky law of restraints will evolve easily into a more rational system. In judicial sale for reinvestment lies the best hope of overcoming the objectionable features of all restraints. So long as restraints on life estates are permitted, abolition of the doctrine permitting reasonable restraints on the fee would be an ineffectual gesture.

APPENDIX *1*

KENTUCKY PERPETUITIES ACT OF 1960

KY. ACTS 1960, C. 167

Section 1. [381.215 Adoption of common law rule against perpetuities.]¹ No interest in real or personal property shall be good unless it must vest, if at all, not later than twenty-one years after some life in being at the creation of the interest. It is the purpose of this section to enact the common law rule against perpetuities, except as hereinafter modified by this Act.

Section 2. [381.216 Wait-and-see doctrine; reformation.] In determining whether an interest would violate the rule against perpetuities the period of perpetuities shall be measured by actual rather than possible events; provided, however, the period shall not be measured by any lives whose continuance does not have a causal relationship to the vesting or failure of the interest. Any interest which would violate said rule as thus modified shall be reformed, within the limits of that rule, to approximate most closely the intention of the creator of the interest.

Section 3. [381.217 Exception in the case of pension trusts.] A trust created by an employer as part of a stock bonus plan, pension plan, disability or death benefit plan or profit-sharing plan, for the exclusive benefit of some or all of his employes, to which contributions are made by such employer and employes, or both, for the purposes of distributing to such employes the earnings or the principal, or both earnings and principal, of the fund so held in trust, shall not be deemed to be invalid as violating the rule against perpetuities, but such a trust may continue for such time as may be necessary to accomplish the purposes for which it may be created.

Section 4. [381.218 Abolition of fee simple determinable and possibility of reverter.] The estate known at common law as the fee simple determinable and the interest known as the possibility of reverter are abolished. Words which at common law would create a fee simple determinable shall be construed to create a fee simple subject to a right of entry for condition broken. In any case where a person would have a possibility of reverter at common law, he shall have a right of entry.

Section 5. [381.219 Termination after thirty years of rights of entry created after July 1, 1960.] A fee simple subject to a right of entry for condition broken shall become a fee simple absolute if the specified contingency does not occur within thirty years from the effective date of the instrument creating such fee simple subject to a right of entry. If such contingency occurs within said thirty years the right of entry, which may be created in a person other than the person creating the interest or his heirs, shall become exercisable notwithstanding the rule against perpetuities. This section shall not apply to rights of entry created prior to July 1, 1960.

Section 6. [381.221 Termination and preservation of forfeiture restrictions created before July 1, 1960.] (1) Every possibility of reverter and right of entry created prior to July 1, 1960, shall cease to be valid or enforceable at the expiration of thirty years after the effective date of the instrument creating it, unless before July 1, 1965, a declaration of intention to preserve it is filed for record with the county clerk of the county in which the real property is located.

(2) The declaration shall be entitled "Declaration of Intention to Preserve Restrictions on the Use of Land," and shall set forth:
- (a) the name of the record owner or owners of the fee in the land against whom the possibility of reverter or right of entry is intended to be preserved;
- (b) the names and addresses of the persons intending to preserve the possibility of reverter or right of entry;
- (c) a description of the land;
- (d) the terms of the restriction;
- (e) a reference to the instrument creating the possibility of reverter or right of entry and to the place where such instrument is recorded. The declaration shall be signed by each person named therein as intending to preserve the possibility of reverter or right of entry and shall be acknowledged or proved

---

[1] Section numbers and headings for the Kentucky Revised Statutes, which have been supplied by the reviser of statutes, are inserted in brackets.

in the manner required to entitle a conveyance of real property to be recorded. The county clerk shall record the declaration in the record of deeds and shall index it in the general index of deeds in the same manner as if the record owner or owners of the land were the grantor or grantors and the persons intending to preserve the possibility of reverter or right of entry were the grantees in a deed of conveyance. For indexing and recording the clerk shall receive the same fees as are allowed for indexing and recording deeds.

Section 7. [381.222 Exceptions to KRS 381.219 and 381.221.] Sections 5 and 6 of this Act shall not apply to any possibility of reverter or right of entry contained in a deed, gift or grant from the Commonwealth or any political subdivision thereof; nor shall they apply where both the fee simple determinable and the succeeding interest, or both the fee simple subject to a right of entry and the right of entry, are for public, charitable or religious purposes; nor shall they affect any lease present or future or any easement, right of way, mortgage or trust, or any communication, transmission, or transportation lines, or any public highway, right to take minerals, or charge for support during the life of a person or persons, or any restrictive covenant without right of entry or reverter.

Section 8. Section 381.220 of the Kentucky Revised Statutes is repealed.

Section 9. [381.223 Application of KRS 381.215 to 381.223.] Except as provided in Section 6, this Act shall apply only to inter vivos instruments and wills taking effect after July 1, 1960, and to appointments made after July 1, 1960, including appointments by inter vivos instrument or will under powers created before July 1, 1960.

APPENDIX 2

ANALYSIS OF KENTUCKY PERPETUITIES CASES

TABLE 1

CASES CONSISTENT WITH ORTHODOX
PERPETUITIES DOCTRINE IN RESULT

Armstrong v. Armstrong, 53 Ky. (14 B. Mon.) 269 (1853)
Atty. Gen. v. Wallace's Devisees, 46 Ky. (7 B. Mon.) 611 (1847)
Barnes v. Graves, 259 Ky. 180, 82 S.W.2d 297 (1935)
Barren County Bd. of Educ. v. Jordan, 249 S.W.2d 814 (Ky. 1952)
Bates v. Bates, 314 Ky. 789, 236 S.W.2d 943 (1950)
Beall v. Wilson, 146 Ky. 646, 143 S.W. 55 (1912)
Board of Nat'l Missions v. Harrel's Trustee, 286 S.W.2d 905 (Ky. 1956)
Bowling v. Grace, 219 Ky. 496, 293 S.W. 964 (1927)
Brumley v. Brumley, 28 Ky. L. Rep. 231, 89 S.W. 182 (1905)
Cambron v. Pottinger, 301 Ky. 768, 193 S.W.2d 412 (1946)
Campbell v. Campbell, 313 Ky. 249, 230 S.W.2d 918 (1950)
Carter's Trustee v. Gettys, 138 Ky. 842, 129 S.W. 308 (1910)
Chenowith v. Bullitt, 224 Ky. 698, 6 S.W.2d 1061 (1928)
Clay v. Anderson, 203 Ky. 384, 262 S.W. 604 (1924)
Commonwealth v. Pollitt, 25 Ky. L. Rep. 790, 76 S.W. 412 (1903)
DeCharette v. DeCharette, 264 Ky. 525, 94 S.W.2d 1018, 104 A.L.R. 1455 (1936)
Egner v. Livingston County Bd. of Educ., 313 Ky. 168, 230 S.W.2d 448 (1950)
Emler v. Emler's Trustee, 269 Ky. 27, 106 S.W.2d 79 (1937)

Epperson v. Clintonville Cemetery Co., 303 Ky. 852, 199 S.W.2d 628 (1947)
Fayette County v. Morton, 282 Ky. 481, 138 S.W.2d 953 (1940)
Fayette County Bd. of Educ. v. Bryan, 263 Ky. 61, 91 S.W.2d 990 (1936)
First Nat'l Bank v. Purcell, 244 S.W.2d 458 (Ky. 1951)
Ford v. Yost, 300 Ky. 764, 190 S.W.2d 21 (1945)
Gillespie v. Winston's Trustee, 170 Ky. 667, 186 S.W. 517 (1916)
Goodloe's Trustee v. Goodloe, 292 Ky. 494, 166 S.W.2d 836 (1942)
Gray v. Gray, 300 Ky. 265, 188 S.W.2d 440, 160 A.L.R. 633 (1945)
Haydon v. Layton, 128 S.W. 90 (Ky. 1910)
Jefferson County Bd. of Educ. v. Littrell, 173 Ky. 78, 190 S.W. 465 (1917)
Kasey v. Fidelity Trust Co., 131 Ky. 609, 115 S.W. 739 (1909)
Maddox v. Keeler, 296 Ky. 440, 177 S.W.2d 568, 162 A.L.R. 578 (1944), noted 33 Ky. L.J. 118 (1945)
Miller v. Miller, 151 Ky. 563, 152 S.W. 542 (1913)
Mitchell v. Deegan, 301 Ky. 587, 192 S.W.2d 715 (1946)
Moore's Trustees v. Howe's Heirs, 20 Ky. (4 T.B. Mon.) 199 (1827)
Page v. Frazier's Ex'rs, 77 Ky. (14 Bush) 205 (1878)
Pullins v. Bd. of Educ. of Methodist Church, 25 Ky. L. Rep. 1715, 78 S.W. 457 (1904)
Russell v. Meyers, 202 Ky. 593, 260 S.W. 377 (1924)
Saulsberry v. Saulsberry, 290 Ky. 132, 160 S.W.2d 654 (1942)
Smith v. Fowler, 301 Ky. 96, 190 S.W.2d 1015 (1945)
Sorrell v. Tenn. Gas Transm. Co., 314 S.W.2d 193 (Ky. 1958)
Texas Eastern Transm. Corp. v. Carman, 314 S.W.2d 684 (Ky. 1958)
Vokins v. McGaughey, 206 Ky. 42, 266 S.W. 907 (1924)

TABLE 2

CASES HOLDING CONTRARY TO
ORTHODOX PERPETUITIES DOCTRINE[1]

Bach v. Pace, 305 S.W.2d 528 (Ky. 1957)
    Deed of land to W for life, remainder in fee to grandchildren of grantor. Grantor had grandchildren living at date of deed (Record, Exhibit A). Held: remainder to grandchildren void. *Contra*, 6 Am. L. Prop. § 24.25; Gray § 379; Simes & Smith § 1270, example 5, see also n. 69, 1959 pocket part. Orthodox view: class closing at W's death saves gift.
Coleman v. Coleman, 23 Ky. L. Rep. 1476, 65 S.W. 832 (1901)
    Devise in trust to pay income to W for life, then to T's children; at end of twenty-five years to distribute corpus to T's children then

[1] In some of these cases the holdings could be made consistent with orthodox doctrine if an unusual construction were given the dispositive language.

living, with the heirs of any deceased child taking his share. Held: entire devise void. *Contra*, 6 Am. L. Prop. § 24.19, case 22a (1958 supp.); Carey & Schuyler, Illinois Law of Future Interests § 480 (1941); 5 Powell ¶ 772; 4 Restatement of Property § 378; 1 Scott, Trusts § 62.10 (2d ed. 1956); Simes & Smith § 1391; *cf.* Gray §§ 410-10.5. Orthodox view: gifts of income vest immediately; all interests in corpus will vest in interest with possession postponed at or before the death of T's children. Interests not invalid because trust may last beyond perpetuity period.

Curtis v. Citizens Bank, 318 S.W.2d 33 (Ky. 1958)
Devise in trust to pay income to A, B, and C (T's children) and distribute to each one-third of his share of the corpus at age forty, one-third at forty-five, one-third at fifty. If any child dies before distribution, "his issue to take equally his share per stirpes" at time he would have taken it had he lived. Held: entire trust void. *Contra*, 6 Am. L. Prop. § 24.19; Carey & Schuyler, Illinois Law of Future Interests § 480 (1941); 5 Powell ¶ 784 nn.81, 92; 4 Restatement of Property § 386, ill. 7, see also § 389, ill. 2. Orthodox view: all gifts will vest in interest with possession postponed within the period. If gift to T's grandchildren void because subject to condition precedent of surviving, striking down gift to T's children is very harsh application of infectious invalidity. Case criticized by Sparks, 35 N.Y.U.L. Rev. 410 (1960).

Fidelity & Columbia Trust Co. v. Tiffany, 202 Ky. 618, 260 S.W. 357 (1924)
Devise in trust of $10 a month to invest and accumulate income for each of T's grandchildren living at his death or born within ten years thereafter. As each grandchild arrived at age twenty-two, trustee directed to pay him the amount invested and accumulated for his benefit; "if one or more of my said grandchildren shall die before attaining age twenty-two, then" his share to be divided among the other grandchildren who have not attained twenty-two. Held: all gifts to grandchildren void. *Contra*, 6 Am. L. Prop. § 24.28, case 44; 5 Powell ¶ 784; 4 Restatement of Property § 385; Simes & Smith § 1266. Per capita gift to living grandchildren will vest in possession, if at all, within their own lives. Per capita gift to afterborn grandchildren should vest in interest on birth with possession postponed. See authorities cited under Curtis v. Citizens Bank *supra*. See also authorities cited under Holoway v. Crumbaugh *infra*.

Fidelity Trust Co. v. Lloyd, 25 Ky. L. Rep. 1827, 78 S.W. 896 (1904)
Devise in trust to pay income to T's children, with share of income of any child dying to go to his children; at end of forty years to distribute corpus among "those who shall then be the heirs of my body." Held: entire trust void. Under orthodox doctrine the gift of corpus is void, but the gift of income to T's children and grandchildren is valid. See authorities cited under Coleman v. Coleman

supra. There is no reason to apply doctrine of infectious invalidity in this case. 6 Am. L. Prop. § 24.48; 5 Powell ¶ 789; Simes & Smith §§ 1262, 1263.

Ford v. Yost, 299 Ky. 682, 186 S.W.2d 896 (1945)
Devise in trust to pay income to A and his children, and at end of thirty years to turn over property to A for life, remainder to A's children in fee. Held: there could be no "vesting" [in possession?] for thirty years. "The provisions of the trust offend the rule . . . and are void." *Contra*, 6 Am. L. Prop. § 24.67; 5 Powell ¶ 773; 4 Restatement of Property § 378; 1 Scott, Trusts § 62.10(2) (2d ed. 1956); Simes & Smith §§ 1391, 1393. Orthodox view: the gift to A's children vests in interest at A's death with possession postponed. Interests not void because trust may last beyond perpetuity period. (On a second appeal, Ford v. Yost, 300 Ky. 764, 190 S.W.2d 21 (1945), the court eliminated the provision for holding in trust and upheld the beneficial interests.)

Holoway v. Crumbaugh, 275 Ky. 377, 221 S.W.2d 924 (1938)
Devise to A's children whenever born; if any child dies without issue him surviving, his share to X. A had three children, all born before T's death. None were born subsequently. Held: gift over to X void. *Contra*, 6 Am. L. Prop. § 24.47, case 72; 4 Restatement of Property § 384, ill. 2, com. g. The gifts over on death of each child are on separate divesting contingencies. Therefore, under orthodox view, the gifts over on death of each of these three children living at T's death are valid.

Hussey v. Sargent, 116 Ky. 53, 75 S.W. 211 (1903)
Devise in trust to pay income to A in amount necessary to support his children, accumulate excess, and pay over accumulated income and corpus to A's children when his daughter Emily reaches thirty-five, or if dead, when she would have reached thirty-five had she lived. Held: gift to A's children violates Rule; contingencies not separated. *Contra*, authorities cited under Coleman v. Coleman and Curtis v. Citizens Bank *supra*. Gift to A's children vests in interest with possession postponed at A's death under orthodox view; in any event the gift on the first contingency is valid.

Laughlin v. Elliott, 202 Ky. 433, 259 S.W. 1031 (1924)
Deed to A for life, then to B for life, then to grandchildren of A in fee. A had grandchild living at date of deed. Held: remainder in fee void. *Contra*, 6 Am. L. Prop. § 379; Simes & Smith § 1270, example 5, see also n. 69, 1959 pocket part. Orthodox view: class closing at death of A and B saves gift.

Letcher's Trustee v. Letcher, 302 Ky. 448, 194 S.W.2d 984 (1946)
Devise to A for life, then in trust to the children of B, then to church forever, but if church ceases to maintain church house, to synod. Held: gifts to children of B, to church, and to synod all void. *Contra* as to children of B and church, 6 Am. L. Prop. §§ 24.3, 24.19 (case 16); Gray § 205; 5 Powell ¶ 772; 4 Restatement

of Property § 378, ill. 1, § 370, com. o; Simes & Smith § 1233. Orthodox view: gift to church immediately vests in interest with possession postponed; gift to children of B vests at death of A and B, if not before. Trust not invalid because might last beyond perpetuity period. *Contra* as to gift to synod, 6 Am. L. Prop. § 24.40; 5 Powell ¶ 770; 4 Restatement of Property § 397; Simes & Smith § 1280.

Lindner v. Ehrich, 147 Ky. 85, 143 S.W. 778 (1912)
Devise in trust to A for life, then to A's children for their lives, remainder in fee to A's grandchildren. Held: gift to A's grandchildren void (orthodox); preceding life estate increased to a fee (unorthodox). *Contra* on latter point, 6 Am. L. Prop. § 24.47; Gray § 248; 5 Powell ¶ 790; 4 Restatement of Property § 403. Invalid interest passes to T's heirs under orthodox view.

Ludwig v. Combs, 58 Ky. (1 Met.) 128 (1858)
Deed providing that children of slave Martha should be free when they reached twenty-five. Martha had no children when deed was executed. Held: deed of freedom void under Rule against Perpetuities. Application of the Rule to grants of freedom, keeping property in fetters, violates the fundamental reason for the Rule. If, however, a grant of freedom is subject to the Rule and is treated like a gift of a stated sum of money to each person described by a class designation, the decision is correct. But in that case, Davis v. Wood, 56 Ky. (17 B. Mon.) 86 (1856), is wrong. It held a devise of freedom to all Beck's children and grandchildren born after testator's death, to take effect twenty-six years after testator's death, did not create a perpetuity. Whether or not a grant of freedom to slaves is within the Rule is not today a pressing problem.

Maher v. Maher 139 F. Supp. 294 (E.D. Ky. 1956), noted 9 Okla. L. Rev. 440 (1956); further litigation dismissed for lack of jurisdiction, Maher v. Maher, 154 F. Supp. 804 (E.D. Ky. 1957).
Devise to A for life, then to A's children for their lives, remainder in fee to A's grandchildren per stirpes. Held: gift to A's grandchildren void (*but see* 4 Restatement of Property § 389, com. c); A's children take a fee. *Contra* on latter point, authorities cited under Lindner v. Ehrich *supra*. Criticized by Sparks, 32 N.Y.U.L. Rev. 419, 429 (1957).

Patterson v. Patterson, 135 Ky. 339, 122 S.W. 169 (1909)
Deed in fee from G to turnpike company, providing that when land ceased to be used for a tollhouse, it would "revert back to" X, Y, and Z (not the grantor). Held: executory interest in X, Y, and Z valid. *Contra*, 6 Am. L. Prop. § 24.62, cases 94, 95, 96; 5 Powell ¶ 767; Simes & Smith § 1241.

Stevens v. Stevens, 21 Ky. L. Rep. 1315, 54 S.W. 835 (1900)
Devise in trust for forty years, to pay income to T's minor children in such amounts necessary for their support, maintenance, and education. As each child reached twenty-one, his share of any

accumulated income to be paid to him; thereafter his share of income to be paid to him annually. At expiration of forty years, corpus "is to be divided equally between my living children or issue of my said children"; if all children die without surviving issue, corpus is to be divided among T's heirs. (Facts from Record, p. 2; Brief for Appellee, p. 1.) Held: entire devise void. *Contra*, authorities cited under Coleman v. Coleman and Curtis v. Citizens Bank *supra*. Orthodox view: income gift to children vests immediately. All interests in corpus will vest in interest with possession postponed at or before the death of T's children (lives in being).

Street v. Cave Hill Investment Co., 191 Ky. 422, 230 S.W. 536 (1921)
Devise of land to four churches for ninety-nine years, then land to be sold and proceeds divided among the churches then in existence. Held: ninety-nine-year term violated mortmain statute; term passed to T's heirs. Gift at end of ninety-nine-year term to churches then in existence held valid. *Contra* as to gift at end of ninety-nine-year term, Gray §§ 320.1, 210, 201; 5 Powell ¶ 767; 4 Restatement of Property § 374, ill. 7, see also § 370, com. h. Gift is contingent on churches being in existence after ninety-nine years—too remote.

Thornton v. Kirtley, 249 S.W.2d 803 (Ky. 1952)
Devise in trust for fifty years to pay income to T's three children, and on death of each child his share of the income to his issue per stirpes; at end of fifty years in fee to those persons receiving the income, with five shares of stock to be held in further trust in perpetuity to maintain cemetery lots. Held: all gifts invalid. *Contra* as to five-share trust to begin after fifty years, 6 Am. L. Prop. § 24.20; 4 Restatement of Property § 370, com. h, ill. 2; Simes & Smith § 1236. The gift is either a vested remainder or a "vested" executory interest to take effect at a specific date. Invalidity of prior gift should not cause it to fail. 6 Am. L. Prop. § 24.51. *Contra* as to income gifts to children, 6 Am. L. Prop. § 24.19, case 22a (1958 supp.); 5 Powell ¶ 772; 1 Scott, Trusts § 62.10(2) (2d ed. 1956); Simes & Smith §§ 1391, 1393; *cf.* Gray §§ 410-10.5.

Trosper v. Shoemaker, 312 Ky. 344, 227 S.W.2d 176 (1950)
Deed to A in fee, providing that if A, his heirs, or assigns failed to buy oil and gas from grantor, his heirs, and assigns, then grantor had right of entry upon repayment of purchase price of $3,000. Held: grantor retained valid right of entry, not void option. *Contra*, 6 Am. L. Prop. § 24.56; 4 Restatement of Property § 394, com. c; Simes & Smith § 1245.

Tyler v. Fidelity & Columbia Trust Co., 158 Ky. 280, 164 S.W. 939 (1914)
Devise in trust for A for life, then to B for life, then to A's children for their lives, remainder in fee to A's grandchildren per capita. Held: remainder in fee void; preceding life tenants take a fee. *Contra*, authorities cited under Lindner v. Ehrich *supra*.

U. S. Fidelity & Guaranty Co. v. Douglas' Trustee, 134 Ky. 374, 120 S.W. 328 (1909)
> Devise in trust to A for life, then in equal shares for each child of A for life, and upon death of any child to pay the share of corpus on which he had been receiving the income to his issue per stirpes. Held: devise to A's grandchildren void. *Contra*, 6 Am. L. Prop. § 24.29; Gray §§ 391, 392, 395 n.3; 4 Restatement of Property § 389; Simes & Smith § 1267. Doctrine of severed shares saves the gift to issue of any child of A in being at T's death. All children of A were in being at T's death, and so under orthodox view entire gift is valid.

TABLE 3

DOUBTFUL CASES UNDER ORTHODOX
PERPETUITIES DOCTRINE

Brown v. Columbia Finance & Trust Co., 123 Ky. 775, 97 S.W. 421 (1906)
> Exercise of special power of appointment held invalid. Gray § 522 n.1 says case was "erroneously decided," on assumption court refused to apply "second look" doctrine. However, case is also explicable on ground donee had only a power to appoint in fee. See Barnes v. Graves, 259 Ky. 180, 82 S.W.2d 297 (1935).

Curd's Trustee v. Curd, 163 Ky. 472, 173 S.W. 1148 (1915)
> Devise to A's grandchildren held invalid; A's children, as holders of preceding estate, take the fee. Incorrect if instrument construed to give A's children a life estate, increased into a fee by invalid gift over. See Lindner v. Ehrich, Table 2 *supra*.

Duncan v. Webster County Bd. of Educ., 205 Ky. 86, 265 S.W. 489 (1924)
> Holding defeasible fee becomes absolute when executory interest is struck out as void. Incorrect if grant was of a determinable fee. See Brown v. Independent Baptist Church, 325 Mass. 645, 91 N.E.2d 922 (1950).

Farmer's Nat'l Bank v. McKenney, 264 S.W.2d 881 (Ky. 1954)
> Holding trust for "as long as the law allows" void for uncertainty. Compare 6 Am. L. Prop. § 24.13; 4 Restatement of Property § 370, com. n, ill. 4. See p. 9 *supra*.

Johnson v. Pittsburgh Consol. Coal Co., 311 S.W.2d 537 (Ky. 1958)
> Court declined both to classify interest over after fee defeasible after 999 years and to say if it violated perpetuity rule. "In the event the coal remains unmined 999 years after the date of the instrument, future generations may be called upon to deal with the problem." *Id.* at 539. Application of wait-and-see? (Court assumed it was possible to classify interest as either a reversionary interest or an executory interest.)

Johnson's Trustee v. Johnson, 25 Ky. L. Rep. 2119, 79 S.W. 293 (1904)
   Void age limitation struck from will. Cy pres? See p. 51 *supra*.
Ligget v. Fidelity & Columbia Trust Co., 274 Ky. 387, 118 S.W.2d 720 (1938)
   Gift to A's grandchildren *per stirpes* held void. But see 4 Restatement of Property § 389, com. c.
McGaughey v. Spencer County Bd. of Educ., 285 Ky. 769, 149 S.W.2d 519, 133 A.L.R. 1474 (1941)
   Holding "contingent reversion" void; defeasible fee becomes absolute. Compare 6 Am. L. Prop. § 24.62; 5 Powell ¶ 769; Simes & Smith § 1239.
Renaker v. Tanner, 260 Ky. 281, 83 S.W.2d 54 (1935)
   Gift to "heirs" of living persons held void for perpetuity; no explanation given.
Robertson v. Simmons, 322 S.W.2d 476 (Ky. 1959)
   Option in gross held not subject to Rule against Perpetuities, but subject to rule against unreasonable restraints on alienation. Criticized by Sparks, 35 N.Y.U.L. Rev. 412 (1960). Discussed herein at pp. 117-18 *supra*.
Sandford's Adm'r v. Sandford, 230 Ky. 429, 20 S.W.2d 83 (1929)
   Liberal severance of invalid measuring lives for a trust; reversion held to pass to testator's heirs ascertained at termination of trust. Discussed herein at pp. 34-35 *supra*.
Taylor v. Dooley, 297 S.W.2d 905 (Ky. 1957)
   Void interest, which passed to T's heir by intestacy, ordered held in trust for heir's life. Cy pres? See pp. 46-48 *supra*.
Thomas v. Utterback, 269 S.W.2d 251 (Ky. 1954), noted 43 Ky. L.J. 559 (1955)
   Gift to A's grandchildren *per stirpes* held void. But see 4 Restatement of Property § 389, com. c.
Tillman v. Blackburn, 276 Ky. 550, 124 S.W.2d 755 (1939)
   Liberal construction to avoid Rule.
Tuttle v. Steele, 281 Ky. 218, 135 S.W.2d 436 (1939)
   Liberal construction to avoid Rule. Criticized by Gray § 395 n.3; see 6 Am. L. Prop. § 24.29 n.4; 5 Powell ¶ 816 n.26.
West v. Ashby, 217 Ky. 250, 289 S.W. 228 (1926)
   Harsh application of doctrine of infectious invalidity?

TABLE 4

CASES HOLDING INTERESTS VALID UNDER THE REMOTE POSSIBILITIES TEST: THE RESULTS ARE NOT AFFECTED BY THE 1960 PERPETUITIES ACT, SINCE IT IS NOT NECESSARY TO WAIT AND SEE TO SAVE THE GIFTS

Armstrong v. Armstrong, 53 Ky. (14 B. Mon.) 269 (1853)
Atty. Gen. v. Wallace's Devisees, 46 Ky. (7 B. Mon.) 611 (1847)

Board of Nat'l Missions v. Harrel's Trustee, 286 S.W.2d 905 (Ky. 1956)
Cambron v. Pottinger, 301 Ky. 768, 193 S.W.2d 412 (1946)
Clay v. Anderson, 203 Ky. 384, 262 S.W. 604 (1924)
Commonwealth v. Pollitt, 25 Ky. L. Rep. 790, 76 S.W. 412 (1903)
DeCharette v. DeCharette, 264 Ky. 525, 94 S.W.2d 1018, 104 A.L.R. 1455 (1936)
Egner v. Livingston County Bd. of Educ., 313 Ky. 168, 230 S.W.2d 448 (1950)
Emler v. Emler's Trustee, 269 Ky. 27, 106 S.W.2d 79 (1937)
Epperson v. Clintonville Cemetery Co., 303 Ky. 852, 199 S.W.2d 628 (1947)
First Nat'l Bank v. Purcell, 244 S.W.2d 458 (Ky. 1951)
Gillespie v. Winston's Trustee, 170 Ky. 667, 186 S.W. 517 (1916)
Goodloe's Trustee v. Goodloe, 292 Ky. 494, 166 S.W.2d 836 (1942)
Gray v. Gray, 300 Ky. 265, 188 S.W.2d 440, 160 A.L.R. 633 (1945)
Haydon v. Layton, 128 S.W. 90 (Ky. 1910)
Johnson v. Pittsburgh Consol. Coal Co., 311 S.W.2d 537 (Ky. 1958)
Kasey v. Fidelity Trust Co., 131 Ky. 609, 115 S.W. 739 (1909)
Miller v. Miller, 151 Ky. 563, 152 S.W. 542 (1913)
Mitchell v. Deegan, 301 Ky. 587, 192 S.W.2d 715 (1946)
Moore's Trustees v. Howe's Heirs, 20 Ky. (4 T.B. Mon.) 199 (1827)
Page v. Frazier's Ex'rs, 77 Ky. (14 Bush) 205 (1878)
Russell v. Meyers, 202 Ky. 593, 260 S.W. 377 (1924)
Sorrell v. Tenn. Gas Transm. Co., 314 S.W.2d 193 (Ky. 1958)
Texas Eastern Transm. Corp. v. Carman, 314 S.W.2d 684 (Ky. 1958)
Tillman v. Blackburn, 276 Ky. 550, 124 S.W.2d 755 (1939)
Vokins v. McGaughey, 206 Ky. 42, 266 S.W. 907 (1924)

TABLE 5

CASES HOLDING INTERESTS VOID WHICH ACTUALLY DID, OR VERY PROBABLY WOULD, VEST IN TIME: HOW KRS 381.216 WOULD HAVE SAVED THEM

Some nonfertile octogenarians

(1) *Fact pattern:* T devised property "to A for life, then to A's children for their lives, remainder in fee to A's grandchildren." Instrument litigated after A's death. Either opinion or record discloses that A died without having any more children born after T's death. Remainder in fee would be valid under wait-and-see. See p. 86 *supra*.

Bach v. Pace, 305 S.W.2d 528 (Ky. 1957)
Brown v. Columbia Finance & Trust Co., 123 Ky. 775, 97 S.W. 421 (1906), fact pattern results from exercise of power of appointment
Holoway v. Crumbaugh, 275 Ky. 377, 121 S.W.2d 924 (1938)
Laughlin v. Elliott, 202 Ky. 433, 259 S.W. 1031 (1924)

Letcher's Trustee v. Letcher, 302 Ky. 448, 194 S.W.2d 984 (1946), remainder in fee to a church, rather than to A's grandchildren

Tyler v. Fidelity & Columbia Trust Co., 158 Ky. 280, 164 S.W. 939 (1914)

U.S. Fidelity & Guaranty Co. v. Douglas' Trustee, 134 Ky. 374, 120 S.W. 328 (1909)

(2) *Fact pattern:* Same devise as (1) above. Instrument litigated before A's death. Either opinion or record discloses that A had no more children after T's death and at the time of litigation was at an age where further children were highly improbable. Remainder in fee would almost certainly be valid under wait-and-see. For application of KRS 381.216, see pp. 86-87 *supra*.

Beall v. Wilson, 146 Ky. 646, 143 S.W. 55 (1912), woman age fifty-seven at time of decision

Lindner v. Ehrich, 147 Ky. 85, 143 S.W. 778 (1912), woman age sixty-six at time of decision

Maher v. Maher, 139 F. Supp. 294 (E.D. Ky. 1956), man (widower) age seventy at time of decision

Taylor v. Dooley, 297 S.W.2d 905 (Ky. 1957), woman age fifty-nine at time of decision

Thomas v. Utterback, 269 S.W.2d 251 (Ky. 1954), male age sixty-six and females age seventy-five and seventy-eight at time of decision

Tuttle v. Steele, 281 Ky. 218, 135 S.W.2d 436 (1939), facts unclear but briefs imply A (brother or sister of testator) is dead or beyond age of procreation

A widow not unborn

(3) *Fact Pattern:* T devised property "to A for life, then to A's surviving widow for life, then in fee to A's issue then living." The opinion discloses A's surviving widow was in fact alive at T's death, and thus the gift to issue would be valid under wait-and-see. See p. 85 *supra*.

Chenowith v. Bullitt, 224 Ky. 698, 6 S.W.2d 1061 (1928)

Age contingencies

(4) *Fact pattern:* T devised property "to A for life, remainder in fee to A's children who reach twenty-five." Opinion or record discloses that at A's death all his children were over four years of age. Thus under wait-and-see the gift would be valid. See pp. 84-85 *supra*.

Johnson's Trustee v. Johnson, 25 Ky. L. Rep. 2119, 79 S.W. 293 (1904)

Ludwig v. Combs, 58 Ky. (1 Met.) 128 (1858)

(5) *Fact pattern:* T devised property "to my grandchildren now living and born within ten years of my death who reach twenty-two." It is highly probable that T's grandchildren will reach twenty-two

within twenty-one years of the death of T's children. Thus the gift probably would be valid under wait-and-see. See pp. 84-85 *supra*.
Fidelity & Columbia Trust Co. v. Tiffany, 202 Ky. 618, 260 S.W. 357 (1924)

Trusts for years

(6) *Fact pattern:* T devised property "to pay income to A for life, then to A's children, and twenty-five years from T's death to distribute the property to A's issue then living per stirpes." Opinion or record discloses distribution date would definitely occur within twenty-one years of A's death. Therefore gift of corpus would be valid under wait-and-see. See p. 87 *supra*.
Coleman v. Coleman, 23 Ky. L. Rep. 1476, 65 S.W. 832 (1901)
Ford v. Yost, 299 Ky. 682, 186 S.W.2d 896 (1945); Ford v. Yost, 300 Ky. 764, 190 S.W.2d 21 (1945)
Hussey v. Sargent, 116 Ky. 53, 75 S.W. 211 (1903)

TABLE 6

CASES HOLDING INTERESTS VOID WHICH
DID NOT OR MIGHT NOT VEST IN DUE TIME:
HOW KRS 381.216 WOULD HAVE APPLIED

Some fertile nonoctogenarians

(1) *Fact pattern:* T devised property "to A for life, then to A's children for their lives, then to A's grandchildren in fee." A had a child born after T's death. For application of KRS 381.216, see pp. 86-87 *supra*.
Brumley v. Brumley, 28 Ky. L. Rep. 231, 89 S.W. 182 (1905)
Curd's Trustee v. Curd, 163 Ky. 472, 173 S.W. 1148 (1915)
West v. Ashby, 217 Ky. 250, 289 S.W. 228 (1926)

Trusts for years

(2) *Fact pattern:* T devised property "in trust for forty years to pay income to T's issue per stirpes from time to time living, and at the end of forty years to distribute the corpus to T's issue per stirpes then living." For application of KRS 381.216, see p. 87 *supra*.
Curtis v. Citizens Bank, 318 S.W.2d 33 (Ky. 1958)
Fidelity Trust Co. v. Lloyd, 25 Ky. L. Rep. 1827, 78 S.W. 896 (1904)
Stevens v. Stevens, 21 Ky. L. Rep. 1315, 54 S.W. 835 (1900)
Thornton v. Kirtley, 249 S.W.2d 803 (Ky. 1952)

Perpetual trusts

(3) *Fact pattern:* T devised property "in trust to pay the income to his issue per stirpes forever" (no termination date). Under wait-and-see

the trust may continue for the lives of T's issue living at his death plus twenty-one years. See p. 87 *supra*.
Farmers Nat'l Bank v. McKenney, 264 S.W.2d 881 (Ky. 1954)
Renaker v. Tanner, 260 Ky. 281, 83 S.W.2d 54 (1935)
Sandford's Adm'r v. Sandford, 230 Ky. 429, 20 S.W.2d 83 (1929), similar result without wait-and-see
Smith v. Fowler, 301 Ky. 96, 190 S.W.2d 1015 (1945)

Powers of appointment

(4) *Fact pattern*: T devised property "to A for life, remainder as A by will appoints." A appoints "to B for life, remainder to B's children in fee." B was not in being at T's death. For application of KRS 381.216, see pp. 86-87, 90 *supra*.
Ligget v. Fidelity & Columbia Trust Co., 274 Ky. 387, 118 S.W.2d 720 (1938)

TABLE 7

CASES ON OPTIONS: APPLICATION OF KRS 381.216

(1) *Options unlimited in time.* Held void; would be valid for twenty-one years and void thereafter under KRS 381.216. See p. 88 *supra*.
Maddox v. Keeler, 296 Ky. 440, 177 S.W.2d 568, 162 A.L.R. 578 (1944)
Robertson v. Simmons, 322 S.W.2d 476 (Ky. 1959)
Saulsberry v. Saulsberry, 290 Ky. 132, 160 S.W.2d 654 (1942)

(2) *Option limited to twenty-one years after life in being.* Held valid under KRS 381.216.
Gilbert v. Union College, 343 S.W.2d 829 (Ky. 1961)

(3) *Options personal to optionee and thus limited to life in being.* Held valid; not affected by 1960 Perpetuities Act.
Bates v. Bates, 314 Ky. 789, 236 S.W.2d 943 (1950)
Campbell v. Campbell, 313 Ky. 249, 230 S.W.2d 918 (1950)

TABLE 8

CASES ON RIGHTS OF ENTRY, POSSIBILITIES OF REVERTER, AND EXECUTORY INTERESTS AFTER DETERMINABLE FEES: APPLICATION OF KRS 381.218 AND KRS 381.219

(1) *Rights of entry and possibilities of reverter held valid.* Under KRS 381.218 and 381.219, interest would be treated as right of entry, which is void after thirty years if contingency has not happened. See pp. 99-107 *supra*.

Austin v. Calvert, 262 S.W.2d 825 (Ky. 1953)
Barren County Bd. of Educ. v. Jordan, 249 S.W.2d 814 (Ky. 1952)
Bowling v. Grace, 219 Ky. 496, 293 S.W. 964 (1927)
Devine v. Isham, 284 Ky. 587, 145 S.W.2d 529 (1940)
Egner v. Livingston County Bd. of Educ., 313 Ky. 168, 230 S.W.2d 448 (1950)
Fayette County v. Morton, 282 Ky. 481, 138 S.W.2d 953 (1940)
Fayette County Bd. of Educ. v. Bryan, 263 Ky. 61, 91 S.W.2d 990 (1936)
Hoskins v. Walker, 255 S.W.2d 481 (Ky. 1953)
Jefferson County Bd. of Educ. v. Littrell, 173 Ky. 78, 190 S.W. 465 (1917)
Trosper v. Shoemaker, 312 Ky. 344, 227 S.W.2d 176 (1950)
Webster County Bd. of Educ. v. Gentry, 233 Ky. 35, 24 S.W.2d 910 (1930)
Webster County Bd. of Educ. v. Wynn, 303 Ky. 110, 196 S.W.2d 983 (1946)

(2) *Executory interests held void.* Under KRS 381.219, interest would be treated as a right of entry, which is void after thirty years if contingency has not happened. See p. 108 *supra.*

Duncan v. Webster County Bd. of Educ., 205 Ky. 86, 265 S.W. 489 (1924)
McGaughey v. Spencer County Bd. of Educ., 285 Ky. 769, 149 S.W.2d 519 (1941)

(3) *Executory interest held valid.* Under KRS 381.219, interest would be treated as a right of entry, which is void after thirty years if contingency has not happened. See p. 108 *supra.*

Patterson v. Patterson, 135 Ky. 339, 122 S.W. 169 (1909)

TABLE OF CASES

Adams v. Security Trust Co., 141
Allen v. Allen, 116
Anderson v. Blackburn, 135, 137
Anderson v. Simpson, 119
Armstrong v. Armstrong, 20, 50, 150, 157
Atty. Gen. v. Wallace's Devisees, 57, 150, 157
Austin v. Calvert, 101, 162
Auxier's Ex'x v. Theobald, 125, 132, 135

Bach v. Pace, 8, 32, 45, 81, 151, 158
Baldwin's Coex'rs v. Curry, 18
Bank of Taylorsville v. Vandyke, 140
Baptist Church v. Wagner, 101
Barnes v. Graves, 38, 45, 46, 150, 156
Barren County Bd. of Educ. v. Jordan, 102, 108, 150, 162
Bates v. Bates, 40, 129, 150, 161
Beall v. Wilson, 45, 50, 150, 159
Bedinger v. Graybill's Ex'r, 75
Biltmore Village v. Royal, 111
Birney v. Richardson, 57
Bland's Adm'r v. Bland, 135, 136
Board of Educ. of Taylor County v. Bd. of Educ. of Campbellsville, 100
Board of Nat'l Missions v. Harrel's Trustee, 24, 41, 57, 150, 158
Bonzo v. Nowlin, 112
Bottom v. Fultz, 136, 139
Bowling v. Grace, 96, 150, 162
Brashear v. Macey, 57
Breckinridge v. Breckinridge's Ex'rs, 18
Breckinridge v. Skillman's Trustee, 75
Brock v. Brock, 135

Brock v. Conkwright, 123
Brown v. Columbia Finance & Trust Co., 37, 156, 158
Brown v. Independent Baptist Church, 156
Brownell v. Edmunds, 12
Brumley v. Brumley, 45, 150, 160
Bull v. Ky. Nat'l Bank, 136

Cadell v. Palmer, 56
Calloway v. Smith, 139
Cambron v. Pottinger, 150, 158
Cammack v. Allen, 56, 120, 123, 124
Campbell v. Campbell, 40, 129, 150, 161
Carpenter v. Allen, 126
Carter's Trustee v. Gettys, 60, 63, 150
Cattlin v. Brown, 33
Cecil's Trustee v. Robertson, 139
Chappell v. Chappell, 126
Chappell v. Frick Co., 126
Charlotte Park & Recreation Comm'n v. Barringer, 101
Chenowith v. Bullitt, 10, 38, 45, 64, 150, 159
Citizens Fidelity Bank v. Bernheim Fdn., 83
Clay v. Anderson, 8, 20, 57, 150, 158
Clay v. Security Trust Co., 17
Coleman v. Coleman, 18, 20, 25, 49, 58, 151, 160
Commissioner v. Proctor, 139
Commonwealth v. Pollitt, 104, 150, 158
Consolidated Realty Co. v. Norton's Trustees, 141

Cooper v. Knuckles, 121, 126, 132
County School Bd. v. Dowell, 101
Courts v. Courts' Guardian, 126
Cropper v. Bowles, 123
Cuddy v. McIntyre, 98
Curd's Trustee v. Curd, 2, 18, 45, 46, 156, 160
Curtis v. Citizens Bank, 18, 23, 25, 28, 44, 45, 48, 56, 152, 160

Davidson's Ex'rs v. Kemper, 139
Davis v. Wood, 21, 154
DeCharette v. DeCharette, 37, 150, 158
Dep't of Public Welfare v. Meek, 139
Dep't of Revenue v. Kentucky Trust Co., 101, 105
Devine v. Isham, 100, 162
Dills v. Deavors, 120, 126
Dority v. W. E. Rogers Co., 135
Duncan v. Webster County Bd. of Educ., 108, 116, 156, 162

Edgerly v. Barker, 50, 84
Edwards v. Hammond, 17
Egner v. Livingston County Bd. of Educ., 150, 158, 162
Emler v. Emler's Trustee, 20, 35, 150, 158
England v. Davis, 132
Epperson v. Clintonville Cemetery Co., 42, 151, 158
Ernst v. Shinkle, 122
Erwin v. Benton, 12

Farmers Bank v. Morgan, 18
Farmers Nat'l Bank v. McKenney, 9, 57, 64, 156, 161
Fayette County v. Morton, 96, 151, 162
Fayette County Bd. of Educ. v. Bryan, 96, 100, 101, 151, 162
Festing v. Allen, 17
Fidelity & Columbia Trust Co. v. Tiffany, 18, 23, 28, 33, 45, 47, 152, 160
Fidelity Trust Co. v. Lloyd, 35, 49, 58, 152, 160
First Nat'l Bank v. Purcell, 20, 60, 151, 158
First Owensboro Bank v. Central Trust Co., 135
Fitchie v. Brown, 9
Ford v. Ford, 135, 140
Ford v. So. Nat'l Life Ins. Co., 133
Ford v. Yost (299 Ky. 682), 12, 18, 58, 63, 116, 153, 160
Ford v. Yost (300 Ky. 265), 60, 151, 153, 160
Fox v. Burgher, 117, 122

Francis v. Big Sandy Co., 126, 132
Frazier v. Combs, 119, 121, 126, 132, 133
Fulton v. Teager, 101

Gaites' Will Trusts, Re, 11
George v. George, 135
Gilbert v. Union College, 10, 40, 85, 89, 127, 129, 161
Gillespie v. Winston's Trustee, 8, 20, 141, 151, 158
Goodloe's Trustee v. Goodloe, 10, 22, 29, 38, 64, 85, 151, 158
Grand Rapids Trust Co. v. Herbst, 116
Gray v. Gray, 8, 20, 119, 120, 132, 151, 158
Groger v. Long, 142

Hackett v. Hackett, 140
Haggerty v. City of Oakland, 12
Hale v. Elkhorn Coal Corp., 107, 119, 126, 132
Hamilton v. Jackson, 101
Harkness v. Lisle, 123
Harned v. Dorman, 140
Haydon v. Layton, 151, 158
Henning v. Harrison, 122
Hickman v. Boffman, 56
Highfill v. Konnerman, 125
Hinckley, Estate of, 116
Hite v. Barber, 117, 122
Holoway v. Crumbaugh, 45, 153, 158
Holt's Ex'r v. Deshon, 124
Hooper, Re, 9
Hoskins v. Walker, 110, 162
Howard's Adm'x v. Asher Coal Co., 125, 132
Howell v. Weisemuller, 119
Hubbard v. Hayes, 140
Huffman v. Chasteen, 139
Hussey v. Sargent, 18, 25, 44, 50, 83, 85, 153, 160
Hutchinson v. Loomis, 122, 126

Jefferson County Bd. of Educ. v. Littrell, 96, 151, 162
Johnson v. Dumeyer, 125
Johnson v. Pittsburgh Consol. Coal Co., 74, 98, 112, 156, 158
Johnson's Trustee v. Johnson, 33, 50, 60, 157, 159

Kasey v. Fidelity Trust Co., 42, 98, 151, 158
Kean's Guardian v. Kean, 121, 127, 133
Keith v. First Nat'l Bank, 60, 116
Kelly v. Marr, 141

Kenner v. American Contract Co., 101, 107, 132
Kentland Coal & Coke Co. v. Keen, 107, 116, 126, 132, 143
Kentucky Coal Lands Co. v. Mineral Dev. Co., 101

Lane v. Taylor, 127, 136
Latta v. Louisville Trust Co., 141
Laughlin v. Elliott, 32, 45, 68, 73, 74, 153, 158
Lawson v. Asberry, 98
Lawson v. Lightfoot, 119
Letcher's Trustee v. Letcher, 23, 28, 42, 45, 49, 58, 153, 159
Ligget v. Fidelity & Columbia Trust Co., 22, 29, 34, 37, 38, 46, 64, 157, 161
Lindner v. Ehrich, 32, 45, 46, 154, 159
Lindsay v. Williams, 123
Livingston v. Meyers, 111
Louisville v. Cooke, 127, 135, 136
Louisville Tobacco Warehouse Co. v. Thompson, 139
Lucas v. Hamm, 69
Ludwig v. Combs, 21, 70, 154, 159
Luke v. Marshall, 57

Maddox v. Keeler, 40, 62, 118, 129, 151, 161
Maher v. Maher (207 Ky. 360), 127
Maher v. Maher (139 F. Supp. 294), 32, 34, 46, 47, 154, 159
Malone v. Jamison, 104
Martin v. Harris, 25
Maynard v. Ratcliff, 112
McGaughey v. Spencer County Bd. of Educ., 97, 108, 157, 162
Meade v. Rowe's Ex'r, 135
Merchants Nat'l Bank v. Curtis, 80
Miller v. Miller, 45, 50, 151, 158
Miller's Ex'rs v. Miller's Heirs, 60
Mitchell v. Deegan, 151, 158
Moore's Heirs v. Moore's Devisees, 83
Moore's Trustees v. Howe's Heirs, 20, 57, 151, 158
Morgan's Trust, In Re, 47
Morton's Guardian v. Morton, 119
Muir's Ex'rs v. Howard, 127
Myers v. Davis, 42

Newsom v. Barnes, 61, 116, 133
Nutter v. Russell, 101

Ohm v. Clear Creek Drainage District, 101
Opinion of the Justices, 111

Page v. Frazier's Ex'rs, 56, 151, 158
Patterson v. Patterson, 54, 154, 162
Perry v. Metcalf, 117, 122
Phillips v. Big Sandy Co., 136
Pimbe's Case, 136
Polley v. Adkins, 119, 126
Pond Creek Coal Co. v. Day, 132
Pond Creek Coal Co. v. Runyon, 126, 132, 133
Price v. Virginia Iron Co., 126, 132
Pullins v. Bd. of Educ. of Methodist Church, 42, 98, 151

Ramey v. Ramey, 120
Ramsey v. Holder, 104
Ratliff's Ex'rs v. Commonwealth, 139
Renaker v. Tanner, 35, 45, 64, 73, 157, 161
Rice v. Hall, 40, 129
Robertson v. Simmons, 40, 56, 62, 117, 128, 157, 161
Robsion v. Gray, 117, 119, 120, 122
Rousseau v. Page's Ex'x, 141
Ruh's Ex'rs v. Ruh, 18
Russell v. Meyers, 8, 20, 57, 140, 151, 158

Saffold v. Wright, 122
Sandford's Adm'r v. Sandford, 34, 42, 45, 51, 57, 157, 161
Sanford v. Sims, 101
Saulsberry v. Saulsberry (140 Ky. 608), 117, 122
Saulsberry v. Saulsberry (290 Ky. 132), 40, 62, 126, 129, 151, 161
Savannah School District v. McLeod, 101
Scott v. Ratliff, 104, 136
Scott County Bd. of Educ. v. Pepper, 100
Searcy v. Lawrenceburg Nat'l Bank, 42
Sears v. Coolidge, 38
Second Church v. Le Prevost, 101
Security Trust Co. v. Mahoney, 141
Smith v. Fowler, 34, 42, 151, 161
Smith v. Isaacs, 125
Smith v. Smith, 135
Sorrell v. Tenn. Gas Transm. Co., 39, 151, 158
So. Nat'l Life Ins. Co. v. Ford's Adm'r, 127, 133, 135
Sparrow v. Sparrow, 141
Speckman v. Meyer, 120
Spilman v. Mercer County Nat'l Bank, 135
Stevens v. Stevens, 18, 28, 43, 49, 58, 154, 160

Stewart v. Barrow, 125
Stewart v. Brady, 121, 125
Story v. First Nat'l Bank, 80
Street v. Cave Hill Investment Co., 24, 54, 155

Taylor v. Dooley, 32, 47, 51, 55, 64, 157, 159
Tesdell v. Hanes, 111
Texas Co. v. Bowen, 112
Texas Eastern Transm. Corp. v. Carman, 39, 151, 158
Thomas v. Utterback, 32, 34, 45, 64, 68, 157, 159
Thornton v. Kirtley, 23, 35, 49, 58, 155, 160
Thurman v. Hudson, 105
Tillman v. Blackburn, 35, 157, 158
Todd's Ex'rs v. Todd, 139
Trosper v. Shoemaker, 41, 155, 162
Trustees of Schools v. Batforf, 111
Turner v. Lewis, 126, 132
Tuttle v. Steele, 35, 157, 159
Tyler v. Fidelity & Columbia Trust Co., 32, 45, 57, 155, 159

U.S. Fidelity & Guaranty Co. v. Douglas' Trustee, 20, 34, 45, 56, 64, 156, 159

Vance v. Vance, 111
Vaux, *Re*, 9
Vittitow v. Keene, 141
Vokins v. McGaughey, 39, 151, 158

Walker, Will of, 116
Wallace v. Smith, 125
Ward v. Van der Loeff, 71
Webster County Bd. of Educ. v. Gentry, 102, 162
Webster County Bd. of Educ. v. Wynn, 101, 162
West v. Ashby, 32, 49, 68, 117, 119, 120, 157, 160
Whisman v. McMullan's Ex'r, 142
Wichelman v. Messner, 111
Williams v. Johnson, 100
Winn v. William, 122, 123
Wood, *In Re*, 12

Young v. Young, 120

INDEX

Accumulations, 43, 49
Administrative contingencies: post-1960 law, 88; pre-1960 law, 12
Age contingencies: drafting, 93; reduction by court, 50-51, 84-85; under 1960 act, 84-85, 159; vesting affected by, 11-12, 17, 24-26, 29, 33, 38, 48
Alienation. *See* Restraints on alienation; Suspension of the power of alienation
Alternative contingencies, 45, 50. *See also* Substitutional gifts

Causal relationship. *See* Lives in being
Charitable gifts: exemption preserved by 1960 act, 112; under common law Rule, 23-24, 41-42
Children. *See* Class gifts; Fertility
Class gifts: class closing rule, 32-33, 74; drafting, 94; separability, 34-35; severed shares, 33-34; under 1960 act, 84-87; when vested, 26, 31-33
Confusion in cases, 2-3, 19-30, 52-65, 68-70, 151-57
Consequences of violating Rule, 44-51, 75-76. *See also* Cy pres
Construction: different in perpetuities cases, 14-19; liberal, 35; vested subject to divestment, 26-29; vested with payment postponed, 24-26, 29, 58, 63-65
Cy pres: adoption of, 76, 83-84; illustrations of, 84-91; pre-1960 cases, 42, 50-51

Defeasible fees, 103-104, 108
Determinable fee abolished, 99-106

Drafting suggestions, 91-95
Duration of trusts: drafting, 92-93; permissible duration, 9, 57-65; under 1960 act, 87, 160

Easements, 39
Employee trusts, 42-43
Erroneous cases, 151-57. *See also* Orthodox doctrine not followed
Executory interests: forfeiture restrictions on land use, 103-104, 108, 162; Rule applied to, 20, 23-24, 54

Fertility: application of 1960 act, 86, 159-60; presumptions regarding, 10-11, 75

Gifts over. *See* Substitutional gifts

Infectious invalidity, 46-49, 76

Kentucky Revised Statutes: § 353.300, 140; § 381.180, 135, 137; § 381.210, 101; § 381.215, 6, 78-79, 147; § 381.216, 7, 38, 41, 49, 51, 74, 78-91, 95, 104, 108, 128, 130-31, 147, 158-61; § 381.217, 42-43, 147; § 381.218, 99-106, 148, 161-62; § 381.219, 41, 99, 104, 106-109, 132, 149, 161-62; § 381.220, 12, 43, 52-57, 61-65, 70, 114, 118, 129-30, 149; § 381.221, 99, 109-13, 148; § 381.222, 99, 111-13, 149; § 381.223, 38, 79, 149; § 382.010, 101; § 389.010, 140; § 389.030, 72, 140; § 389.035, 72, 140; § 389.040,

Kentucky Revised Statutes (*continued*): 72, 140; § 389.045, 141; § 394.500, 44; § 395.200, 140; § 426.190, 135, 137

Leases: options in, 39; under 1960 act, 88, 112
Life estates: duration of, effect on vesting remainder, 23, 63-64; in unborn persons, 10-11, 85-86; restraints on, 119, 123-25
Lives in being: under common law Rule, 7-9; under KRS 381.220, 56-57; under 1960 act, 80-81

Options: restraints on alienation, treated as, 127-31; under common law Rule, 39-41, 127-31; under 1960 act, 88-89, 161
Orthodox doctrine not followed, 19-35, 45-46, 48-51, 57-65, 68-70, 151-57

Pension trusts, 42-43
Possibilities of reverter: abolition, 99-106; alienability, 101; defined, 100, 104-105; function of, 96-99; pre-1960 interests terminated, 109-13
Powers of appointment: exercise of, 93; under common law Rule, 22, 36-40; under 1960 act, 38, 90, 161

Reform of Rule against Perpetuities: confusion in cases, 2-3, 68-70, 151-57; forfeiture restrictions exempt, 96; legislative history, 2-5; objections to Rule, 66-78
Reformation. *See* Cy pres
Remainders: *see also* Vest; under 1960 act, 84-87
Remote possibilities test: abolition, 79; defined, 9-14; objections to, 70-75
Restraints on alienation: *see also* Restraints on fees; consequences of violating, 131-34; court sale permitted, 140-42; creditors' rights, 134-40; disabling and forfeiture restraints distinguished, 115-16, 131-34; distinguished from Rule against Perpetuities, 114; distinguished from rule against suspension of power of alienation, 114-18; equitable interests, restraints on, 127, 133-35, 140-41; life estates, restraints on, 119, 123-25; options as restraints, 127-31; remainders, retraints on, 119-20

Restraints on fees: critique of doctrine, 142-45; forfeiture for violation, 131-32; reasonable restraints allowed, 120-27
Reversion, 104-106
Reverter. *See* Possibility of reverter
Right of entry: alienability, 101; distinguished from executory interest, 103-104, 108; distinguished from option, 40-41; distinguished from possibility of reverter, 100-102; termination of, post-1960, 106-109, 132, 161-62; termination of, pre-1960, 109-13; to enforce restraint on alienation, 132

Separability, 34-35
Statutes. *See* Kentucky Revised Statutes
Substitutional gifts, 18, 24-29
Suspension of the power of alienation: by options, 117; distinguished from direct restraints on alienation, 114-18; distinguished from Rule against Perpetuities, 53-56, 114; meaning of KRS 381.220, 52-57; rule against, repealed, 70, 78, 149; trust duration affected by, 61-65, 116-17

Trusts: discretionary, 139-40; duration of, 57-65, 87, 160; employee, 42-43; for term of years, 58, 87, 160; indestructible, 59-60; pension, 42-43; restraints on equitable interests, 127; revocable, 36; sale of corpus, 140-41; spendthrift, 135
Twenty-one years: meaning under KRS 381.220, 56-57; reformation to vest within, 88

Vest: *see also* Age contingencies, Orthodox doctrine; confusion in meaning, 28-30, 63-65, 76-78; indefeasibly in interest, 21-24; in interest subject to divestment, 18-19, 27-28; in interest subject to open, 26, 31-33; in interest with possession postponed, 17, 24-26; in possession, 19-21; meaning of, 14-30, 58-59, 63-65, 76-78
Violation of Rule. *See* Consequences of violating Rule

Wait-and-see doctrine: appraisal, 70-75; how long we wait, 81-83; illustrations of how applied, 84-91, 157-61; legislation, 2, 79; measuring lives, 80-81
Widow, unborn, 10, 85, 89, 159

www.ingramcontent.com/pod-product-compliance
Lightning Source LLC
Chambersburg PA
CBHW021830300426
44114CB00009BA/393